Digitalization and the Use of New Technologies in International Arbitration

Chinese and Comparative Law Series

VOLUME 13

The titles published in this series are listed at *brill.com/ccls*

Digitalization and the Use of New Technologies in International Arbitration

By

Magdalena Łągiewska

BRILL | NIJHOFF

LEIDEN | BOSTON

Library of Congress Cataloging-in-Publication Data

Names: Łągiewska, Magdalena, author.
Title: Digitalization and the use of new technologies in international arbitration / by Magdalena Łągiewska.
Description: Leiden ; Boston : Brill/Nijhoff, 2024. | Series: Chinese and comparative law series, 2213-4875 ; volume 13 | Includes bibliographical references and index.
Identifiers: LCCN 2024023185 (print) | LCCN 2024023186 (ebook) | ISBN 9789004700703 (hardback) | ISBN 9789004700710 (ebook)
Subjects: LCSH: Arbitration and award–Technological innovations. | Arbitration (International law) | International commercial arbitration.
Classification: LCC K2400 .L34 2024 (print) | LCC K2400 (ebook) | DDC 341.5/22–dc23/eng/20240527
LC record available at https://lccn.loc.gov/2024023185
LC ebook record available at https://lccn.loc.gov/2024023186

Typeface for the Latin, Greek, and Cyrillic scripts: "Brill". See and download: brill.com/brill-typeface.

ISSN 2213-4875
ISBN 978-90-04-70070-3 (hardback)
ISBN 978-90-04-70071-0 (e-book)
DOI 10.1163/9789004700710

This book is printed on acid-free paper and produced in a sustainable manner.

Contents

List of Figures IX

Introduction 1

1 General Approach to Digitalization in International Dispute Resolution 7
1 Introduction 7
2 Law and Technology 7
3 Technology and Dispute Resolution 10
4 Notion of Digitalization 15
5 Types of International Dispute Resolution 17
5.1 *International Commercial Arbitration* 18
5.1.1 Geneva Protocol 18
5.1.2 Geneva Convention 20
5.1.3 New York Convention 20
5.1.4 UNCITRAL Model Law 21
5.1.5 Delocalized Arbitration 21
5.2 *International Investment Arbitration* 22
5.3 *International Commercial Mediation* 23
5.4 *International Negotiation* 25
6 Twofold Approaches to the Use of New Technologies in International Arbitration 25
7 Online Arbitration 27
8 Conclusion 29

2 New Technologies in Arbitral Tribunals: An Overview 31
1 Introduction 31
2 IT Tools in Arbitral Tribunals 31
2.1 *Online Filing System* 33
2.1.1 AAA-ICDR 34
2.1.2 ICC Case Connect 36
2.1.3 WIPO eADR 37
2.1.4 SCC Platform 38
2.1.5 E-Arbitration-T 40
2.1.6 ICSID 40
2.2 *Remote Hearings* 41
2.2.1 Definition of Remote Hearings 41
2.2.2 Regulations on Remote Hearings 44

2.2.3 Seoul Protocol on Video Conferencing in International Arbitration 45
2.2.4 Twofold Standpoint on Remote Hearings 48
2.2.5 Right to a Hearing in International Arbitration 48
2.2.4 Need of Handling Remote Hearings 52
2.2.5 Challenges Related to Remote Hearings 53
2.2.6 Remote Hearings and Post-Arbitration Problems 58
2.3 *Electronically Stored Information* 61
3 Significance of AI in Arbitration 64
3.1 *Definition of AI* 64
3.2 *AI in International Arbitration: General Approach* 66
3.3 *AI Arbitrator's Selection Tools* 73
3.4 *ChatGPT in International Arbitration: a Game-Changer?* 75
3.5 *Risks of AI* 80
4 Conclusion 81

3 Advantages of Digitalization in International Arbitration 83
1 Introduction 83
2 Rule of Law and Access to Justice 83
3 Transparency 85
4 Efficiency, Flexibility, and Low Costs 87
5 Effectiveness and Convenience 90
6 Enhanced Diversity in International Arbitration 92
7 Conclusion 93

4 Challenges Related to Digitalization in International Arbitration 94
1 Introduction 94
2 Electronic Arbitration Agreement: An Overview 95
2.1 *Electronic Consent to Arbitration* 95
2.2 *Accessibility of the Arbitration Agreement* 96
2.3 *Electronic Form of the Arbitration Agreement* 97
3 Seat of Arbitration 101
4 Procedural Challenges 103
5 E-proceedings 104
6 E-evidence in Arbitration 106
6.1 *Definition of Electronic Evidence* 106
6.2 *Definition of Blockchain* 108
6.3 *Collecting of E-evidence* 111
6.4 *E-evidence before an Arbitral Tribunal* 112
6.4.1 Admissibility of E-evidence 112
6.4.2 Illegally Obtained or "Hacked" Evidence 114
6.4.3 Blockchain as Evidence 117

7 Digital Arbitral Award 122
7.1 *Form of the Digital Arbitral Award* 122
7.2 *Enforcement of the Digital Arbitral Award* 126
8 Cybersecurity 127
9 Data Protection 140
10 Inability to Observe Parties' Demeanour and Credibility 144
11 Conclusion 145

5 Future of International Arbitration 148
1 Introduction 148
2 Digitalization of International Arbitration in View of the UN Sustainable Development Goals 148
2.1 *Definition of the UN Sustainable Development Goals* 148
2.2 *Digitalization and 16th SDGs* 150
3 From "Smart Courts" to "Smart Arbitration" 154
4 Green Arbitration 163
5 AI-arbitrators: Pipe Dream or Realistic Future? 167
6 Blockchain-based Arbitration 173
6.1 *Definition of Blockchain-based Arbitration* 173
6.2 *Types of Blockchain-based Arbitration* 175
6.3 *Challenges Related to Blockchain-based Arbitration* 178
7 Conclusion 180

Final Conclusions and Recommendations 181

References 187
Index 206

Figures

1 How machine learning works? 68
2 Overview of AI 70
3 United Nations' Sustainable Development Goals 151
4 Idea of selecting a court by smart contract creators 176

Introduction

David Gauke once said during the AI Summit in London in 2019 that "technological revolution is no longer on the horizon – it is here".[1] Therefore, it has become a widespread practice in international dispute resolution to handle cases remotely. This means that all participants are not present in the same place, instead they could participate in the proceedings through phone or video. Before the outbreak and then the spread of the COVID-19 pandemic, parties very often agreed to conduct some aspects of proceedings in such a way. In fact, the reason behind choosing the remote solutions is based upon convenience, cost savings as well as other efficiencies such as environmental concerns or even the necessity of a case. The latter refers to some obstacles to obtaining a visa for travelling to arbitral tribunal, for instance. The COVID-19 pandemic even sped up the process of going online. Therefore, many arbitral proceedings were handled fully online as a matter of necessity.[2]

There are many benefits, but also some concerns and threats stemming from the online hearings. To name a few, some practical legal issues that can result from remote hearings refer to the arbitral tribunal's authority to handle a case remotely given the objection of a party and due process concerns. In addition, some challenges concern efficient, effective, and fair arbitral proceedings held remotely along with concerns on witness misconduct, cybersecurity, and data protection issues.[3] New cyber risks emerge, and they could influence different types of stakeholders, including competitors, hackers, investigative journalists the opponent party, among others. This entails those different actors who could have an interest in acquiring arbitration-related data transferred online for the sake of influencing, controlling, or even challenging the outcome of entire proceedings.[4]

Digitalization changes the faces of international dispute resolution. Even if it provides many benefits compared to traditional mechanisms of dispute settlement (offline proceedings), it also may cause new concerns and lead to threats. This book aims to primarily identify new technologies widely used in

1 See: D. Gauke, Lord Chancellor and Sec'y of State for Just., House of Commons, Statement at The Artificial Intelligence in Legal Services Summit (June 4, 2019).

2 S.P. Finizio, *Remote hearings in international arbitration* [in:] *Specialized arbitration: Emerging international trends and practices*, eds. C. Balyan. Y. Samant, Gurgaon 2022, p. 355.

3 *Ibidem.*

4 K. Baetens, *Cyber hack challenges in international arbitration*, "Linkaters" 22.04.2021, https://www.linklaters.com/en/insights/blogs/arbitrationlinks/2021/april/cyber-hack-challenges-in-arbitration. Accessed on 04.04.2023.

 | DOI:10.1163/9789004700710_002

international arbitration along with advantages and challenges related to the digitalization of international disputes. Such analysis is necessary to assess whether the binding legal framework of international commercial arbitration provides a pro-technology approach.

One must note that certain questions have been already addressed and resolved, but there is still a considerable amount of uncertainty. Therefore, a thorough analysis of the connections between dispute resolution and digital technologies is lacking. The primary purpose of this scientific research is to formulate pertinent questions rather than solely providing predetermined answers that reflect the potential risks and benefits of technology.

Notably, the COVID-19 pandemic should be seen as a landmark in the development of online dispute-resolution mechanisms. In fact, it also verified already adopted solutions and paved the way for introducing new tools to adjust quickly to new challenges and reality.

The subject of this dissertation, and at the same time the main research question, is to answer how digital law upholds the use of new technologies in international arbitration. In addition, this analysis aims to create of a list of recommendations regarding the use of new technologies in international commercial arbitration. For this purpose, the following research problems have been identified, which will allow the achievement of the assumed scientific goal. The first one relates to determining the relationship between new technologies and dispute resolution, particularly in international arbitration. In other words, an attempt to answer the question of whether digitization and the use of new technologies are the appropriate directions for the development of international dispute resolution. Secondly, what solutions within digitization and which new technologies have been adopted by arbitration tribunals? It is worth noting here whether existing legal regulations enable the use of such solutions in international arbitration. Thirdly, whether the process of digitization and the introduction of new technological solutions is beneficial from the perspective of international arbitration. In what way do new technologies guarantee fundamental rights arising from international conventions and international arbitration law? Fourthly, what challenges and threats arise from digitization and the use of new technologies, and whether existing legal and international solutions regulate these issues. Fifthly, whether there are legal solutions in the field of green arbitration, AI-arbitrators, and blockchain-based arbitration. How does technological progress in international arbitration relate to the achievement of sustainable development goals?

Finding answers to the following research questions will be helpful given the conducted research:

1. What is the relation between international law and new technologies?
2. How do new technologies affect dispute resolution mechanisms?
3. Are digitization and the use of new technologies the appropriate direction for the development of international dispute resolution?
4. Which forms of IT tools and innovation-driven technologies are widely used in international arbitration?
5. What is the legal background of IT tools?
6. What are the main challenges related to the use of IT tools in international arbitration?

The solution to the outlined research problems will allow for proving the main thesis of the dissertation, according to which international law in the field of international commercial arbitration lags behind technological changes. The process of adopting a new international convention regulating the issues of digitization and the use of new technologies in international arbitration would be time-consuming to the extent that the existing problems would become outdated or exacerbated. Therefore, in the case of conventions concerning international commercial arbitration, it is necessary to reinterpret existing provisions in the context of ongoing technological advancements. Bearing in mind the specificity of international law and addressing current issues, leading international institutions and arbitration tribunals have updated their arbitration rules and adopted a series of regulations in the form of "soft law" to fill the existing gap and create a framework for the functioning of arbitral tribunals in the digital environment.

It should be noted that the substantive scope of the work does not cover detailed regulations concerning international investment arbitration due to the broad thematic scope of the study. The focus has therefore been primarily on international commercial arbitration, with only auxiliary references to the solutions adopted in investment arbitration to demonstrate that digitization and the use of new technologies are also common in this field.

Given the chosen research subject, there has been no attempt so far to create recommendations and conduct a comprehensive analysis of the digitization process and the use of new technologies in international arbitration. It is worth mentioning that in Polish literature, there have only been attempts to analyze the solutions adopted during the COVID-19 pandemic in the field of international commercial arbitration. It is worth mentioning the special issue of the "Arbitration Bulletin" from December 2020, which was dedicated to the topic of new technologies in institutional arbitration. The "Bulletin" consists of 7 articles that highlight the use of IT in cases decided by arbitration tribunals.

It is worth remembering that the COVID-19 pandemic has only proven that arbitration has the potential to quickly adapt to changing socio-economic circumstances and the challenges associated with them. Technological progress is so dynamic that the solutions and recommendations presented in the dissertation are up to date at the time of writing the work.

The outlined research questions and main theses of the dissertation determine the adopted structure of the work. Therefore, the monograph has been divided into five chapters, each ending with a summary and partial conclusion. Based on the research results indicated in each section, final conclusions and recommendations have been formulated.

The first chapter of the monograph presents the relationship between "law and technology", "technology and dispute resolution", as well as the concept of digitization and types of international dispute resolution and the concept of online arbitration. This analysis was necessary to indicate that new technologies are increasingly present in dispute resolution, and even contribute to the emergence of a new type in the form of online arbitration. Nonetheless, there are no international legal solutions that would regulate this issue.

The second chapter sets forth what kind of new technologies are used in arbitration courts. Therefore, attention was paid to IT tools in leading arbitration institutions such as the American Arbitration Association, the International Chamber of Commerce in Paris, WIPO in Geneva, SCC in Stockholm, E-Arbitration-T as a European solution and ICSID. The selection of these arbitration institutions was motivated by their level of internationalization and the innovativeness of the solutions adopted regarding the use of modern dispute resolution platforms. Thanks to these platforms, it is possible to file cases online and attach necessary documentation. In the subsequent part of the analysis, remote hearings using IT tools were examined, and practical issues were identified.

The analysis was conducted based on the existing provisions in international arbitration law. It was necessary to determine whether the existing provisions of the 1958 New York Convention on the Recognition and Enforcement of Foreign Arbitral Awards and the UNCITRAL Model Law on International Commercial Arbitration allow for remote proceedings. This analysis leads to the conclusion that international regulations are general enough that they do not explicitly prohibit the use of new technologies in arbitration proceedings. Nonetheless, significant changes have taken place at the level of arbitration institutions themselves, which have amended their rules and adapted them to the new reality. The Seoul Protocol on Video Conferencing in International Arbitration is also noteworthy as it contains a range of practical solutions for conducting online proceedings. Important provisions are also introduced by the International Bar Association's Rules on the Taking of Evidence in International Arbitration, which address the production of documents in electronic form.

Finally, the analysis also examines the use of artificial intelligence in international arbitration. The technology is sufficiently developed that artificial intelligence can be helpful in the day-to-day work of not only arbitral tribunals but also arbitrators themselves. While the UNCITRAL Model Law along with the rules and guidelines of arbitration institutions do not prohibit the use of AI-supported tools in international arbitration, there are no more detailed regulations as to the limits of the use of artificial intelligence in international arbitration.

The third chapter highlights the advantages of digitization and the use of new technologies in international arbitration. Thus, the discussion resolves around greater access to justice, transparency, efficiency, flexibility and low costs, effectiveness, and convenience, and enhances diversity in international arbitration. The conducted analysis leads to the conclusion that the digitization process and the use of new technologies should respect the basic principles and rights under international conventions and international arbitration law (e.g. access to justice, right to be heard, due process, etc.).

The fourth chapter analyzes numerous challenges related to digitization and the use of new technologies in arbitration. Thus, this includes examining topics such as the electronic arbitration agreement, the seat of arbitration in case of online proceedings, procedural challenges, e-proceedings, e-evidence, digital arbitral award, cybersecurity and data protection issues, as well as an inability to observe parties' demeanour and credibility. This analysis leads to the conclusion that it is necessary to reinterpret the provisions of international conventions to take full advantage of modern technologies. In the absence of relevant regulations, the rules of arbitration institutions contain more detailed provisions in this regard.

The fifth chapter discusses digitization and the use of new technologies in international arbitration in the context of the Sustainable Development Goals and highlights new trends such as green arbitration, AI-arbitrators, and blockchain-based arbitration. This analysis leads to the conclusion that once again there is a lack of detailed international legal solutions. Instead, international arbitral tribunals adopt their own rules to keep up with the ongoing changes as a result of the development of technology. "Soft law" solutions are also commonly used in this context.

The result of the scientific considerations undertaken in the monograph and the research issues addressed is the construction of a list of recommendations for further digitization and the use of new technologies in international arbitration. Many issues have not yet been regulated either by international conventions, rules of arbitration institutions or other "soft law" instruments.

Regarding the research methods used in the monograph, first and foremost, the legal-dogmatic method should be mentioned. This research method enabled the interpretation of the legal provisions and their application. The use of this research method was crucial for the presentation and attempt to answer the research questions. The comparative method was also employed, allowing for a comparison of solutions adopted in different rules of arbitration institutions. The criteria for selecting specific arbitration institutions were dictated by the innovativeness of the adopted solutions. As for the choice of countries whose solutions have been analyzed (People's Republic of China and United States of America), it also results from technological innovations on a global scale. Additionally, the functional method was also used as an auxiliary method to demonstrate the "law in action".

The dissertation uses a substantive interpretation, which allowed for interpreting following established rules, and a doctrinal interpretation by presenting the position presented in the literature on the subject.

Given that the issues of digitization and the use of new technologies in international arbitration are the subjects of a few publications in Polish literature, mainly in the form of articles, the work is largely based on English-language sources.

CHAPTER 1

General Approach to Digitalization in International Dispute Resolution

1 Introduction

This chapter explores the relationship between "law and technology" and "technology and dispute resolution" along with the concept of digitalization and different forms of international dispute resolution. In addition, it also introduces two approaches to the use of new technologies in international arbitration and the concept of online arbitration which is a new type of dispute resolution facilitated by advancing technologies. This chapter aims to answer three research questions such as "What is the relation between international law and new technologies?", "how do new technologies affect dispute resolution mechanisms?" and "are digitization and the use of new technologies the appropriate direction for the development of international dispute resolution?"

2 Law and Technology

The law itself cannot be described as a stable product. One could even say after Rudolph Ihering that "Law is not a pure theory, but a living force".[1] Additionally, following Zygmunt Bauman and his theory of liquid modernity, it is noteworthy that there is a dichotomous and metaphorical transition in view of the traditional (aka solid) society and fluid modernity. Therefore, once he said:

> What all these characteristics of fluids show, in simple language, is that liquids, unlike solids, do not maintain their shape easily. Fluids, so, do not fix space or arrest time. Solids have clear spatial dimensions and neutralize impact and, therefore, reduce the significance of time (effectively resist its flow or make it irrelevant), fluids do not stick to any shape and are constantly ready (and prone) to change it; thus, for them, what counts

1 A. Cavalcanti Andrade de Araújo, *Connecting Law to New Technologies: Perspectives and Challenges*, [in:] *Internet and New Technologies Law. Perspectives and Challenges*, eds. D. Szostek, M. Załucki, Nomos 2021, p. 36.

> is time more than the space that they have to occupy; space that, after all, only fill 'for a moment'. In a sense, solids suppress time; liquids, on the contrary, time is what matters. In describing solids, we can ignore time entirely; when describing fluids, leaving time out would be a serious mistake.[2]

Given this perspective, the law itself, as a social science, is exposed to changes due to the impact of new technologies. This means that the law very often must reissue its main foundations to fit the new normal. In fact, regardless of some sceptical views on ongoing shifts, it seems obvious that the information age will influence paradigm changes. In addition, this digital era will set forth both benefits and harms for traditional law. One could even say that digitalization and the use of artificial intelligence (AI), robots, law techs, and legal techs would become a natural consequence of development. Therefore, these new tools and achievements will assist the law in many relevant issues. Nonetheless, it is noteworthy that many new and unknown problems will appear because of such innovation-driven changes. Practically, they will challenge not only human but also technical and professional law capacities.[3]

Therefore, it should be noted that both lawyers and legal institutions must constantly adjust to technological changes. Such a readjustment concerns their activities and more specifically the following issues: 1. the development of new functions that need new skills (which leads to new positions, in some kinds of hybrid professionals); 2. new skills require that lawyers learn basic technological vocabulary; 3. new skills and specializations would change the lawyer's environment (work in groups concerning complexes cases analyzed from interdisciplinary perspectives will be a new normal).[4]

Even if there are many definitions of law in literature, it is noteworthy to explore the relationship between "law and technology" as a new arising phenomenon. One could even say that such a relationship is not only simple but also complex.

According to "Black's Law Dictionary" "Law" could be defined as the "regime that orders human activities and relations through the systematic application of the force of politically organized society, or through social pressure, backed by force, in such a society".[5] Law, in turn, is understood as a set of rules which

2 *Ibidem*; cf. Z. Bauman, *Modernidade Líquida*, Zahar 2001.
3 A. Cavalcanti Andrade de Araújo, *Connecting Law to New* ..., p. 37.
4 *Ibidem*.
5 S.W. Brenner, *Law in an Era of "Smart" Technology*, Oxford 2007, p. 7. Cf. S. Wronkowska, Z. Ziembiński, *Zarys teorii prawa*, Poznań 2001, p. 46; *Black's Law Dictionary*, Minnesota 2004.

are adopted for the sake of governing institutions. This means that modern societies launched such institutions which have the power to apply, interpret and enforce these rules.[6]

There are many definitions of "technology". Under the "Chambers Dictionary", "technology" is defined as "the practice of any or all of the applied sciences that have practical value and/or industrial use".[7] Given the "Oxford English Dictionary", "technology" is understood as "the application of scientific knowledge for practical purposes".[8] Ron Westrum defines "technology" as the "objects, techniques, and knowledge that allow human beings to transform and control the inanimate world".[9] Some scholars (i.e. Susan Brenner) consider that this definition pays attention to the more expansive conception of knowledge. In general, many definitions concentrate on instrumental formulations of the concept that is on technology as applied science.[10] Hence, technology itself has the aim to create a certain product, to generate a service or even to lead to a determined result. Therefore, the aim of technology could be summarized as generating new results or even generating "old results by using fewer or less costly inputs".[11]

Nonetheless, there is a certain interaction between law and technology, most notably in cases when legal rules and regulations foster or impede the growth of technology. Sometimes society also intervenes, especially when technology leads to unfavourable results. Therefore, society seeks to apply legal rules with the aim to contain or change such results.[12]

In fact, nowadays, it is common to analyze law instrumentally. This means that the law itself is rather seen as a tool, an instrument which is necessary to achieve social goals. Following Kieran Tranter, "thinking like a lawyer means being able to manufacture arguments about law involving terms such as 'mischief', 'policy', and 'intent of the legislators'".[13] Legal research and legal scholarship are defined mostly in terms of the effectiveness of various law

6 D. Gifford, *Law and Technology: Interactions and Relationships*, "Minnesota Journal of Law, Science & Technology" 2007, vol. 8, issue 2, p. 571.

7 S.W. Brenner, *Law in an Era ...*, p. 8. Cf. *The Chambers Dictionary*, Edinburgh 2003, p. 1556.

8 *Ibidem*. Cf. *Concise Oxford English Dictionary*, New York 2002, p. 1471.

9 *Ibidem*, p. 9; Cf. R. Westrum, *Technologies & Society: The Shaping of People and Things*, Belmont 1990, p. 7.

10 S.W. Brenner, *Law in an Era ...*, p. 9.

11 D. Gifford, *Law and Technology ...*, p. 571.

12 *Ibidem*, pp. 571–572.

13 K. Tranter, *From Law and Technology to Law as Technology* [in:] K. Tranter, *Living in Technical Legality*, Edinburgh 2018, p. 33.

tools, including regulations, rights, and codes, among others.[14] It is noteworthy, however, that the law-making process is relatively slow and lengthy compared to emerging new technologies. Therefore, it creates a distance between technological innovation and legal changes. This could have an impact on legal certainty or even result in some ambiguous environment with unacknowledged or unpredicted rights and responsibilities. Hence, such a development of new technologies and further their diffusion impact users' behaviours. In addition, it also triggers a market demand. One could even say that such a temporal gap or even loophole in legal regulations gives more time for necessary analysis. In fact, il also helps to make better policy decisions and implement them properly. Such a slow pace in adopting new laws could not be classified as a weakness to warn against from the outset.[15]

Therefore, new innovation-driven technologies offer human beings' new tools along with new ways of handling old things. In addition, such technologies also offer things to do.[16] However, this begs the question of how, and when the law itself should adapt in the wake of technological changes. On the one hand, if the changes in legal regulations are relatively slow, they could result in risks concerning human health, and environmental risks along with some concerns related to privacy and individual rights. On the other hand, legal changes could lead to an unfavourable environment for both the economy and some technological improvements. Hence, one could even say that in case of too fast or ill-conceived legal changes, they could cause much harm by demolishing expectations or restraining more advanced technological innovations. As such, legal responses concerning technological changes influence not only the economy, but also further technological development and social welfare.[17]

3 Technology and Dispute Resolution

Currently, one of the most noteworthy changes in the dispute resolution mechanisms is the use of Information and Communications Technologies (ICTs). Therefore, ICTs are widely applied not only for the sake of interacting with each other, doing business but also resolving disputes. It must be

14 *Ibidem.*

15 E. Palmerini, *The interplay between law and technology, or the RoboLaw project in context*, pp. 16–17.

16 R. Brownsword, *Law, Liberty, and Technology* [in:] *The Oxford Handbook of Law, Regulation and Technology*, ed. Roger Brownsword et al., Oxford 2016, p. 41.

17 G.N. Mandel, *Legal Evolution in Response to Technological Change* [in:] *The Oxford Handbook of Law, Regulation and Technology*, ed. R. Brownsword et al., Oxford 2016, p. 225.

acknowledged that alongside the digital age, which is speeding up the process of globalization, traditional means of resolving disputes, mostly concerning arbitration have been adjusted to the new reality. One must note that innovative applications and technologies (i.e. ICTs) have been already incorporated into arbitral proceedings. In addition, the wholly virtualized or even digitized arbitral proceedings may be handled in the foreseeable future. Even though these solutions are interesting and worth watching, such use and integration of ICTs in arbitral proceedings also require some changes, most notably concerning new mandatory regulations and legal requirements not only at the national States level but also international one. Practically, the use of new technologies challenges the seat of arbitration or even place(s) of recognition and enforcement of arbitral awards.[18]

Indeed, it is noteworthy that disputes nowadays are becoming more international and even complex. Additionally, they involve multiparty proceedings. To decrease the excessive duration of the arbitral proceedings alongside related costs, information technologies (IT) are needed to tackle these problems. Although there are many obvious advantages of using IT in arbitration, some arbitrators are sceptical towards such new-innovation-driven technologies because of possible violations of procedural rights while using these IT tools. In fact, notwithstanding such an attitude, the use of new technologies seems to be inevitable. Therefore, the way of solving disputes throughout the arbitral proceedings would be changed as well.[19]

The COVID-19 pandemic paved the way for considering alternative mechanisms to settle disputes in an efficient, timely and cost-effective way. In fact, the current crisis also led to many changes in business relationships and the renegotiation of contracts to find amicable methods of dispute resolution. Considering international arbitration, the COVID-19 pandemic sped up the process of finding innovative ways of solving disputes based on the use of new technologies. As a result, many arbitral institutions worldwide adopted guidelines and tools to allow remote hearings. In addition, they also entered into more close collaborations and thirteen arbitral institutions even issued the so-called Joint Statement on Arbitration and COVID-19.

---

18 M.S. Abdel Wahab, E. Katsh, *Revolutionizing Technologies and the Use of Technology in International Arbitration: Innovation, Legitimacy, Prospects and Challenges* [in:] *Arbitration in the Digital Age: The Brave New World of Arbitration*, ed. M. Piers, C. Aschauer, Cambridge University Press 2018, p. 43.

19 G. Kaufmann-Kohler, T. Schulz, *The Use of Information Technology in Arbitration* (December 5, 2005), JusLetter, December 2005, pp. 3–4, available at SSRN: https://ssrn.com/abstract=924878. Access on 11.03.2023.

At the outset, it is noteworthy to explain threefold interactions between technology and dispute resolution mechanism (with a special focus on arbitration). Such an interaction is not even a question of the future, but it is happening nowadays. This begs the question of how to integrate such technology into arbitration to make it better. There is no doubt that technology will change the arbitration itself and the way we arbitrate. The directions of possible changes and improvements belong to the international arbitration community which is entitled to decide on how this happens. Although the international community was always much more concerned about the efficiency of the arbitral proceedings and the overall quality of arbitration, there is a new trend focusing on the optimization of such proceedings. Therefore, some stakeholders also pay attention to the duration and costs of arbitration alongside the transparency and predictability of such factors. This entails the new challenge of how technology could be used to achieve these goals.[20]

The first interaction requires that the parties and arbitrators make use of innovation-driven technologies, including online and electronic tools for the sake of supporting the entire arbitral proceedings. Given this solution, both costs and time are saved due to communication held merely through emails and online submissions. The parties concerned have access to online platforms or even "drop boxes" where they can easily upload the relevant documents. Furthermore, it is worth adding that procedural hearings have been more often conducted via telephone or videoconference, whereas witness hearings or hearings on the merits are still handled in a traditional physical way. On the one hand, this kind of hearing requires advance planning and significantly impacts the costs of the entire arbitral proceedings. This also begs the question of whether these traditional hearings would change into remote ones. If so, how these new changes would impact the principles of fairness and due process in arbitration? In fact, such innovation-driven technologies and changes should comply with the already existing standards in handling arbitral proceedings and therefore such tools could also be in line with the security standards.[21]

The second interaction refers to the full development of online dispute resolution mechanisms. Given this perspective, it is necessary to launch and

20 M. Piers, C. Aschauer, *Foreword* [in:] *Arbitration in the Digital Age. The Brave New World of Arbitration*, eds. M. Piers, C. Aschauer, Cambridge 2018, p. IX.

21 *Ibidem*, p. IX. See more: H. Alessa, *The role of Artificial Intelligence in Online dispute Resolution: A brief and critical overview*, "Information & Communications Technology Law" 2022, Vol. 31, issue 3, pp. 319–342.

use platforms dedicated to Online Dispute Resolution (ODR).[22] ODR systems could probably become a landmark in the digital revolution.[23] Hence, online arbitration has the aim to handle a dispute likewise in a traditional arbitral tribunal. This means that the arbitral award rendered by the tribunal is binding upon the parties. In addition, such an award is also enforceable, unless challenged by the parties and overruled by court.[24] It is noteworthy that at the beginning the out-of-court dispute settlement mechanisms were classified as alternative dispute resolution (ADR). One of the features of ADR requires that "they depart from the absolute application of the provisions pertaining to a specific normative system in favour of equitable forms of resolving conflicts between the parties".[25] Compared to traditional court litigation, arbitration is much more flexible and gives the parties the opportunity to select arbitrators, and methods of submitting and receiving pieces of evidence, among others.[26] ODR is widely considered to be a form of ADR. Therefore, a dispute is settled through arbitration, mediation, or conciliation.

It is worth adding that ODR platforms are widely available and there are multifarious shapes and sizes of them. They can also serve different purposes to handle disputes. Indeed, the ODR platforms ensure a relatively simple, fast, flexible, and efficient way to solve disputes. Despite these positive aspects of ODR platforms, there are some challenges ahead. One of the pressing questions concerns how to properly ensure that the fundamental principles of arbitral proceedings are preserved. It is noteworthy that the ODR platforms could meet the requirements concerning the following principles, namely fairness, due process, transparency, accountability, independence, impartiality, efficiency, and effectiveness.[27]

Currently, the ODR platforms are widely used in cases of low-value transactions which are mostly far away from traditional court litigation. It seems to

22 *Ibidem.*

23 It is worth adding that first electronic courts were launched in Japan and Poland, respectively. These courts are based upon blockchain technologies. To illustrate, the so-called "blockchain arbitration court" functions within the Polish Chamber of Commerce for Blockchain and New Technologies. Given its features, this arbitral tribunal has the aim to "provide an efficient, fast and industry-specific way of binding dispute resolution". See: *The Arbitration Court of the Blockchain and New Technologies Chamber of Commerce*, https://www.blockchaintribunal.org/. Accessed on 05.01.2023.

24 P. Polański, J. Gołaczyński, *Online Dispute Resolution and the Form of an Arbitration Agreement*, , [in:] *Internet and New Technologies Law. Perspectives and Challenges*, eds. D. Szostek, M. Załucki, Nomos 2021, p. 209.

25 *Ibidem*, p. 210.

26 *Ibidem.*

27 M. Piers, C. Aschauer, *Foreword ...*, p. x.

be an interesting solution to cross-border e-commerce disputes. To illustrate, the European Union introduced the first ODR platforms for consumers in 2015 as a kind of a trial. As already mentioned, the ODR platforms provide multiple ways of dispute resolution, including three stages such as negotiation, facilitated settlement and adjudication. Therefore, the ODR proceedings begin with a notice of claim made via an ODR platform. The next step concerns a technology-enabled negotiation, most notably in the form of a double-blind bidding or visual-blind bidding. Given this stage, an algorithm would be responsible for either generating some suggestions or even automatically settling a monetary claim provided that the parties' proposal/offer complies with the range of agreements accepted by them. The result would be obtained within a certain time limit and further, the ODR system starts the facilitated settlement procedure. Hence, the ODR administrator is responsible for appointing a neutral intermediary for the sake of communicating with the parties to settle disputes. In case of no consensus between the parties, the next stage begins with the dispute resolution mechanism, namely arbitration, third-party binding decision or expert determination, among others. One could even say that the final stage resembles the traditional adjudication held by a judge, an arbitrator, or an expert. This entails that this stage requires a human being to handle disputes, that is to weigh the arguments of each party and to issue a decision based on thereof.[28]

The third interaction concerns the use of artificial intelligence (AI) in arbitration. Therefore, one must note that "data mining is gradually finding its way into the field of law. Systems exist whereby case law and doctrine are selected out of huge databases in order to generate a first opinion on a question of law. And just around the corner are systems which learn and therefore create such opinions themselves in order to solve legal issues".[29] Even if the use of AI seems to be very interesting and innovative, many new questions arise as a result of such new technologies. For instance, how strongly will we rely on the decision suggested by the AI-based software compared to decisions made by an arbitrator? Will such innovations influence the distinction between AI arbitration and human arbitration contrary to the currently existing difference between institutional and *ad hoc* arbitration? (discussed further).[30]

Finally, it is worth adding that the technology itself should not be considered as a menace to arbitration, but rather a challenge to make it better. As such, the concept of the "Fourth Party" emerged. One must note that "Fourth

28 *Ibidem*.
29 *Ibidem*, p. XI.
30 *Ibidem*.

Party" represents technology as "something that is an influence on the process of communication and negotiation, something that adds value to the Third Party [i.e. the mediator or the arbitrator], something that typically does not replace the Third Party but can displace her, in the sense that the Third Party operates with an ally or assistant alongside".[31] In the case of ODR mechanisms, the effectiveness of the Fourth Party stems from the synergetic relationship between the efficiency of the Internet itself and the transformative effect that computers can have on humans, most notably in terms of communication.[32]

4 Notion of Digitalization

The term "digitalization" has become a buzzword commonly applied to describe different changes linked to the use of modern information and communication technologies (ICT). Even if the term itself has not been well defined thus far, digitalization is mostly used to clarify transformation towards a post-industrial information society.[33] Therefore, "digitalization" is understood in terms of various changes linked to ICT which appear in society. This notion is mostly used to describe some small-scale shifts concerning working methods alongside business models and large-scale disruptions within industries and societies. The latter meaning considers the transformation aiming at a post-industrial information society.[34]

One could even say that "digitalization" includes multifarious types of activities undertaken for the sake of enhancing the use of computer technologies and the Internet. As such, "digitalization" means the enlargement of different services throughout the Internet and the conversion of traditional paper-based documents into digital ones.[35]

New technologies impact not only the lives of every human being but also international courts and broadly speaking international dispute resolution mechanisms. It should be stressed, however, that courts are widely recognized as core public institutions. This means that they should implement such new

---

31 D. Protopsaltou, T. Schultz, N. Magnenat-Thalmann, *Taking the Fourth Party further? Considering a shared virtual workspace for arbitration*, "Information & Communications Technology Law" 2006, Vol. 15, issue 2, p. 158.

32 *Ibidem*.

33 R. Koulu, *Law, Technology and Dispute Resolution. Privatisation of Coercion*, New York 2019, p. 40.

34 *Ibidem*, p. 40.

35 W. Pfadt, *Cyfryzacja* [in:] *Leksykon prawa nowych technologii. 100 podstawowych pojęć*, ed. A. Krasulski, Warszawa 2021, p. 31.

technologies in law and legal practice responsibly. In fact, on the one hand, such a stance refers to the appropriate focus on problem-solving and the facilitation of court proceedings in a relatively quick and unexpensive way. On the other hand, such innovation-driven technologies should also ensure the human character of the courts.[36]

At the outset, it is noteworthy that courts are human institutions. This entails that people create courts. In addition, courts should also fulfil their primary role as public governmental power, that is judicial power. Given such a theory, judicial power is considered a manifestation of equality before the law, impartiality (including substantive and apparent) and the fair and appropriate determination of facts and laws, among others. By way of explanation, the statement "courts are human" means that they not only involve human reasoning but also emotion.[37]

Therefore, the notion of "online dispute resolution" (ODR) appeared as a result of ongoing technological changes. ODR stems from an online environment and was created in response to the vacuum concerning online disputes. There was no adequate authority to handle such cases. Therefore, ODR mechanisms had the aim to offer "new and better ways to resolve the disputes that arise in connection with [network] use".[38]

At the outset, the developer of ODR mechanisms sought to imitate the traditional ADR proceedings by providing online equivalents. Hence, a natural consequence of such actions was to "create an online mirror of the 'live' or offline process".[39] Nonetheless, it occurred relatively difficult to easily copy and transfer ADR mechanisms into an online setting. This led to the establishment of fully independent processes equipped with features dedicated solely to ODR mechanisms. It is noteworthy that these solutions differ significantly from the traditional dispute settlement methods. On the one hand, there is no face-to-face interaction. On the other hand, all disputes are automatically recorded online. Additionally, such online mechanisms are based on the intelligence of the machine. It should be stressed that many of these innovation-driven technologies faced challenges which were even seen as a kind of shortcomings. Currently, the former challenges are considered benefits. To illustrate, the lack of face-to-face interaction could be regarded as an advantage by employing asynchronous communication. Therefore, this solution ensures time to

---

36 J. Allsop Ao, *Technology and the future of the courts*, "University of Queensland Law Journal" 2019, Vol. 38, issue 1, p. 1.

37 *Ibidem*, p. 2.

38 E. Katsh, O. Rabinovich-Einy, *Digital justice*, Oxford 2017, p. 33.

39 *Ibidem*, p. 33.

consult and conduct research prior to replying. Some concerns regarding privacy issues based on documentation could be useful in terms of quality control along with dispute prevention efforts. Lastly, the intelligence of the machine could also lead to better and increased efficiency achieved thanks to automation. Therefore, ODR mechanisms could help to handle an increasing number of relatively small-scale disputes.[40]

5 Types of International Dispute Resolution

Arbitration as a dispute resolution mechanism was used for hundreds of years. This mechanism of dispute settlement is rooted mostly in international and commercial contexts. By way of explanation, arbitration means an institution which is based upon an agreement reached between the two parties concerned.[41] Therefore, arbitration itself refers to the proceedings where the dispute is handled by a third independent and neutral entity. Overall, one could even say that such an arbitrator has no active role in view of assisting the parties in the course of the proceedings. This entails that the arbitrator solely conducts hearings and following the facts proved in a certain case issues an arbitral award.[42] The arbitrator plays a role likewise a judge in a typical litigation proceeding in court.[43]

It should be stressed that the COVID-19 pandemic significantly affected the dispute resolution landscape. Both courts and arbitral institutions had to accommodate some pandemic-related measures for the sake of ensuring social distancing. In addition, these measures also aimed at facilitating remote hearings to constantly handle arbitral disputes. Interestingly, international arbitration was much more flexible to parties compared to national courts worldwide. The chief feature of arbitral proceedings, namely the party autonomy, was of crucial significance for fostering a spirit of compromise. It is worth adding that, in the case of international arbitration, both virtual and remote

40 *Ibidem.*

41 *Online arbitration. Club des jurists report. Working group chaired by Thomas Clay, Professor at the Faculty of Law at the Sorbonne (Paris-I University)*, Paris 2019, p. 6. See more about the history of arbitration: D. Centner, M. Ford, *A Brief Primer on the history of arbitration*, [in:] *Arbitration and the surety*, eds. A. Belleau, L. McGrew Brewer, L.P. Jortner, M. Oertel, Chicago 2020, pp. 1–9.

42 D. Carneiro, P. Novais, J. Neves, *Conflict Resolution and its Context. From the Analysis of Behavioural Patterns to Efficient Decision-Making*, "Law, Governance and Technology Series" Vol. 18, Series Editors: P. Casanovas, G. Sartor, Springer 2014, p. 26.

43 *Ibidem*, p. 27.

proceedings have been already present before the spread of the COVID-19 pandemic. Therefore, several procedural hearings have been conducted remotely through telephone conferencing or even specially dedicated online platforms. Given these solutions, it was possible to accommodate participants stemming from different countries and locations along with decreasing costs and time limitations.[44]

5.1 *International Commercial Arbitration*

In international commercial arbitration, the disputing parties seek the assistance of an impartial and independent third party.[45] In the context of modern era, the Montevideo Convention from 1889 signed by different Latin American states was considered the first international commercial arbitration treaty. Similarly to other efforts undertaken in the field of international arbitration, there were merely a few signatories to this convention and thus limited practical impact of this international instrument. Nevertheless, this convention is widely considered a landmark and an initial step in the development of international commercial arbitration framework. In the wake of this Convention, the 1899 Hague Convention on the Pacific Settlement of Disputes and the 1907 Hague Convention on the Pacific Settlement of International Disputes were adopted. Indeed, "it remained, however, for later developments, in the 1920's, to lay the foundations of the contemporary legal framework for international commercial arbitration".[46]

5.1.1 Geneva Protocol

Through the development of businesses in the first decades of the 20th century, there was a need for legislation which could allow the use of arbitration in handling both domestic and international commercial cases. Therefore, arbitration was seen as not only reliable but also effective and fair mechanisms in the context of international disputes. As such, within the framework of newly established International Chamber of Commerce in 1923, major trading nations concluded the so-called Geneva Protocol on Arbitration Clauses in Commercial Matters. One must stress that this Protocol, albeit underappreciated, contributed significantly to the advancement in terms of contemporary

44 B. Hatami Alamdari, *The Question of Remote Hearings in International Commercial Arbitration*, [in:] *The Impact of Covid on International Disputes*, eds. S. Lalani, S.G. Shapiro, "International and Comparative Business Law and Public Policy" Vol. 2, Leiden-Boston 2022, p. 141.

45 See: D. Carneiro, P. Novais, J. Neves, *Conflict Resolution and its Context. From the Analysis of Behavioural Patterns to Efficient Decision-Making*, Cham 2014, p. 26.

46 G. Born, *International Commercial Arbitration*, Wolters Kluwer 2019, p. 58.

international commercial arbitration law. Therefore, this Protocol is widely seen as a common ground for modern international arbitration process given which Contracting States have to recognized, although imperfectly, the enforceability of both international arbitration agreements and awards. Likewise, this Protocol also played a crucial role in identifying the party autonomy to launch arbitral proceedings.[47]

In addition, it is noteworthy that the Geneva Protocol stated that:

> Each of the Contracting States recognizes the validity of an agreement whether relating to existing or future differences between parties subject respectively to the jurisdiction of different contracting states by which the parties to a contract agree to submit to arbitration all or any differences that may arise in connection with such contract relating to commercial matters or to any other matter capable of settlement by arbitration, whether or not the arbitration is to take place in a country to whose jurisdiction one of the parties is subject.[48]

This framework was supplemented by addition provision expressed in Article 4 of the Protocol. Therefore:

> The tribunals of the Contracting Parties, on being seized of a dispute regarding a contract made between persons to whom Article 1 applies and including an arbitration agreement whether referring to present or future differences which is valid by virtue of the said article and capable of being carried into effect, shall refer the parties on the application of either of them to the decision of the arbitrators.[49]

Indeed, the provisions of the Geneva Protocol have already laid the grounds for developing principles of the contemporary international commercial law such as the presumptive validity of agreements to handle arbitration in the case of future disputes, the concept of handling commercial disputes and recognize international arbitral awards likewise the domestic ones, among others. These provisions are rooted even in the contemporary international commercial arbitration law.[50]

---

47 *Ibidem*, p. 59.

48 Geneva Protocol, Article 1.

49 *Ibidem*, Article 4.

50 G. Born, *International Commercial Arbitration ...*, p. 60.

5.1.2 Geneva Convention

In the wake of Geneva Protocol, the so-called Geneva Convention for the Execution of Foreign Arbitral Awards was adopted in 1927. Given the deficiencies of the Geneva's Protocol covering these issues, the latter Convention focuses on the enforceability of arbitral awards. Therefore, it required Contracting State to recognize and enforce "foreign" arbitral awards alongside forbid substantive judicial review of the merits of such awards. One must note, however, that this Convention "placed the burden of proof in recognition proceedings on the award-creditor, requiring it to demonstrate both the existence of a valid arbitration agreement, concerning an arbitrable subject matter, and that the arbitral proceedings had been conducted in accordance with the parties' agreement".[51]

Even though this Convention was not perfect, both Protocol and Convention are considered a landmark in shaping current legal framework for international commercial arbitration.

5.1.3 New York Convention

The chief aim of the New York Convention, adopted in 1958,[52] is to ensure the recognition and enforcement of arbitration agreements and awards. Indeed, through its remarkable effectiveness, this Convention has been positioned as a cornerstone and landmark in the development of international arbitration system, thereby safeguarding the stability of global contractual relationships. In addition, this Convention has a broader scope, namely the promotion of international trade through an efficient and unbiased mechanism for resolving disputes.[53] Therefore, it has been even designed to transcend geographical boundaries and strengthen the trustworthiness of contracts. One must note, however, that the United Nations (UN) played a crucial role in promoting the implementation of this Convention. It has been stressed by the UN Secretary-General who noted in 1998 that:

> This landmark instrument has many virtues. It has nourished respect for binding commitments, whether they have been entered into by private

51 *Ibidem*, pp. 61–62.

52 See: P. Sanders, *New York Convention on Recognition and Enforcement of Foreign Arbitral Awards*, "Netherlands International Law Review" 1959, Vol. 6, issue 1, pp. 43–59. DOI: https://doi.org/10.1017/S0165070X00027005

53 See more: A.H. Qureshi, *The World Trade Organization and the Promotion of Effective Dispute Resolution: In Times of a Trade War* [in:] *International Organizations and the Promotion of Effective Dispute Resolution. AIIB Yearbook of International Law 2019*, ed. P. Quayle, Gao Xuan, Leiden-Boston 2019, pp. 145–162.

> parties or governments. It has inspired confidence in the rule of law. And it has helped ensure fair treatment when disputes arise over contractual rights and obligations [...]. International trade thrives into cross-border commercial transactions or make international investments.[54]

5.1.4 UNCITRAL Model Law

International commercial arbitration is defined as "a means by which international business disputes can be definitively resolved, pursuant to the parties' agreement, by independent, non-governmental decision-makers, selected by or for the parties. Applying neutral judicial procedures that provide the parties an opportunity to be heard".[55]

UNICTRAL Model Law on International Commercial Arbitration was adopted in 1985 with amendments in 2006. The UNCITRAL Model Law aims to aid countries in updating and modernizing their legislation in view of the procedural aspects of international commercial arbitration. It should be noted that when the UNCITRAL Model Law was adopted, there was no need for a new unifying or harmonizing convention. Instead, the international community decided to follow the trends of the time. Therefore, the idea was to adopt more flexible solutions, which would allow both individual preferences and the needs of the addressees to be taken into account (so-called soft law). It should be added that although the UNCITRAL Model Law is not formally binding on individual states, it plays an important role in international commercial arbitration. It represents a model standardization of the fundamental legal issues in international commercial arbitration. As such, it should serve as a guide for national legislators when codifying or reforming existing arbitration laws (discussed further).[56]

5.1.5 Delocalized Arbitration

One must note that international commercial arbitration is an effective tool in terms of preventing business loses. Through the so-called delocalization, parties have more freedom from local and national legal systems. Therefore, they can in some kind ignore the procedural legal protections stemming from the national laws. As such, international commercial arbitration is not linked to any specific jurisdiction. In addition, according to the 1958 New York Convention,

54 M. Paulsson, *The 1958 New York Convention in Action*, New York 2016, pp. 117–134.

55 G. Born, *International Commercial Arbitration ...*, pp. 64–65.

56 M. Łągiewska, *Prawo arbitrażowe Chińskiej Republiki Ludowej na tle ustawy modelowej UNCITRAL o międzynarodowym arbitrażu handlowym – zagadnienia wybrane*, „Folia Iuridica Universitatis Wratislaviensis" 2023, Vol. 12(1), pp. 50–51.

courts which function in the background have the aim to both recognize and enforce arbitral awards. Nonetheless, despite such independence, "it is argued that there is the need for national courts interference in international commercial arbitration to make certain justice is meted out".[57] Besides, Georgios I. Zekos even stresses that the arbitral tribunal is deemed to decide all issues for the sake of ensuring an effective dispute resolution method. Given that, instead of two ineffective systems, exists one which is well equipped and thus well-functioning.[58]

The effectiveness of such a system results from the applicability of the rule of delocalized arbitration in AI arbitration and e-arbitration. Such a delocalized arbitration stems from the agreement concluded by the parties. Both the general principles of commercial arbitration and related procedure still apply in the case of delocalized arbitration. Likewise, it is bound by international conventions.[59] Lastly, it is noteworthy that:

> Delocalized arbitration goes to the root of the arbitration process as the autonomy of parties is the sole reason behind arbitration. Without allowing parties to decide which procedural rules will be applicable, there will be no purpose left behind in the arbitration. In modern times, when e-arbitration and other forms of technologically advanced arbitration have come to the fore, delocalized arbitration is the need of the hour.[60]

5.2 *International Investment Arbitration*

International investment arbitration refers to dispute resolution settlement involving different states. This entails that the so-called "investor-State arbitration" concern a dispute resolution mechanism given which a foreign investor may file a case in its own name against the host State. The entire process is handled by an adjudicatory body which holds a position of an arbitral tribunal such as the ICSID or UNCITRAL arbitration.[61]

---

57 G.I. Zekos, *Advanced Artificial Intelligence and Robo-Justice*, Cham 2022, p. 322.

58 See more: G.I. Zekos, *Development on courts' involvement in arbitration. Volume 1: the rule of law*, New York 2019; G.I. Zekos, *Development on courts' involvement in arbitration. Volume 2: the rule of law*, New York 2019.

59 C. Ceil, *Theory of Delocalization in International Commercial Arbitration*, available at SSRN: https://papers.ssrn.com/sol3/papers.cfm?abstract_id=3521053., pp. 5–6.

60 *Ibidem*, p. 12.

61 G. Kauflmann-Kohler, M. Potestà, *Special Issue: Investor-State Dispute Settlement and National Courts. Current Framework and Reform Options. European Yearbook of International Economic Law*, Springer 2020, p. 5.

The current legal framework for international investment arbitration is based on the ICSID Convention along with the first BITs from the 1960s. Indeed, the ICSID Convention was adopted in 1965 under the auspices of the World Bank. Therefore, this Convention provides twofold dispute resolution mechanisms, namely conciliation and arbitration. These mechanisms can be used either by foreign investors or host States. Given the arbitration rules included therein, "the ICSID Convention allows a Contracting Party and a national of another Contracting Party (thus, to the exclusion of domestic investors) to settle their disputes arising out of an investment through arbitration, provided the parties have separately consented to it".[62]

This entails that the 1965 ICSID Convention requires the so-called "dual-consent". As such, according to the Preamble, "no Contracting State shall by the mere fact of its ratification, acceptance or approval of this Convention and without its consent be deemed to be under any obligation to submit any particular dispute to conciliation or arbitration".[63]

5.3 *International Commercial Mediation*

The term mediation is commonly deemed ambiguous in definition and scope. It should be noted that it falls under the broader concept of alternative dispute resolution (ADR). Due to changing circumstances, a more comprehensive approach is necessary to address ADR mechanisms. Notably, there are concerns regarding the limited familiarity with mediation within the business sector. Furthermore, numerous solicitors do not recommend this method of resolving international disputes to their clients. Consequently, it leads to a comparatively low degree of trust in mediation processes. Thus, enhancements are necessary. This raises the issue of whether public authorities should make use of mediation procedures for commercial disputes a requirement.[64]

Mediation has a longstanding cultural and historical significance, offering unique advantages over ADR methods. The process is based on the parties' cooperation, facilitated by an impartial mediator who possesses no authority to dictate or offer advice on the final outcome. With its distinct features like adaptable, self-governing, and informal procedures, mediation is highly

---

62 *Ibidem*, p. 12. See more: Liang Wenwen, *The World Bank and the Creation of the International Center for Settlement of Investment Disputes: Legality and Legitimacy* [in:] *International Organizations and the Promotion of Effective Dispute Resolution. AIIB Yearbook of International Law 2019*, ed. P. Quayle, Gao Xuan, Leiden-Boston 2019, pp. 103–120.

63 ICSID Convention, https://icsid.worldbank.org/sites/default/files/ICSID_Convention_EN.pdf. Accessed on 12.05.2024.

64 K.F. Gómez, *The Role of Mediation in International Commercial Disputes. Reflections on some Technological, Ethical, and Educational Challenges* [in:] *Mediation in International Commercial and Investment Disputes*, ed. C. Titi, K.F. Gómez, Oxford 2019, pp. 4–6.

attractive to commercial disputants on an international scale. The mediation process must prioritize the parties' consent in every stage, from initiation to organization and mediator selection. This ensures that the parties retain complete control throughout the entire process, and they can withdraw from mediation if they become displeased with the ongoing procedures. Substantial party autonomy is essential to the numerous advantages of this ADR mechanism. Tailored and informal mediation procedures offer an efficient and cost-effective way to resolve disputes. It is important to note that a clear and logical structure, precise word choice, grammatical correctness, and objectivity should be maintained throughout the writing. They also help maintain relationships between the disputing parties, as the remedies and outcomes are flexible and considerate.[65]

Throughout the development of blockchain technology, numerous legal disputes have arisen. It is significant to note that such disputes are characterized by unique features relating to commercial contracts. Considering the specifics of these disputes, offline mediation is not an optimal solution. There is a developing approach to tackle such problems through dispute resolution platforms such as the Decentralized Arbitration and Mediation Network (DAMN) and new protocols released by conventional ADR providers, notably JAMS. Consequently, it is essential to use „smart ADR mechanisms", including mediation, to address difficulties linked to „smart contracts".[66] International commercial mediation has greater potential compared to non-jurisdictional e-initiatives and innovative software options.[67]

The Singapore Mediation Convention (SMC) primarily deals with achieving final settlement agreements for international commercial disputes through mediation. Voluntarily made pre-mediation agreements are excluded, but it is not beyond a state's right to make them legally binding according to their domestic laws. This approach acknowledges mediation's voluntary nature and its ability to facilitate negotiations. One must note, however, that the mediation process emphasizes the importance of voluntary participation, as compulsory mediation is often less effective. In addition, in the mediation setting, these pre-mediation agreements are considered contracts, whereby the parties agree in good faith but are not legally obliged to engage in mediation.[68]

---

65 Chen Meng, *The Reforming Chinese Chapter of International Dispute Resolution under the Belt and Road Initiative*, "The Pacific Review" 2021, vol. 34, no. 3, https://doi.org/10.1080/09512748.2019.1677749, p. 477.

66 K.F. Gómez, *The Role of Mediation ...*, p. 9.

67 *Ibidem.*

68 Yun Zhao, *The Singapore mediation convention: A version of the New York convention for mediation?*, "Journal of Private International Law" 2021, Vol. 17, issue 3, p. 541.

It is important to note that the Singapore Mediation Convention (SMC) applies to international mediated settlement agreements in commercial disputes. An agreement is considered international if the businesses of the parties are located in different countries, or if the state in which their businesses are located differs from the state in which a significant portion of the obligations under the settlement agreement is most closely linked.[69]

It is worth noting that the term „commercial" has not been defined in the Singapore Mediation Convention. As a result, this term varies depending on the regulations associated with individual domestic regimes. Despite the lack of an explicit definition, it should be understood broadly. Furthermore, it is interesting to note that the SMC does not provide a legal definition of mediation. Given that, the mediation can be understood as either evaluative or facilitative. Thus, this choice does not affect the application of the SMC as long as there is proof that the settlement agreement resulted from mediation.[70]

5.4 *International Negotiation*

Negotiation is widely considered the least formal method of settling commercial disputes. Parties involved prefer direct communication in order to achieve a mutually acceptable solution. Despite being unstructured, legislation regarding negotiation remains limited. The success of the parties relies solely on their willingness to negotiate, leaving no other factors at play. On one hand, the negotiating parties are free to determine the course of the negotiation process. In doing so, information concerning the dispute remains confidential between the involved parties. On the other hand, an informal negotiation process may present challenges due to difficulties in direct communication. Such challenges can potentially reduce the likelihood of reaching an agreement during the negotiation. It could also be a consequence of an unrealistic perception of the strengths and weaknesses of the parties involved.[71]

6 Twofold Approaches to the Use of New Technologies in International Arbitration

Some scholars express their sceptical standpoint on the integration of new technologies in international arbitration. They even argue that such a process

69 United Nations Convention on International Settlement Agreements Resulting From Mediation (Singapore Mediation Convention), Article 1(1), https://uncitral.un.org/sites/uncitral.un.org/files/singapore_convention_eng.pdf. Accessed on 12.05.2024.

70 Yun Zhao, *The Singapore mediation convention ...*, p. 543.

71 T. Gaultier, *Cross-Border Mediation: A New Solution for International Commercial Dispute Settlement?*, "NYSBA International Law Practicum" 2013, Vol. 26, no. 1, p. 44.

will pose many new challenges ahead. Based on the key features of the arbitration proceedings, namely confidentiality and the private nature of international arbitration significantly limits available data for analysis. By contrast, others assert that international arbitration aligns with emerging technologies, including cryptocurrencies or "decentralized digital assets" given the "neutrality, cross-border enforceability and the flexibility to tailor specific arbitration rules".[72]

Therefore, there are twofold approaches to the use of new technologies within the framework of international arbitration. Given the first category, technological tools cannot play a crucial role and thus have an impact on the decision-making process or forecasting the outcome of legal or arbitral proceedings. Rather, such new technologies aim to streamline and optimize the efficiency of the arbitral workflow. To name a few, it refers to online signatures, electronic filing cases along with videoconferencing tools.[73]

The second category, in turn, encompasses tools that are designed not only to forecast but also to influence the outcome of arbitral proceedings (i.e. Context by LexisNexis, and Arbitrator Intelligence, among others). The latter has the aim "to increase transparency, accountability, and diversity in arbitrator selection by making key information about arbitrators' past decision-making more generally available through the publication of AI Reports".[74]

Briefly, one could even say that these two opposite approaches represent traditional and modern approaches to the use of new technologies in international arbitration. Indeed, the first one considers such use merely in terms of efficiency, whereas the second seeks to benefit from new technologies in the entire arbitral proceedings. In practice, there are no obstacles to making use of new technologies for the sake of smoothening the entire arbitral proceedings. Nevertheless, in the case of "business-to-business" international arbitrations, parties together with their lawyers are less likely to benefit from new technologies because of their highly risk-averse standpoint.[75]

Considering the second category, one must note that it has gained significant attention in recent times. Zhen Qin stresses that "having confidentiality as one of international arbitration's 'selling points' has imposed limitations on the accuracy of data analytics tools. Nevertheless, supporters of using data

---

72 Zhen Qin, *The Use of New Technologies in International Arbitration*, "The American Review of International Arbitration. Columbia Law School" 25.02.2019, https://aria.law.columbia.edu/the-use-of-new-technologies-in-international-arbitration/. Accessed on 20.06.2023.

73 *Ibidem.*

74 *Ibidem.*

75 *Ibidem.*

analytics in international arbitration have argued that we can still be confident in the small data samples available."[76]

7 Online Arbitration

The Internet together with Information Technology[77] has not only emerged but also evolved in a relatively short time. Therefore, due to these factors, globalization was even facilitated and accelerated. As a result, the new world of technology significantly impacted our lives, including the legal framework which is no exception at all. It is not even surprising bearing in mind that laws, jurisprudence, and legal systems of countries are available online.[78]

Technology started playing a much more important role in the case of dispute resolution mechanisms, mostly with regard to international commercial arbitration. There are, however, twofold problems concerning the use of such technologies. On the one hand, one could ask about the degree of such use of modern technologies (both tools and software applications). On the other hand, this also begs the question of what the balance between the human factor and the use of artificial intelligence (AI) in arbitral proceedings is.[79]

There are three types of ODR schemes based on innovative technologies which could be summarized as follows: 1. Technology-assisted ODR mechanisms; 2. Technology-based ODR mechanisms and 3. Technology-facilitated online dispute prevention (ODP) guarantees. The first one refers to a mechanism where the technology is limited merely to adequate and secure communication and information exchange. The second approach fully benefits from innovation-driven and even cutting-edge technologies to resolve disputes. The last one makes use of technology "to reduce the risk of potential e-disputes and incontrovertibly enhances trust and security in e-business".[80] Therefore, because of an increasing number of new technologies emerging, international

---

76 *Ibidem.*

77 See more: R. Susskind, D. Susskind, *Future of the Professions: How Technology Will Transform the Work of Human Experts*, Oxford 2015, pp. 145–187.

78 M.S. Abdel Wahab, E. Katsh, *Revolutionizing Technologies and the Use of Technology in International Arbitration: Innovation, Legitimacy, Prospects and Challenges* [in:] *Arbitration in the Digital Age: The Brave New World of Arbitration*, ed. M. Piers, C. Aschauer, Cambridge University Press 2018, p. 35.

79 *Ibidem*, p. 36.

80 *Ibidem*. Cf. M.A. Wahab, *The Global Information Society and Online Dispute Resolution: A New Dawn for Dispute Resolution*, "Journal of International Arbitration" 2004, Vol. 21, issue 2, pp. 167–168.

arbitration has also been affected by this new trend. Since the 1990s, there has been a significant shift towards a digital world which has also integrated and increased the use of technology in arbitration.[81] Nonetheless, this also begs the question of to what extent international arbitration has been affected by such cutting-edge technologies and how they have been integrated thus far.

Alongside the accessibility of data through the Internet, there is an increasing number of international commerce. Therefore, millions of transactions are held thanks to electronic communication. Nonetheless, disputes still arise, and they are still settled by arbitration proceedings. It is noteworthy to mention a few practical problems with the arbitration itself. To name a few, Carrington once shared his colleague's experience on international arbitration. The arbitrator had to travel more than 20 times from the US to Asia merely to hear witnesses. In addition, these witnesses also had to travel from different locations situated both in Asia and North America. As a result, such arbitration generated enormous costs of proceedings. The use of innovation-driven technologies such as means of teleconferencing could be easily adapted to arbitration. This entails, however, some practical problems related to cyberspace. Importantly, the legal framework for international arbitration has been launched far before the emergence of digital society.[82]

One could even say after Morek that "the major legal challenges faced by arbitration in online settlings do not depend on the 'origin' of a dispute".[83] As such, there is no practical matter whether the dispute itself concerns the Internet or e-commerce, or anything else. The question is whether the proceedings could be moved from the "real world" to the "virtual one" based on the content. This leads to twofold approaches and different models.

Given the first one, although the parties concluded a paper-based arbitration agreement, they opt for online arbitration[84] to reduce the costs of proceedings and secure expedient procedures. To address this practical problem, many arbitral institutions worldwide have already introduced special tools providing an opportunity to file a case online and administrate it in such a way. This entails that any dispute could be easily handled fully or partially via means of a "virtual world".[85]

81 *Ibidem*, p. 36.

82 S. Halla, *Arbitration going online - new challenges in 21st Century?*, "Masaryk University Journal of Law and Technology" 2011, Vol. 5, issue 2, p. 216.

83 *Ibidem*, p. 217.

84 See more: F.F. Wang, *Online arbitration*, Routledge 2018.

85 S. Halla, *Arbitration going online...*, p. 217.

The second approach refers to the situation when the contract is concluded online via the exchange of emails. Therefore, the arbitration clause is also included in such a contract.[86]

Therefore, this begs the question of whether such an arbitration agreement included in the exchange of emails or even standard terms of "click-wrap" contracts is valid. What are the requirements related to the guarantee of due process and equal treatment of parties[87] while handline proceedings online? These questions will be answered in the following sections of the book. Overall, it is worth adding that online arbitration can apply in the case of online disputes and offline disputes. Recently, this type of arbitration has been used mostly in e-commerce disputes.

8 Conclusion

This chapter explained the conceptual framework that will be used in the work, as well as the organization of such terminology. This chapter demonstrated that law, as a social science, is subject to many changes resulting from the use of new technologies. Therefore, it must somehow adapt to the new reality. "Law and technology" is a relatively new phenomenon that arises from ongoing globalization and innovative changes. Nonetheless, it is important to note that this relationship, although seemingly straightforward, is an extremely complex phenomenon in practice. It is worth mentioning, for example, the law-making process, which is relatively slow and lengthy compared to the pace of technological development. In practice, this leads to a deepening gap between technological innovations and legal changes.

The COVID-19 pandemic has contributed to even faster changes driven by the health crisis. Considering the need to ensure social distancing, it was necessary to adopt solutions that would limit face-to-face meetings in favour of online proceedings. As a result, new technologies have been significantly used in international dispute resolution. Furthermore, new technologies already offer the possibility of transferring the entire proceedings to the digital world. Nonetheless, opinions on this matter are divided.

86 *Ibidem.*

87 See more: D. Fernández Arroyo, B. Sousa Rodrigues, *An Arbitrator's Perspective: Between Equal Treatment and the Good Administration of Transnational Justice in Online Arbitration* [in:] *Online Dispute Resolution. New Challenges*, ed. D. Moura Vicente, E. Dias Oliveira, J. Gomes de Almeida, Baden-Baden 2022, pp. 37–58.

On one hand, the more traditional environment advocates for the use of such technologies, as long as they improve the efficiency of proceedings and reduce costs. On the other hand, some see new technologies as the future and would like to adapt new technological solutions to the widest possible extent in international dispute resolution. This is evidenced, for example, by the development of new concepts such as online dispute resolution and online arbitration, which already provide such possibilities. However, it should be emphasized despite the increasing presence of new technologies in dispute resolution, there is currently a lack of international legal frameworks to cover these issues thus far.

CHAPTER 2

New Technologies in Arbitral Tribunals: An Overview

1 Introduction

This chapter discusses the incorporation of new technologies in arbitral tribunals. It specifically focuses on the use of IT tools in prominent arbitration institutions such as the American Arbitration Association, the International Chamber of Commerce in Paris, WIPO in Geneva, SCC in Stockholm, E-Arbitration-T as a European solution, and ICSID.

These institutions are well-renown given their international presence and eagerly adopt innovative solutions for using modern platforms in dispute resolution. Further, this chapter seeks to answer what solutions within digitization and which new technologies have been adopted by arbitration tribunals. Therefore, it pays attention to the remote hearings and practical challenges related to this form of arbitral proceedings. Finally, it analyzes the significance of artificial intelligence in arbitral tribunals.

2 IT Tools in Arbitral Tribunals

Given the Latin paremia, *Judex non calculate*, which means that "the judge does not calculate". One could even say that lawyers in general are not too familiar with mathematics. It should be stressed that information technology (IT) is underappreciated in legal contexts. IT is very often misunderstood, mistrusted, or even misused.[1] Despite some scepticism towards new technologies, technology itself became an immanent part of the future international arbitration. On the one hand, technology ensures paperless, cost-efficient, and relatively fast alternatives compared to traditional stages of international arbitral proceedings. This entails that both arbitrators and counsels should have basic technological competences along with awareness of cybersecurity and data protection issues. Such expectations are deemed based on the ongoing digitalization of the legal industry, including dispute resolution mechanisms

1 G. Kaufmann-Kohler, T. Schulz, *The Use of Information ...*, p. 6.

 | DOI:10.1163/9789004700710_004

in general and international arbitration in particular. Such changes should be in line with the existing requirements regarding the ethical obligations of arbitrators, mostly considering the confidentiality of arbitral proceedings and the arbitrator's duty of competence. On the one hand, it should be stressed, however, that the notion of "duty of competence" has not been defined and included in ethical codes thus far. On the other hand, there is a certain context resulting from the evolution of lawyer's ethics which requires an understanding of basic technologies and their role in this profession. This entails that lawyers, including arbitrators, are required to keep abreast of new innovation-driven technologies along with their benefits and risks.[2]

The use of IT in arbitration cannot be reduced merely to computers. This term refers to different actions, including the use of handheld devices (such as personal digital assets or smart phones), simple word processing, online legal research, billing software, shared calendaring, automated interest calculation, automated conflict of interest checking, e-mailing, videoconferencing, and more exotic technologies like 3D virtual reality".[3]

Therefore, it seems worthwhile to name the basic types of IT software which are used throughout the arbitral proceedings. Firstly, IT is helpful in terms of transmitting messages and files via electronic networks. To realize this function, emails, and web-based means, namely, web interfaces and bulletin boards can be used. Secondly, IT tools allow us to have meetings from afar. This means that given innovation-driven technologies, parties are allowed to take part in actual meetings online which can be handled throughout chat rooms, videoconferences, or even synchronous communications. Thirdly, IT helps to handle properly documents. To illustrate, IT is useful to search for specific words within documents and copy and paste some sections of the documents alongside the introduction of hyperlinks to link documents. Fourthly, IT enables the creation of new documents. It is certainly important given that the process of drafting an arbitral award is based upon the "copy-pastes" stemming from the parties' briefs and some documentary evidence. In addition, arbitrators from different locations can also collaborate while drafting an arbitral award thanks to the IT tools. Fifthly, the process of managing documents in electronic files is much easier compared to traditional paper-based documents. Sixthly, the IT tools also sped up the managing cases. For instance, the progress tracking

2 *Leveraging Technology for Fair, Effective and Efficient International Arbitration Proceedings*, "ICC Dispute Resolution Services, Commission on Arbitration and ADR", Paris 2022, p. 7, https://iccwbo.org/wp-content/uploads/sites/3/2022/02/icc-arbitration-and-adr-commission-report-on-leveraging-technology-for-fair-effective-and-efficient-international-arbitration-proceedings.pdf.

3 *Ibidem*, p. 8.

software exposes the stage of a given case alongside the next expected actions that should be undertaken and the deadline. Seventhly, thanks to IT tools, parties can easily virtually present arguments and facts by sharing some slideshows, video depositions and video presentations. These new ways of presenting stances are widely used in the course of arbitral proceedings. Indeed, such visual presentations are better remembered compared to purely traditional oral presentations. Lastly, IT also allows tracking of the virtual desktop. Hence, it is possible not only to record and store documents but also presentations, oral statements, videoconferencing exchanges, etc. On the one hand, this solution facilitates the process of handling disputes, on the other hand, it can lead to some violations concerning data. Anyone who has access to a computer can easily reproduce such data.[4]

2.1 *Online Filing System*

One of the most significant implications of the COVID-19 pandemic in international arbitration refers to the adoption of electronic-only submissions. Even though electronic submissions along with the electronic case management systems were widely applicable in many arbitral institutions worldwide, the COVID-19 pandemic even sped up the process. Therefore, the hard-copy submissions became "a matter of the past".[5] To illustrate, at the beginning of March 2020, arbitral institutions realized that the hard-copies requirements are highly influenced by quarantine and lockdowns as a result of the COVID-19 pandemic. The ICSID even stressed that it was "further steps to reduce reliance on paper-filings in its cases". Therefore, the ICSID required "only an electronic copy of a request for arbitration ... and any accompanying documents".[6] Furthermore, ICSID "encourage[d] parties to submit all written submissions ... electronically," with arbitrators "also encouraged to use electronic copies of case-related documents".[7] It is worth mentioning the statement by the ICSID Secretary-General Meg Kinnear who said that "given the state of information technology – and the ease with participants in ICSID cases have adapted to online file sharing in recent years – it made sense to make electronic filing the norm".[8]

4 *Ibidem*, p. 9.

5 K.M. Young, J.A. Ivers, K. Schroeder, *The Impact of Covid-19 on International Arbitration Procedure*, [in:] *The Impact of Covid on International Disputes*, eds. S. Lalani, S.G. Shapiro, "International and Comparative Business Law and Public Policy" Vol. 2, Leiden-Boston 2022, p. 86.

6 "ICSID Makes Electronic Filing its Default Procedure," ICSID, last modified March 16, 2020, https://icsid.worldbank.org/news-and-events/news-releases/icsid-makes-electronic-filing-its-default-procedure. Accessed 12.05.2024.

7 *Ibidem*.

8 *Ibidem*.

Considering the request for arbitration, prior to the outbreak of the COVID-19 pandemic, most arbitration rules required the submission of hard copies. To illustrate, according to the Article 23 of the International Centre of Investment Disputes (ICSID) Arbitration Rules, "every request … shall be filed in the form of a signed original accompanied by the following number of additional copies: (a) before the number of members of the Tribunal has been determined: five; (b) after the number of members of the Tribunal has been determined: two more than the number of its members."[9]

Nonetheless, it should be stressed that other arbitral institutions, including the Hong Kong International Arbitration Centre (HKIAC), the London Court of International Arbitration (LCIA), the Singapore International Arbitration Centre (SIAC), the World Intellectual Property Organization (WIPO), among others, allow to submit the request for arbitration both in electronic and hand-copies.[10]

It is worth analyzing different solutions adopted by leading arbitral tribunals.

2.1.1 AAA-ICDR

The AAA-ICDR (American Arbitration Association – International Centre for Dispute Resolution) is widely recognized as a secure online platform which allows parties to handle their case online. It provides a solution to manage every aspect of the case-related documents through the AAA-ICDR. In addition, panellists can easily follow their cases online and access necessary information. The so-called Case Shield, developed and introduced by AAA-ICDR, is a cloud-based virtual desktop solution which has been designed to provide arbitrators and mediators with a "uniform, secure, and easy-to-use environment to manage their case".[11] Indeed, this tool ensures enhanced protection in terms of cybersecurity issues. Therefore, more advanced mechanisms have been introduced to prevent phishing attempts, ransomware, problems with access control, passwords, encryption, along with patch management. Case Shield also offers disaster recovery in case of lost, damaged, or stolen computers. This tool is accessible from any location for most computers' marks and models.[12]

Another tool developed by AAA is known as AAA WebFile. Given this tool, individuals involved either in AAA or ICDR cases can securely manage every

9 ICSID Arbitration Rules, Rule 23; see also ICSID (Additional Facility) Arbitration Rules, Article 3(3) ("The request shall be accompanied by five additional signed copies …").

10 K.M. Young, J.A. Ivers, K. Schroeder, *The Impact of Covid-19 …*, p. 87.

11 *AAA-ICDR Technology Services*, "American Arbitration Association", https://www.adr.org/TechnologyServices/aaa-icdr-software-and-online-tools. Accessed on 11.06.2023.

12 *CaseShield. Cyber threaths are on the rise. Is your case information safe?*, "American Arbitration Association", https://go.adr.org/Case-Shield. Accessed on 11.06.2023.

aspect of their case since the initial filing, through additional claims or counterclaims on existing cases and case-related financial functions. They can also upload, download, and review all case-related documents. Furthermore, parties can access the panellists' resumes and thus rank them for potential selection. Thanks to AAA WebFile, parties have access to the summary of case information, event calendar and all contacts related to a particular case.[13]

Recently, AAA WebFile provides a new type of service, namely Hearing Exhibits which is "an easy-to-use, accessible, and secure space for parties to upload their hearing exhibits for the arbitrator".[14] Given this tool, it is possible to minimize or even eliminate costly and time-consuming preparation of physical exhibits by uploading PDF files up to 75 MB and other file types up to 16 MB. As such, it also leads to the reduction of risks related to the process of sending flash drives or hard copies through email. In terms of security, AAA WebFile benefits from a next-generation firewall and the so-called 256-bit encryption.[15]

One must note that Hearing Exhibits are activated upon the parties' agreement to use this tool. Through access to this space, all the participants of proceedings (including parties and arbitrators) can view hearing exhibits. They can also upload multiple files simultaneously which can be seen in real time. In addition, once a file document is uploaded, participants are notified about this fact with an email.[16] The Hearing Exhibits also provide some special features for the parties. To name a few, it allows to designate documents as joint exhibits. It is also possible to filter and privately flag such exhibits.[17]

Another tool provided by the AAA-ICDR concern the Panelist eCenter. Indeed, this Center serves likewise AAA WebFile in the case of panellists. Therefore, it not only enables panellists to manage their cases online in a more efficient way but also offers multiple functionalities. Such functions can be summarized as follows: performing case-related financial tasks, submitting and monitoring payments and deposit requests, uploading, downloading, and reviewing case documents, creating, and fulfilling case-related tasks. The latter enables completing the online oath which is necessary in case of disclosure process when invited to serve on a specific case. Just like in AAA WebFile,

---

13 *AAA-ICDR Technology Services …*

14 *AAA WebFile. New Hearing Exhibits Feature*, "American Arbitration Association", https://www.adr.org/aaa-webfile-hearing-exhibits?utm_source=website-adr&utm_medium=tech-services-software-and-online-tools-page&utm_campaign=website_hearing-exhibits-webfile. Accessed on 11.06.2023.

15 *Ibidem.*

16 *Ibidem.*

17 *Ibidem.*

panellists have access to the summary of a case, and event calendar along with a comprehensive list of all contacts related to the case.[18]

Finally, AAA-ICDR introduced a tool supporting a successful draft of the dispute resolution clause. The so-called Clause Builder ensures guidance to parties on available options to properly customize the clause (in terms of arbitration, mediation, or arbitration-mediation) in cases of commercial, construction, employment, international, and healthcare disputes. Clause Builder offers a range of options such as the number and selection process of arbitrators, the extent of information exchange (involving the so-called eDiscovery options) along with the location of hearings, the possibility of documents-only proceedings, the form of the arbitral award, among others.[19]

2.1.2 ICC Case Connect

The International Chamber of Commerce (ICC) in Paris encourages parties to submit their application file electronically. To spur online filing, the ICC introduced the so-called ICC Case Connect which is a secure online case management system. ICC Case Connect is a new system launched in October 2022 with the aim of connecting parties, arbitral tribunals, and the ICC Secretariat. This system was launched for the sake of facilitating communication and document-sharing. Therefore, it provides a secure and dedicated online space available for all the parties concerned. Nonetheless, it should be noted that cases registered by October 2022 are managed by this system. Both the parties and arbitral tribunals can easily determine the extent to which they would like to benefit from this system. Furthermore, the system offers its service at no additional charge in case of arbitrations conducted by the ICC in Paris. Interestingly, although the ICC Case Connect is dedicated to handling new cases submitted to this arbitral tribunal, there are some exceptions to make use of it even for cases registered prior to October 2022. There are three situations when it is possible when: "(i) the case file has not yet been transferred to the arbitral tribunal, (ii) all participating parties to the arbitration agree to its usage and/ or (iii) where use of the platform will provide a clear benefit to the proceedings".[20]

Considering the procedure to submit a request via the ICC Case Connect, the Claimant's representative should first contact the administrative or support

18 *Ibidem.*

19 *Ibidem.*

20 *File your Request via ICC Case Connect*, "ICC International Court of Arbitration", https://iccwbo.org/dispute-resolution-services/arbitration/file-your-request-via-icc-case-connect/#case-before-2022. Accessed on 19.02.2023.

staff to create an ICC case Connect account. Further, they can complete the form online and thus upload the Request for arbitration. After payment of the filing fee, the ICC Court Secretariat will notify all the parties concerned about the requests. Interestingly, Claimants have even a choice to decide whether they prefer to notify respondents about the case electronically or in a traditional way through the delivery of hard copies.[21]

The Secretary General of the ICC International Court of Arbitration and the Director for ICC Dispute Resolution Services (DSR) stress that "The trusted technology offered by ICC Case Connect provides easy-to-use, secure file-sharing. By digitising ICC Arbitration processes and eliminating often repetitive administrative actions for each case, our goal is to increase operational efficiency for all involved".[22] In addition, it is noteworthy that this system has been introduced to achieve ICC goals concerning digital solutions.

2.1.3 WIPO eADR

WIPO eADR is also a case management system developed by the WIPO Center at no cost. This tool was introduced for the sake of facilitating communication in cases handled under the WIPO Mediation, Arbitration, Expedited Arbitration or Expert Determination Rules.

Firstly, given this system, both the parties and neutrals (including mediators, arbitrators and even experts) can easily share documents and access the relevant information on the case via a single and secure portal. This platform pays attention to security issues. For that reason, all information submitted to WIPO eADR is protected by the firewall and safely encrypted. To ensure better data protection, the users are requested to go through the authentication process upon submitting their username, password and one-time passcodes received on a mobile device. All the IT systems provided by WIPO have already been certified with ISO/IEC 27001 to comply with international standards on security.[23]

Secondly, the WIPO eADR is useful to provide parties and neutrals secure communications via an online docket. Interestingly, such communications are available in multifarious formats. To name a few, it is possible to upload stand-alone files into the system or a special hierarchical filing structure. Once

21 *Ibidem.*

22 *ICC launches ICC Case Connect: Secure online case management made easy*, "ICC International Court of Arbitration" 12.10.2022, https://iccwbo.org/media-wall/news-speeches/icc-launches-icc-case-connect-secure-online-case-management-made-easy/. Accessed on 19.02.2023.

23 *WIPO eADR*, "World Intellectual Property Organization", https://www.wipo.int/amc/en/eadr/wipoeadr/. Accessed on 19.02.2023.

a submission is made by any party involved, the other participants of the proceedings are notified through email alerts.

Thirdly, the platform provides a search facility which means that all communications are sortable and easily accessible through certain categories. It also allows you to make a free text search.

Fourthly, all users can send messages in a special "Message Board" and each person would be notified about it.

Fifthly, the WIPO eADR system provides the so-called case overview which includes basic information about the case itself such as case number, parties' names, status of the disputed case, type of dispute resolution clause, applicable law, and seat of arbitration, among others.

Finally, it is noteworthy that WIPO paid attention to cybersecurity issues while launching its online platform. Therefore, one could even say that confidentiality and data protection are the key issues therein. This means that all the WIPO cases are handled according to the confidentiality requirements provided by the WIPO Rules.[24] It should also be stressed that the WIPO Center pays attention to personal data processing while following the best international practices in this regard. To achieve this goal, WIPO complies with the Personal Data Protection and Privacy Principles that have been adopted by the United Nations High-Level Committee on Management in October 2018.[25]

2.1.4 SCC Platform

The Stockholm Chamber of Commerce (SCC) Platform was introduced in 2019 as a secure and easy-to-use cloud-based platform. It has the aim to facilitate all communication in disputed cases. Indeed, each new case has its own dedicated and secure workspace, namely the "case site" on the SCC Platform. This entails that all parties, legal representatives along with arbitrators and case administrators can access case-related documents and information at any time once needed. They merely need to log into their accounts. In addition, all parties can also upload, share, and print case materials such as procedural decisions, pleadings, and evidence. The SCC Platform was designed in such a way as to ensure not only a safe but also a streamlined process.[26]

The SCC platforms provide many different features, including a search function, a calendar to keep track of significant dates and deadlines in ongoing

24 *Ibidem.*

25 *Case Filing Guidelines*, "World Intellectual Property Organization", https://www.wipo.int/amc/en/arbitration/filing/#pd. Accessed on 19.02.2023.

26 *Case management*, "SCC Arbitration Institute" https://sccarbitrationinstitute.se/en/case-management. Accessed on 20.06.2023.

arbitral proceedings, the option to set reminders, a notice board which enables to share of practical information with the parties involved, and archiving capabilities. The latter is helpful to store procedural materials once the arbitral proceedings are fully completed. In addition, one of the main advantages of this platform is prompt and round-the-clock communication. Therefore, communication between parties, lawyers, and arbitrators is easier and more efficient. This is crucial in case of time zone differences as well as in situations when face-to-face meetings are importantly limited.[27]

It is also noteworthy that the SCC Platform pays attention to security and digital information-sharing during arbitral proceedings. Therefore, due to the implementation of such innovation-driven tools, the SCC Platform eliminates the necessity of relying on less secure methods, including emails or other means to transfer sensitive or large files. To ensure the highest level of protection in terms of security, the SCC Platform benefits from solutions adopted by HighQ which is a globally renowned provider of secure digital innovations in the legal industry.[28]

As such, cloud-based storage provides that all documents are stored therein within highly secure facilities. Interestingly, there are backup facilities in different locations which ensure redundancy. In addition, both primary and backup facilities are in Germany. Therefore, they ensure heightened security measures. To ensure the highest level of protection, all data pertaining to arbitral proceedings undergo special military-grade encryption. While uploading, each file undergoes scanning to detect any malware or viruses. The system itself benefits from multiple security measures such as "two-factor authentication, a single encrypted https entry point, web application firewalls, intrusion detection, log file monitoring, anti-virus, code scanning technologies, etc.".[29] Indeed, the system also provides solutions to minimize potential risks caused by human error. Such solutions are important given preserving both security and confidentiality.[30]

To sum up, given the features of the SCC Platform, it pays attention to cybersecurity issues and thus provides the best standard of services. Indeed, military-grade encryption along with regular scanning for the sake of detecting malware and viruses are necessary to ensure high-quality services and attract more parties to handle their case in the digital world.

27 *Ibidem.*
28 *Ibidem.*
29 *Ibidem.*
30 *Ibidem.*

2.1.5 E-Arbitration-T

E-Arbitration-T has been created as a modern online platform dedicated to supporting European arbitration and mediation centres. This tool has the aim to provide innovation-driven technologies such as applications, online networks, and integration systems along with online training services. E-Arbitration-T is widely recognized as a mechanism providing a reliable and alternative system for handling disputes. To illustrate, in the case of arbitration, this tool offers online services that are flexible and could easily adapt to diverse types of cases. In addition, this tool provides a certain level of security and confidentiality as well which are of crucial importance for the arbitral proceedings. These features are achieved thanks to the use of multimedia, including interactive text, and video conferencing tools, among others. Furthermore, throughout the ODR chain, all the parties concerned, namely claimants, respondents, arbitrators, translators, and experts could easily contact via this special channel. This means that the E-Arbitration-T tool also improves B2B relationships between different actors of arbitral proceedings via direct contact.

Therefore, E-Arbitration-T is a software system useful given large and small arbitration and mediation centres. It ensures cost-effective proceedings by making use of technological innovations. This means that this platform provides ADR tribunals with a certain set of applications to better control not only procedures and operations but also case management. Practically, E-Arbitration-T has the aim to provide electronic support in case of automation of ADR procedures (by introducing an intelligent case management system), track the documents and evidence submitted, and ensure the real-time interactions between the parties concerned along with the high- security measures and integrity. The latter aspect refers to the electronic signatures and some other forms that could be used to authenticate electronically parties, payments and so on.

2.1.6 ICSID

The International Centre for Settlement of Investment Disputes (ICSID) was very open to online filing. To achieve this goal the ICSID even introduced the so-called default procedure on 16 March 2020. Given this procedure, it is possible merely to submit an electronic copy of a request for arbitration or post-award application alongside the necessary documents. Likewise, the same rules apply in case of a request for conciliation or fact-finding proceeding. Throughout this step, the ICSID decided to reduce its reliance on paper-filings.[31]

31 *ICSID Makes Electronic Filing its Default Procedure*, "ICSID News & Events" 13.03.2020, https://icsid.worldbank.org/news-and-events/news-releases/icsid-makes-electronic-filing-its-default-procedure. Accessed on 19.02.2023.

Furthermore, it is noteworthy that the ICSID opts for electronic submissions in all documentation such as witness statements and expert reports. Similarly, arbitrators, conciliators and *ad hoc* Committee members are supposed to make use of electronic copies while handling disputes.[32]

ICSID benefits from leveraging information technology and thus its proceedings have become much more efficient and environmentally friendly than even. Therefore, the ICSID significantly makes use of electronic filing, most notably of emails and the special dedicated online file-sharing platforms. It is also worth recalling the standpoint of the ICSID's Secretary General who said that "Given the state of information technology—and the ease with which participants in ICSID cases have adapted to online file sharing in recent years—it made sense to make electronic filing the norm" and further confirmed that "The result will be cost and time-savings to parties".[33]

Therefore, the solutions adopted by ICSID are the most pro-innovative technology compared to others in international commercial arbitration.

2.2 *Remote Hearings*

Remote hearings[34] have become commonplace because of the COVID-19 pandemic. International arbitral tribunals had to exit from their comfort zone and adjust to the new normal. Given the travel restrictions and social distancing measures, parties, counsels, and arbitrators had to abandon traditional face-to-face hearings and introduce remote ones. One could even say that the COVID-19 pandemic is a game-changer in international arbitration.[35]

2.2.1 Definition of Remote Hearings

Remote hearings should be defined as hearings conducted thanks to information and communication technologies (ICTs). Such technologies aim to facilitate communication between the parties stemming from two or more locations. This communication could be achieved through telephone or videoconferencing. Some researchers even look forward to the future and point out futuristic technology like telepresence.[36] Nonetheless, it should be stressed that international arbitral tribunals use mostly videoconference links while dealing with remote hearings. Therefore, it is indispensable to use "technology

32 *Ibidem.*

33 *Ibidem.*

34 See more: L.F. Pires de Sousa, *A Judge's Perspective: Online Hearings, especially the Gathering and Assessment of Evidence* [in:] *Online Dispute Resolution. New Challenges*, ed. D. Moura Vicente, E. Dias Oliveira, J. Gomes de Almeida, Baden-Baden 2022, pp. 87–106.

35 M. Scherer, *Remote Hearings in International Arbitration: An Analytical Framework*, "Journal of International Arbitration" 2020, Vol. 37, issue 4.

36 *Ibidem.*

which allows two or more locations to interact simultaneously by two-way video and audio transmission, facilitating communication and personal interaction between these locations".[37]

It is noteworthy that very often the term "remote" hearings is interchanged with "virtual" or "online". Given the computer science, the former wording is understood as "not physically present as such but made by software to appear to be so from the point of view of a program or user".[38] Practically, the term "virtual" points out something which neither really nor physically exists. In addition, the notion of "virtual arbitrators" appears in literature while discussing whether human arbitrators could be replaced or supported by artificial intelligence (AI). Given international arbitration, hearings conducted in several locations refer to the situation where the participants of the proceedings exist but are not present in the arbitral tribunal. Therefore, the term "remote hearings" is much more appropriate. Hence, all the parties concerned together with counsels and arbitrators make use of communication technologies to interact with each other. For that reason, the term "virtual hearings" could lead to many misunderstandings and should be avoided.[39]

Likewise "virtual", the term "online hearings"[40] is ambiguous. On the one hand, it can easily be recognized and confused with online dispute resolution mechanisms. On the other hand, it also resembles "online courts". Nonetheless, there is a relatively huge difference between ODR, and online courts compared to "remote hearings". The former means that the cases are handled beyond the physical courtrooms thanks to the use of computer technologies. In addition, there is no hearing (understood as an exchange of arguments or evidence in the course of proceedings) in the majority of cases at all. As Richard Susskind stresses, "this means that … participants need [not] be available at the same time for a case to progress" and "as with email and text messages, those who are involved do not need to be on tap simultaneously – arguments, evidence and decisions can be sent without sender and recipient being physically or

---

37 *Ibidem*. Cf. Hague Conference on Private International Law, *Guide to Good Practice on the Use of Video-Link under the Evidence Convention*.

38 M. Scherer, *Remote Hearings in International …*, p. Cf. G. Kaufmann-Kohler, T. Schultz, *The Use of Information …*; P. Panjwani, *The Present and Near Future of New Technologies in Arbitration* (Report on the Club Español de Arbitraje's Third Annual Conference), "Spain Arb. Rev." 2018, pp. 21–33.

39 M. Scherer, *Remote Hearings in International …*

40 See more: P. Perales Viscasillas, *An Arbitrator's Perspective: Online hearings in Arbitration: the taking of Evidence* [in:] *Online Dispute Resolution. New Challenges*, ed. D. Moura Vicente, E. Dias Oliveira, J. Gomes de Almeida, Baden-Baden 2022.

virtually together at the same time".[41] Therefore, neither "virtual" nor "online" is the appropriate wording to explain the significance of "remote" hearings.

It is worth adding, however, that remote hearings became a new normal in international arbitration. This means that they do not belong and cannot be classified as a truly innovative and new phenomenon. Both the case management conferences and procedural hearings are conducted remotely, most notably in case of expedited or emergency arbitrator proceedings. Likewise, witnesses and experts also testify in such a way. Interestingly, the International Centre for Settlement of Investment Disputes (ICSID) confirmed that most of the hearings were conducted through videoconference in 2019.[42] This means that the arbitral tribunals made use of ICTs even prior to the COVID-19 pandemic.

Finally, following Maxi Scherer, it is noteworthy to distinguish three different types of remote hearings that can be handled in international arbitration. Given the degree of remoteness, there are semi-remote or fully remote hearings. The former recognizes one main venue of arbitral proceedings and several remote ones. To illustrate, the tribunal together with the parties involved could be present in a certain place, whereas witnesses and experts could testify remotely by videoconferencing. The latter, in turn, recognizes that there is no main venue, but each participant is in a different location. Practically, fully remote hearings are less popular in international arbitration due to some challenges that need to be addressed. Such challenges concern not only technical issues to allow a huge number of participants to join hearings remotely but also fully transplanting the "offline" hearings' features into a "virtual" world. This challenge requires to rethink the fundamental basics of the process itself.[43]

According to the second classification, the remote hearings could be divided based on the content of the handled proceedings. In the majority of cases, as discussed above, remote hearings are available for witnesses or experts who are deemed to testify in arbitral tribunal. Nonetheless, it is also possible that one or even both parties concerned (or maybe their representatives) take part in proceedings in a remote way. It could also concern one or both co-arbitrators.[44]

Given the third classification, remote hearings could concern merely a part or the entire proceedings. This means that there are different possible

41 R. Susskind, *Online courts and the future of justice*, New York 2019, p. 60.

42 M. Scherer, *Remote Hearings in International ...*

43 *Ibidem.*

44 *Ibidem.*

combinations between hearings conducted fully in a physical venue, semi-remotely or remotely.[45]

2.2.2 Regulations on Remote Hearings

This analysis leads to the question of whether there are any specific regulations related to remote hearings provided. It is noteworthy that the pandemic could not be classified as a harbinger of the "remote hearings" as a completely new phenomenon. Even before the spread of the pandemic, some arbitral tribunals have already made use of remote hearings.[46] To illustrate, according to Article 28(4) of the United Nations Commission on International Trade Law (UNCITRAL) Arbitration Rules, both witnesses and experts may be heard remotely. On the contrary, there are no such provisions in the case of other parts of the hearings (concerning the legal arguments, for instance).[47] To name a few, the London Court of International Arbitration (LCIA)[48] provided that "[a]s to form, a hearing may take place by video or telephone conference or in person (or a combination of all three)".[49] Likewise, the Swiss Chambers' Arbitration Rules stipulate that "[t]he arbitral tribunal may direct that witnesses or expert witnesses be examined through means that do not require their physical presence at the hearing (including by videoconference)".[50] Another example refers to the ICC Rules 2017. Even if these Rules did not explicitly grant the possibility of handling remote hearings, under Appendix VI concerning the expedited procedure, "[w]hen a hearing is to be held, the arbitral tribunal may conduct it by videoconference, telephone, or similar means of communication".[51]

45 *Ibidem.*
46 P. Panjwani, *The Impact of the COVID-19 Pandemic on International Arbitration Practices. Greener Arbitrations with Reduced Due Process Paranoia?*, [in:] *The Impact of Covid on International Disputes*, eds. S. Lalani, S.G. Shapiro, "International and Comparative Business Law and Public Policy" Vol. 2, Leiden-Boston 2022, p. 33.
47 UNCITRAL Arbitration Rules, Article 28(4).
48 See more: J. van Haersolte-van Hof, R. Holland, *What makes for Effective Arbitration? A Case Study of the London Court of International Arbitration Rules* [in:] *International Organizations and the Promotion of Effective Dispute Resolution. AIIB Yearbook of International Law 2019*, ed. P. Quayle, Gao Xuan, Leiden-Boston 2019, pp. 28–39.
49 "LCIA Arbitration Rules (2014)," London Court of International Arbitration, in effect as of October 1, 2014, Article 19.2 ("LCIA Arbitration Rules 2014").
50 Swiss Chambers' Arbitration Institution Rules, in effect as of 2012, Article 25(4).
51 "2017 Arbitration Rules," International Chamber of Commerce, adopted March 1, 2017, Appendix VI, Article 3(5) ("ICC Rules 2017"), http://www.arbiter.com.sg/pdf/rules/ICC%20Arbitration%20(2017)%20and%20Mediation%20(2014)%20Rules%20(ENG).pdf. Accessed on 12.05.2024.

2.2.3 Seoul Protocol on Video Conferencing in International Arbitration

There are many challenges related to remote hearings. Therefore, it is worth recalling the Seoul Protocol on Video Conferencing in International Arbitration ("Seoul Protocol").[52] This Protocol is widely considered to be a response to the increasing number of videoconferencing in international arbitration. It was drafted for the sake of identifying potential issues concerning videoconferencing. The Protocol itself could be divided into three chief parts addressing different types of problems, namely due process, confidentiality, and practical difficulties.

2.2.3.1 *Due Process*

Considering due process[53] and most notably fairness and impartiality, the Protocol emphasizes "fair, equal, and reasonable right of access to the Parties and their related persons, as appropriate. Similarly, cross-border connections should be adequately safeguarded so as to prevent unlawful interception by third parties, for example, by IP-to-IP encryption".[54] Therefore, this provision aims to ensure that both parties enjoy equal chances in setting forth their case in the course of witness examination. This means that the videoconferencing should ensure a neutral location and thus realize the right to access all the parties involved.[55] Following this goal, "The Tribunal may terminate the video conference at any time if the Tribunal deems the video conference so unsatisfactory that it is unfair to either Party to continue".[56] In addition, the Protocol also considers the technical requirements agreed by the parties. This means that parties, by mutual consent, could reduce the possible risk concerning unfairness against parties. Hence, it refers to the situation where "witnesses have access to lesser technical capabilities and know-how".[57] There are also

52 See more: M. Durban, *„Protokół seulski" dotyczący wideokonferencji w międzynarodowym arbitrażu handlowym,* "Biuletyn Arbitrażowy. Nowe technologie w arbitrażu instytucjonalnym" 2020, no. 26.

53 See more: J. Serralda Hierro, *An Arbitration Center's Perspective: Due Process in Online Dispute Resolution* [in:] *Online Dispute Resolution. New Challenges*, ed. D. Moura Vicente, E. Dias Oliveira, J. Gomes de Almeida, Baden-Baden 2022, pp. 65–86.

54 Article 2.1c of the Seoul Protocol on Video Conferencing in International Arbitration.

55 J. Hong, J.H. Hwang, *Safeguarding the Future of Arbitration: Seoul Protocol Tackles the Risks of Videoconferencing*, "Kluwer Arbitration Blog" 06.04.2020, https://arbitrationblog.kluwerarbitration.com/2020/04/06/safeguarding-the-future-of-arbitration-seoul-protocol-tackles-the-risks-of-videoconferencing/. Accessed on 09.01.2023.

56 Article 1.7. of the Seoul Protocol on Video Conferencing in International Arbitration.

57 J. Hong, J.H. Hwang, *Safeguarding the Future ...*

some references to witnesses who could be unfairly guided by off-screen individuals. To avoid this kind of situation, the Protocol states that:

> During the course of the video conference, the only persons present in the Remote Venue shall be the Witness giving evidence (with his/her counsel, if applicable), interpreters, paralegals to assist with the documents, and representatives from each Party's legal team on a watching brief. Each Party shall provide the identities of every individual in the room to the other Party/Parties and to the Tribunal prior to the video conference and the Tribunal shall take steps to verify the identity of each individual present at the start of the video conference.[58]

Finally, considering the relation between due process and videoconferencing, the Seoul Protocol pays attention that "All documents on the record which the Witness will refer to during the course of his/her evidence must be clearly identified, paginated and made available to the Witness".[59] This provision was formulated for the sake of ensuring that the hearings are transparent based on the preservation of evidence disclosed during the proceedings.

2.2.3.2 *Confidentiality*

The Seoul Protocol also addresses issues related to confidentiality and videoconferencing. On the one hand, the information technologies are cost- and time-effective. On the other hand, such videoconferences could easily lead to breaches of confidentiality and security due to inappropriate measures. Even if international arbitration seems to be resistant to cybersecurity breaches, there are some violations. To illustrate, hackers targeted not only the Philippines' Department of Justice but also a law firm representing this country and the website of the Permanent Court of Arbitration in the 2015 Philippines-China territorial dispute over the South China Sea.[60]

Another problem refers to the common use of videoconferencing service providers, namely Zoom[61] which did not comply with the security duties. Anyone who had a link to the call was able to join the meeting and thus view the video call. Given international arbitration, the lack of more specific measures

---

58 Article 3.1. of the Seoul Protocol on Video Conferencing in International Arbitration.

59 Article 4.1. of the Seoul Protocol on Video Conferencing in International Arbitration.

60 J. Hong, J.H. Hwang, *Safeguarding the Future ...*

61 See more: S. Cohen, *Draft Zoom Hearing Procedural Order*, "Transnational Dispute Management", https://www.transnational-dispute-management.com/journal-advance-publication-article.asp?key=1815.

to ensure better protection of confidentiality could result in many breaches or even violations. Therefore, one party could even gain some details about the disputed case, trade secrets or any other type of confidential information that should be kept secret.

To address such challenging problems, the Seoul Protocol provides a few recommendations that could be summarized as follows: duty to ensure security during the video call fulfilled by both the arbitral tribunal and the parties. Articles 2.1c and 2.2 specifically provide that a Venue should meet several minimum standards to ensure the high-level of confidentiality. In addition, only witnesses and relevant individuals should be present during the testimony via videoconference. To ensure better protection of cybersecurity, such individuals must properly identify.[62] There is also one recommendation concerning the prohibition to record the videoconference if there is no arbitral tribunal. The Seoul Protocol also pays attention to the specific time limit. Given that, "Any recordings of the video conference shall be circulated to the Tribunal and the Parties within 24 hours of the end of the video conference".[63]

This analysis leads us to the conclusion that remote hearings should also provide the highest standard of arbitral proceedings. Indeed, such proceedings must necessarily comply with measures to ensure confidentiality which is crucial in the context of international arbitration.

2.2.3.3 *Practical Difficulties Concerning the Videoconferencing*

In addition to due process and confidentiality issues, there are some other practical difficulties concerning videoconferencing. Aside from the confidentiality, "there can be disruptions to the momentum of hearings due to delays, power outages and disconnection during videoconferences".[64] The Seoul Protocol does not remain silent about these issues. It provides guidelines concerning the Test Conferencing and Audio-Conferencing Backup to avoid or at least decrease possible interruptions during the arbitral proceedings.

Overall, one could even say that this protocol was the first contribution covering issues related to remote hearings during the COVID-19 pandemic. In the wake of these guidelines issued by the Korean Commercial Arbitration Board, other leading arbitral institutions adopted similar rules. For instance, the ICC published "Guidance Note on Possible Measures Aimed at Mitigating the Effects of the COVID-19 Pandemic" (aka "ICC Guidance Note") on 19 April

62 Article 3.1. of the Seoul Protocol on Video Conferencing in International Arbitration.

63 Article 8.2. of the Seoul Protocol on Video Conferencing in International Arbitration.

64 J. Hong, J.H. Hwang, *Safeguarding the Future ...*

2020 and the Hong Kong International Arbitration Centre (HKIAC)[65] issued "Guidelines for Virtual Hearings" (aka "HKIAC Guidelines") on 14 May 2020.[66]

2.2.4 Twofold Standpoint on Remote Hearings

One could even say that remote hearings are permitted merely in situations stipulated by law and cannot be applied freely. Given the above, certain specific circumstances are allowing to benefit from remote hearings during the arbitral proceedings which means that such innovation cannot be allowed in all forms. Therefore, following the UNCITRAL Arbitration Rules, remote hearings are prohibited when it comes to legal arguments and hearings on the merits of the dispute, namely in the case of non-emergency or non-expedited arbitration.

Some scholars point out (i.e. Maxi Scherer) that there are no convincing arguments not permitting handling remote hearings on legal arguments, whereas witnesses and experts could testify in such a way.[67] The latter situation is surprising because remote witness or expert testimony could lead to many additional difficulties and obstacles concerning their reliability. It is also relatively difficult or even impossible to assess whether these persons testify freely without being under pressure. Interestingly, due to the lack of specific regulations on remote hearings both in national laws and institutional arbitration rules, it seems necessary to refer to the party's rights to a hearing and the arbitral tribunal's power to determine procedural matters in case of arbitral proceedings.

2.2.5 Right to a Hearing in International Arbitration

First and foremost, it should be stressed that a party's right to a hearing is widely considered to be one of the most fundamental principles of international arbitration nowadays. The right to physical hearing stems from the right

65 See more: M. Gearing, J. Liu, *The Contributions of the Hong Kong International Arbitration Centre to Effective International Dispute Resolution* [in:] *International Organizations and the Promotion of Effective Dispute Resolution. AIIB Yearbook of International Law 2019*, ed. P. Quayle, Gao Xuan, Leiden-Boston 2019, pp. 40–55.

66 B.O. Giupponi, *"Virtual" Dispute Resolution in International Arbitration. Mapping Its Advantages and Main Caveats in the Face of COVID-19*, [in:] *The Impact of Covid on International Disputes*, eds. S. Lalani, S.G. Shapiro, "International and Comparative Business Law and Public Policy" Vol. 2, Leiden-Boston 2022, p. 72.

67 M. Scherer, *Remote Hearings in International* .... See more: Monteiro Pires C., Diniz de Ayala M., *A Lawyer's Perspective: Virtual Hearings* [in:] *Online Dispute Resolution. New Challenges*, ed. D. Moura Vicente, E. Dias Oliveira, J. Gomes de Almeida, Baden-Baden 2022.

to be heard and is linked to equal treatment. The latter, in turn, originates from the human right to a fair trial.[68] No one undermines this right itself but rather seeks to find the answer to whether such a hearing should be handled physically according to the binding provisions and principles. There is no unequivocal answer thus far. Some scholars point out that "remote hearing" does not fulfil all requirements to be determined as "a hearing". Such a theory stems from "the assumption that hearings must be oral (principle of orality) and allow for a simultaneous exchange of arguments or evidence (principle of immediacy)".[69]

Nonetheless, this statement seems to be unfounded as there is no clear justification for the lack of recognition in the case of remote hearings. There are three chief arguments to disprove this theory. Firstly, it is possible to express arguments in remote hearings likewise in physical hearings. The only difference concerns the fact that the former makes use of new technologies which allow to transmit the audio and voice. Secondly, both types of hearings ensure the possibility to exchange arguments or evidence in the course of proceedings simultaneously. This means that all participants, namely parties, counsel, witnesses, experts, and arbitrators could make "a live discussion" and express their opinions. Following the above-mentioned principle of orality and immediacy as an explanation to consider differently both types of proceedings (physical or remote) seem to be inadequate. One could even say that "as long as a remote hearing allows for the exchange to be oral and synchronous, it seems difficult to argue that this is not hearing".[70]

For instance, according to the UNCITRAL Notes on Organizing Arbitral Proceedings (2016), an oral hearing is mostly a result of the parties' written submissions. Even if the majority of hearings are handled in person, the procedural ones, including the first procedural meeting are very often conducted remotely (via telephone or videoconference).[71] Given these UNCITRAL Notes, such consultations concerning the organizing of arbitral proceedings can be handled through correspondence or telecommunications. The latter term

68 B.O. Giupponi, *"Virtual" Dispute Resolution …*, p. 65. See: A. Santos Abrantes Geraldeas, *A Judge's Perspective: Guarantees of a Fair Trial and Online Dispute Resolution* [in:] *Online Dispute Resolution. New Challenges*, ed. D. Moura Vicente, E. Dias Oliveira, J. Gomes de Almeida, Baden-Baden 2022, pp. 21–36.

69 M. Scherer, *Remote Hearings in International …*

70 *Ibidem.*

71 *Oral Hearing – UNCITRAL Arbitration*, "International Centre for Settlement of Investment Disputes", https://icsid.worldbank.org/procedures/arbitration/uncitral/oral-hearing. Accessed on 07.01.2023.

refers to telefax, conference telephone calls or any other electronic means.[72] In addition,

> If it is up to the arbitral tribunal to decide whether to hold hearings, the decision is likely to be influenced by factors such as, on the one hand, that it is usually quicker and easier to clarify points at issue pursuant to a direct confrontation of arguments than on the basis of correspondence and, on the other hand, the travel and other cost of holding hearings, and that the need of finding acceptable dates for the hearings might delay the proceedings. The arbitral tribunal may wish to consult the parties on this matter.[73]

Both substantive and evidentiary hearings[74] were mostly conducted face-to-face. Hence, one could even say that handling an entire arbitral proceeding remotely was relatively rare.[75]

Nonetheless, the situation has changed after the outbreak of the COVID-19 pandemic. Many arbitral institutions adjusted their rules to facilitate remote hearings. To illustrate, the International Chamber of Commerce (ICC) introduced the so-called digitalized requests for arbitration. The London International Court of Arbitration (LCIA), in turn, launched a special virtual platform dedicated to electronically filing arbitration applications. In the wake of ongoing changes resulting from the COVID-19 pandemic, arbitration institutions also published guidelines on remote hearings. Therefore, given the new situation resulting from the pandemic, remote proceedings are concerned with both procedural and substantive issues. Such a trend was visible among parties and arbitrators. Some scholars (i.e. Hatami Alamdari) stressed that full or semi-remote hearings will last longer and probably they become a new normal even in post-pandemic times.[76]

Considering the second approach, it is noteworthy that in the lack of any agreement by the parties, the arbitral tribunal may "conduct the arbitration

---

72 UNCITRAL Notes on Organizing Arbitral Proceedings 2012, https://uncitral.un.org/sites/uncitral.un.org/files/media-documents/uncitral/en/arb-notes-e.pdf, p. 2. Accessed on 07.01.2023.

73 *Ibidem.*

74 See more: P. Perales Viscasillas, *An Arbitrator's Perspective: Online hearings in Arbitration: the taking of Evidence* [in:] *Online Dispute Resolution. New Challenges*, ed. D. Moura Vicente, E. Dias Oliveira, J. Gomes de Almeida, Baden-Baden 2022, pp. 107–132.

75 H. Lal, J. Kaiding, L. Defranchi, *Virtual Hearings in International Construction Arbitration: Evolution or Mitigant?*, "Construction Law Journal" 2021, Vol. 37, no. 2, pp. 129–141.

76 B. Hatami Alamdari, *The Question of Remote ...*, p. 142.

in such manner as it considers appropriate" and "decide all procedural and evidential matters". Therefore, it has the power to organize the proceedings in general, and testimony of evidence in particular. This begs the question of whether arbitrators could benefit from their power to handle remote hearings without the consent of the parties or even against them. In other words, this question is based upon the autonomy of the arbitrator while ordering this type of proceedings. On the one hand, arbitration itself could be defined as a consensual method of dispute settlement stemming from an all-party agreement. Nonetheless, it can cause many problems, most notably in case one party is against participating remotely in hearings.[77] Therefore, can an arbitrator order such a remote hearing without the consent of the party concerned? This situation requires that one party seeks to convince the arbitrator about the necessity to handle a face-to-face hearing. However, it is not possible because of pandemic restrictions, for instance.[78] Given that, would this lead to frustration with the arbitration agreement? To fully answer this question, it is indispensable to analyze different situations and theories linked to the nature of arbitration agreements, namely jurisdictional, contractual, mixed or hybrid and autonomous.

The first theory, widely known as jurisdictional, recognizes that the State of the seat of arbitration has supervisory power in the majority of cases. The contractual theory focuses mainly on a valid arbitration agreement which is deemed to be a basis for the arbitration itself. Hybrid theory, in turn, assumes that there is a certain mixture between contractual and jurisdictional theories. Finally, the autonomous theory acknowledges that there is an autonomous arbitral institution which is free from any constraints based on *lex fori* and its legitimacy stems from a transnational legal order.[79]

If the arbitral tribunal decided that the remote hearing would be appropriate for procedural and evidentiary reasons, the parties must participate in such proceedings. In addition, they must act in good faith. In addition, they also must follow the orders of the arbitral tribunal where there are no procedural requirements established by the involved parties. Similarly, it is crucial for the parties to strictly comply with the agree-upon procedure, even if the arbitrator decides to make changes which contradict their initial preferences. Such a fundamental principle stems from the majority of national laws and

77 See more: C. Monteiro Pires, Diniz de Ayala M., *A Lawyer's Perspective: Virtual Hearings* [in:] *Online Dispute Resolution. New Challenges*, ed. D. Moura Vicente, E. Dias Oliveira, J. Gomes de Almeida, Baden-Baden 2022, pp. 133–144.

78 B. Hatami Alamdari, *The Question of Remote ...*, p. 143.

79 *Ibidem*, pp. 143–144.

regulations on arbitration. This entails that once an arbitral tribunal has been constituted and the arbitral proceedings have started, the tribunal itself possesses the power to determine the most suitable course of action. Therefore, it is widely accepted that arbitral tribunals make decisions on procedural matters, including hearings either remotely or in person. As such, if the arbitral tribunal believes that a remote hearing would serve the parties' interests, it is incumbent upon the parties to accept this decision and thus abide by the procedures once established.[80]

Finally, it is noteworthy that the right to a hearing or a fair trial[81] is also linked to the recognition and enforcement of arbitral awards. Therefore, Article V.1.b of the 1958 New York Convention provides "non-recognition of an award if the party facing recognition of the award was not given proper notice of the appointment of the arbitration or the arbitration proceedings or was otherwise unable to present his case".[82]

This section confirms that the right to a hearing is important and cannot be violated in any case. Netherless, the arbitral tribunal is empowered to decide whether remote hearings would be a good fit for a certain case.

2.2.4 Need of Handling Remote Hearings

One must note that not all disputes require a hearing during arbitral proceedings. By contrast, it is a common practice to resolve a case based on the written arguments and related documents or even statements that have been submitted by the parties or witnesses. Indeed, many arbitral institutions worldwide provide the opportunity to handle a case without a hearing. It is also widely confirmed in arbitration rules of different institutions globally. To illustrate, in the case of a standard procedure, a hearing can easily be waived based on the mutual consent of both parties. By contrast, the expedited procedure even does not require handling hearings by default, despite many different approaches represented by arbitral institutions. For instance, according to the SAKIG Rules,[83] the expedited procedure has no hearing, "unless the sole arbitrator or the arbitral tribunal considers that the dispute has not been sufficiently

80 *Ibidem*, p. 145.

81 See more: N. Ferreira Lousa, *A Lawyer's Perspective: Guarantees of a Fair Trial and Online Dispute Resolution* [in:] *Online Dispute Resolution. New Challenges*, ed. D. Moura Vicente, E. Dias Oliveira, J. Gomes de Almeida, Baden-Baden 2022, pp. 59–64.

82 United Nations Convention on the Recognition and Enforcement of Foreign Arbitral Awards (New York, June 10, 1958), Art. V.1.b.

83 See more: A. Grabowska-Łysyszyn, *Rozprawa w postępowaniu przed sądem polubownym w dobie pandemii COVID-19. Doświadczenia Sądu Arbitrażowego przy Krajowej Izbie Gospodarczej w Warszawie*, "Biuletyn Arbitrażowy. Nowe technologie w arbitrażu instytucjonalnym" 2020, no. 26.

clarified based on the parties' arguments included in their submissions and the documents or other evidence submitted by them".[84]

Contrary to SAKIG Rules, the expedited proceedings under the SCC Rules provide for a hearing merely upon the request of one of the parties. In addition, the arbitrator himself also should justify such a need to handle a hearing.[85] Lastly, the ICC Rules[86] grant the power to determine whether a hearing is needed within the competence of the arbitral tribunal. Nevertheless, the arbitral tribunal should also consult such a decision with the parties concerned.[87]

One must note, however, that in case of complex disputes or those involving high-volume subject matter, a hearing is an essential part of the entire arbitral proceedings. During such a hearing, the parties' representatives undermine the credibility of the opposing party's experts along with questioning the testimony of their witnesses. Such a hearing provides an opportunity for arbitrators to ask questions and address any uncertainties after reviewing the written arguments of the parties and their statements. Indeed, given the outbreak of the COVID-19 pandemic, many arbitral institutions worldwide opted for remote hearings[88] and thus released guidelines and recommendations on this matter. To name a few, the ICC, CEPANI, Delos, SIAC, and VIAC are among the leaders in this field. Likewise, the Polish SAKIG has also contributed by issuing "Recommendations for Conducting Hearings via Videoconference". As such, this arbitral tribunal stressed the court itself provides the parties with the necessary technical support to handle such remote hearings.[89]

2.2.5 Challenges Related to Remote Hearings

After analyzing different approaches to remote hearings and new provisions regulating these issues, it is worth assessing whether such rules will evolve in the post-pandemic world. Interestingly, remote hearings would not be beneficial without different logistics which are necessary to ensure efficient conduct of the proceedings along with the parties' rights. Considering cost efficiency, online dispute resolution mechanisms have more advantages compared to

84 § 53, ust. 6 pkt 10 Arbitration Rules of SAKIG, https://sakig.pl/wp-content/uploads/2022/06/ARBITRATION-RULES-in-force-1-January-2015-with-changes-from-8-november-2021-in-force-1-april-2022-1-1.pdf.

85 Art. 33(1) of the Rules for Expedited Arbitration, SCC.

86 Art. 3(5) of the Expedited Procedure Rules, Anex VI to the ICC Rules.

87 M. Judkiewicz, *Wady i zalety zdalnego postępowania arbitrażowego*, "Biuletyn Arbitrażowy. Nowe technologie w arbitrażu instytucjonalnym" 2020, no. 26, p. 5.

88 See more: L.F. Pires de Sousa, *A Judge's Perspective: Online Hearings, especially the Gathering and Assessment of Evidence* [in:] *Online Dispute Resolution. New Challenges*, ed. D. Moura Vicente, E. Dias Oliveira, J. Gomes de Almeida, Baden-Baden 2022.

89 M. Judkiewicz, *Wady i zalety* ..., p. 6.

traditional arbitration. There is no need to travel to attend arbitration hearings. The COVID-19 pandemic proved that arbitral proceedings could be held online through different types of online platforms. This means that such remote hearings could be achieved thanks to different paths. Both parties and their legal teams may be present in the arbitral venue, whereas the other party is online.[90]

There are also some challenges related to the technical issues of remote hearing. Therefore, this begs the question of which platform should be used. In addition, the arbitral tribunal should decide whether this type of proceeding would be beneficial for both parties. Practically, it means that the arbitral tribunal should check if all remote participants have a good and stable Internet connection to effectively take part in the proceedings. Aside from the Internet, each participant also needs to have the hardware set up. To properly prepare such remote hearings, the arbitral tribunal should also assess the number of remote connections needed along with the locations and time zones. In fact, throughout the increasing number of parties involved remotely, many technological or practical issues could arise such as the convenient time for handling proceedings for all the participants, for example.[91]

Indeed, it is noteworthy to recall the ICC International Court of Arbitration "Checklist for a Protocol on Virtual Hearings" which consists of guidelines on how to properly hold remote hearings. Prior to handling this type of hearing, it is necessary to agree on the number and list of participants (such as the arbitrators, parties, counsels, witnesses, experts, and interpreters, among others). After confirming the number of participants shared within the virtual room, it should also be confirmed whether there is a need for a 360-degree view for all participants in such a virtual room. Finally, the log-in locations, the points of connection along with the identification methods at the beginning of the videoconference should be confirmed. Such a remote hearing should also consider the different time zones to properly select the date, duration and daily timetable.[92]

Considering the technical issues, the following issues should be consulted before handling remote hearings. The parties should agree on which kind of platform and technology they would like to use. This also requires an analysis

90 B.O. Giupponi, *"Virtual" Dispute Resolution ...*, pp. 71–72.

91 M. Scherer, *Remote Hearings in International ...*

92 Annex I, *Checklist for a protocol on virtual hearings*, "ICC Checklist for a Protocol on Virtual Hearings and Suggested Clauses for Cyber-Protocols and Procedural Orders Dealing with the Organisation of Virtual Hearings", https://iccwbo.org/publication/icc-checklist-for-a-protocol-on-virtual-hearings-and-suggested-clauses-for-cyber-protocols-and-procedural-orders-dealing-with-the-organisation-of-virtual-hearings/. Accessed on 21.01.2023.

of the legal access to these platforms and technologies. Further, the minimum system specifications and technical requirements should be confirmed to ensure smooth connectivity (including both audio and video along with the necessary visibility and lighting where the remote hearing takes place). Some more specific equipment may be needed depending on the location, namely phones, backup computers, and some connectivity boosters/extenders, among others. Before handling such a hearing, a preliminary check is made to assess whether chosen platform and technology are compatible with each other to avoid possible interruptions in the course of proceedings. It is noteworthy, however, that parties may need some tutorial to make them familiar with the technology, platform, applications and/or equipment. The tribunal should also contact in advance with the parties to undertake some contingency measures in the case of "sudden technical failures, disconnection, power outages (alternative communication channels and virtual technical support for all participants)".[93]

There are different approaches to remote hearings. One must note, however, cogent arguments in favour of such proceedings, even if one party objects. Firstly, remote hearings satisfy the principles of immediacy and orality, most importantly in cases when the parties have agreed to delegate the power to an arbitral tribunal to decide on this matter. It is commonly applied in the case of institutional arbitration. Secondly, one must note that not every violation of a party's right to be heard leads to the non-enforcement of the arbitral award. By contrast, under certain circumstances, such an award can be enforced under the 1958 New York Convention despite a breach of the party's right to be heard. Indeed, such a breach would result in rejecting enforcement of an arbitral award once proved that such violations hindered the party from displaying its claims and defences. Therefore, if a party claims that there is a breach of the right to be heard, it must meet a stringent criterion to resist the enforcement of such an award. Finally, once a party would like to assert that such a breach took place during the arbitral proceedings, it must promptly inform the arbitral tribunal with the intention to raise this matter. Nonetheless, if the arbitral tribunal continues the proceedings, the complaining party should raise objections and request a suspension of such proceedings until the breach is rectified.[94]

Despite many advantages of remote hearings in terms of both time and cost savings, an in-person hearing is much more appropriate in case of high-stakes, technically complex disputes which involve many witnesses, and

93 *Ibidem.*

94 T. Menezes, *Remote Hearings in International* Arbitration, "Jus Corpus Law Journal" 2022, Vol. 2, no. 3, pp. 457–458.

experts alongside different time zones. Indeed, this type of case would be more suitable for a conventional in-person hearing or even a combination of both in-person and remote participation, instead of fully remote hearings.[95] Briefly, many challenges related to remote hearings could be summarized as follows.

First, it may be a challenging problem to find an appropriate time slot that works for all participants of the arbitral proceedings. Indeed, this problem arises mostly in the case of different international time zones. This means that not only parties but also legal representatives and arbitrators may have limited time to conduct arbitral hearings. As such, it may cause many disadvantages to the parties, most notably if the arbitral proceedings are deemed to be handled at inconvenient hours (including early mornings or late nights). Practically, too many challenges and conflicts resulting from different time zones may hinder smooth proceedings. Therefore, it is recommended to opt for an in-person hearing instead of a remote one.[96]

Second, all the parties concerned, including arbitrators, legal representatives and the arbitral tribunal should check carefully whether all participants have access to adequate and reliable technology to take part in remote hearings. It is crucial to ensure a right to a fair trial. If one of the parties or their counsel experiences disparities in terms of technological resources, the entire arbitral proceedings would be threatened in terms of integrity and effectiveness.[97]

Third, remote hearings do not provide fully reliable solutions in terms of cross-examination of witnesses. Indeed, it would be more difficult to assess their credibility, most importantly given multiple witnesses. This entails that a well-defined protocol for remote hearings is needed. Therefore, it should properly address possible challenges such as witnesses that may be seen on a screen with inadequate camera angles or poor lighting. These factors may lead to many practical problems on how to assess not only the witness' demeanour but also body language.[98]

To address these problems, arbitral institutions issued guidance on this matter. To illustrate, the AAA-ICDR Model Order and Procedures for a Virtual Hearing via Videoconference is widely recognized as a model or template covering these issues. This means that arbitrators and parties can freely modify its content to adjust it to specific needs given their case. This document provides detailed recommendations for witnesses and exhibits. As such,

95 K. Nagarajan, J.J. East, *Salient Considerations for Remote ...*, p. 108.
96 *Ibidem*, pp. 108–109.
97 *Ibidem*, p. 109.
98 *Ibidem*.

> With the exception of the parties' corporate representatives and expert witnesses, who may attend the entirety of the hearing, all witnesses are to be sequestered until they testify. [If recording video – Witnesses shall be advised in advance by the party calling them that their testimony will be recorded.] B. Witnesses should follow the below practices: i. A witness shall give evidence sitting at an empty desk or table, and the witness' face shall be clearly visible in the video. ii. To the extent possible, the webcam should be positioned at face level, relatively close to the witness (e.g., by positioning a laptop on a stack of books). iii. Witnesses may not use a "virtual background." Instead, the remote venue from which they are testifying must be visible. iv. Witnesses should speak directly to the camera while testifying. v. Witnesses should avoid making quick movements. VI. All non-party or expert witnesses shall sign-off from the [Platform Name] session at the conclusion of their testimony.[99]

In addition, a witness may be asked to provide a 360-degree view of the remote venue to prove that there are no unauthorized persons therein (Point C of this document).[100]

This entails many concerns related to the examination of witnesses during remote hearings. Therefore, a third party may influence a witness by providing instructions concerning their responses. Such a goal could be achieved either by various communication tools or devices stemming from individuals that are present in the same room. To address such concerns, it is recommended that a witness provide a complete view of the room to the arbitrators through the camera. Given such an action, it is possible to maximize visibility and thus have better access to the space. Indeed, new technologies also offer many tools that can easily be used. To name a few, screen-sharing programs such as TeamViewer can be used to present documents to witnesses. This approach based on the appropriate angle of the camera may be helpful to mitigate concerns related to the witness' access to prepared files or other communication platforms during the testimony. To address these concerns, the witness can be present at a certain distance from the camera. Therefore, it would allow for

99 AAA-ICDR Model Order and Procedures for a Virtual Hearing via Videoconference, "American Arbitration Association", https://go.adr.org/rs/294-SFS-516/images/AAA270_AAA-ICDR%20Model%20Order%20and%20Procedures%20for%20a%20Virtual%20Hearing%20via%20Videoconference.pdf. Accessed on 11.06.2023.

100 *Ibidem*, Point. C.

observation and thus be helpful to ensure that the witness does not rely on any notes, phones or other devices to communicate with third parties.[101]

Fourth, despite many positive sides of remote hearings (mostly in terms of their efficiency), participants may also endure considerable mental and physical strain. Indeed, such problems can be manifested through different types of symptoms, including screen fatigue, and physical exhaustion, among others. Practically, it can even lead to mental health deterioration and reduced ability to concentrate. It is noteworthy that such negative effects stem from extended hearings and can potentially influence the overall quality of entire arbitral proceedings.[102]

Finally, when a case is held over multiple days of taking evidence and oral arguments, legal representatives may prefer to benefit from in-person discussions with witnesses and experts. To illustrate, according to the research study by Berkley Research Group, a lack of in-person preparation between counsel and experts may result in decreased quality of mental preparedness. Given this factor, it may be more favourable to conduct in-person hearings instead of remote hearings. If not possible, it is recommended to conduct in-person preparatory meetings at least.[103]

2.2.6 Remote Hearings and Post-Arbitration Problems

Even though there are many challenges and concerns related to remote hearings, it is also crucial to determine whether remote hearings could violate a party's right to defence. As such, this begs the question of whether such remote arbitration could provide grounds for setting aside an arbitral award or even refusing the recognition of such an award and its enforcement under the 1958 New York Convention. One must note that upon parties' refusal to participate in remote hearings or their consent to other electronic procedures, the arbitral tribunal should comply with the parties' willingness. By contrast, the situation becomes even more complex in case of refusal submitted merely by one of the parties. Therefore, the question arises as to whether that party is effectively opposed to the continuation of arbitration in such a virtual format.[104]

One must note that there are no harmonized regulations at the international level to cover these issues. Given that, the determination of whether a hearing must be conducted in a traditional way (namely with the physical presence of the parties) or if a "virtual presence" is sufficient results from the

101 M. Judkiewicz, *Wady i zalety ...*, p. 8.

102 K. Nagarajan, J.J. East, *Salient Considerations for Remote ...*, p. 109.

103 *Ibidem*, pp. 109–110.

104 M. Judkiewicz, *Wady i zalety ...*, p. 9.

procedural rules of the place of arbitration and the specific rules of the arbitral institution. This entails that once a physical presence is needed and a hearing is handled remotely through videoconference, there is a potential risk of challenging the future arbitral award.[105]

Under Article 26 of the ICC Rules, "A hearing shall be held if any of the parties so requests or, failing such a request, if the arbitral tribunal on its motion decides to hear the parties. When a hearing is to be held, the arbitral tribunal, giving reasonable notice, shall summon the parties to appear before it on the day and at the place fixed by it".[106] This regulation suggests that physical presence at the hearing venue is necessary. Nonetheless, the ICC Arbitration Secretariat's Guide clarifies that the arbitral tribunal has the power to decide whether to conduct remote hearings through teleconferencing or video conferencing under specific circumstances.[107] Indeed, according to part VII C of the "2021 Note to Parties and arbitral tribunals on the Conduct of the Arbitration under the ICC Rules of Arbitration":

> The arbitral tribunal must take any decision to hold an evidentiary hearing by remote means of communication rather than by physical attendance after careful consideration of all relevant circumstances, including the nature of the hearing, the possible existence of travel constraints, the planned duration of the hearing, the number of participants and of witnesses and experts to be examined, the size and complexity of the case, the need for the parties to properly prepare for the hearing, the costs and the gains of efficiency that may be expected by resorting to virtual means of communication, and whether rescheduling the hearing would entail unwarranted or excessive delays.

Similarly, the 2021 ICC Arbitration Rules also stipulate that "The arbitral tribunal may decide, after consulting the parties, and based on relevant facts and circumstances of the case, that any hearing will be conducted by physical attendance or remotely by videoconference, telephone or other appropriate means of communication".[108]

---

105 *Ibidem*, p. 9.

106 2021 ICC Rules, Article 26, https://iccwbo.org/dispute-resolution/dispute-resolution-services/arbitration/rules-procedure/2021-arbitration-rules/#block-accordion-26. Accessed on 12.05.2024.

107 J. Fry, S. Greenberg, F. Mazza, The Secretariat's Guide to ICC Arbitration, 2012, pkt 3–993.

108 See Article 26(1) of the 2021 ICC Arbitration Rules.

Likewise, under Article 19.2 of the 2020 LCIA Arbitration Rules:

> The Arbitral Tribunal shall have the fullest authority under the Arbitration Agreement to establish the conduct of a hearing, specifying that as to form, a hearing may take place in person, or virtually by conference call, videoconference or using other communications technology with participants in one or more geographical places (or in a combined form).[109]

Arbitrators are responsible not only for ensuring the proper conduct of arbitral proceedings but also for equal treatment of the parties. This means that during the submission of written pleadings, parties can indicate some difficulties in assessing paper documentation or witnesses. Given the hearing stage, both parties and their legal representatives along with witnesses and experts may face problems resulting from innovation-driven technologies and not reliable Internet connections. In case of any requests upon suspension of proceedings or opposition to conducting virtual hearings, parties must provide detailed justification specifying difficulties they have encountered during the arbitral proceedings. Therefore, the arbitrators themselves play a crucial role in assessing these issues and their impact on the conduct of the dispute. Arbitral proceedings should not take any further steps if one of the parties faces significant difficulties in assessing either documents or technology. Indeed, such obstacles may significantly impede their ability to fully exercise their right to a defence in arbitral proceedings.[110]

Finally, Gary Born stresses that almost every court has decided to reject attempts to invalidate arbitral awards based on objections against the use of videoconferencing or other technology useful in terms of witness and expert testimony. Likewise, remote witness testimony in the recognition proceedings resulted in the same outcome.[111] In addition, "those results are particularly likely to continue to be reached in the future with respect to entirely remote hearings, with a number of national courts conducting their own remote hearings, and with health regulations making the conduct of physical or in-person hearings impossible or unlikely for prolonged periods of time".[112]

---

109 2020 LCIA Arbitration Rules, https://www.lcia.org/Dispute_Resolution_Services/lcia-arbitration-rules-2020.aspx. Accessed on 12.05.2024.

110 M. Judkiewicz, *Wady i zalety* ..., p. 10.

111 M. Hafez, *Remote hearings and the use of technology in arbitration*, "Global Arbitration Review" 21.04.2023, https://globalarbitrationreview.com/review/the-middle-eastern-and-african-arbitration-review/2022/article/remote-hearings-and-the-use-of-technology-in-arbitration. Accessed on 20.06.2023.

112 *Ibidem*; G.B. Born, *Annulment of International Arbitral Awards* [in:] G.B. Born, *International Commercial Arbitration*, Kluwer Law International 2020, p. 3451.

2.3 *Electronically Stored Information*

International arbitration commonly makes use of electronically stored information (ESI) which is also known in the literature as e-disclosure. Through the increasing number of communication and documentation by electronic means, including email, and text messages alongside videoconferencing (via Microsoft Teams or Zoom), there is a growing demand for e-disclosure. This new trend has been even supported by the International Bar Association's Rules on the Taking of Evidence in International Arbitration (the IBA Rules) which explicitly refer to the production of documents in electronic form.[113]

It is worthwhile to stress that ESI is very often overlooked as a subcategory of metadata. ESI can include numerous documents and some other related data. In addition, such information may be stored in a variety of places, including devices which are almost the size of a fingernail. As electronic storage devices become much more available and smaller in size, the amount of ESI and metadata sources have increased significantly. Indeed, such information can be valuable in the course of legal disputes and proceedings.[114]

Electronic documents contain a significant amount of information commonly not visible to users. Such information is called metadata and is recorded by the computer for the sake of storing and retrieving necessary data in the future. Considering metadata, it involves many details on the file (i.e. its name, creation and modification dates, authorship, comments and history, among others).[115]

One must note that the use of e-disclosure and the production of ESI provides not only advantages but also challenges for international arbitration practitioners. On the one hand, the production of ESI could be useful in terms of more comprehensive investigation and examination of the relevant evidence in an ongoing case. On the other hand, ESI can also be more efficiently searched and managed given the available technological tools. Indeed, ESI is more environmentally friendly due to its reduced ecological footprint compared to the traditional paper-based document systems existing in the past.[116]

One of the most significant challenges related to ESI is that it seems to be available in greater quantities compared to paper documents. Furthermore, it may exist in many duplicates across different locations. ESI is likely to be more

113 K. Larkin, J. Sherman, K. Renehan, A. Patel, *Using Technology and e-Disclosure*, "Global Arbitration Review" 03.09.2021, https://globalarbitrationreview.com/guide/the-guide-evidence-in-international-arbitration/1st-edition/article/using-technology-and-e-disclosure. Accessed on 13.04.2023.

114 S.R. Jagusch, *E-disclosure in international arbitration* [in:] *Electronic disclosure in international arbitration*, ed. D.J. Howell, New York 2008, p. 39.

115 *Ibidem*, p. 40.

116 K. Larkin, J. Sherman, K. Renehan, A. Patel, *Using Technology and e-Disclosure* ...

susceptible to manipulation and changes through technology. Therefore, it is much more difficult to detect whether some documents are authentic or not. The production of ESI can also lead to more expensive and time-consuming proceedings. As a result, the costs of the entire international arbitration would probably increase.[117]

Furthermore, there is a growing concern about the hidden nature of metadata. Such a feature may potentially lead to the disclosure of confidential or privileged information. Aside from this, there is a significant burden of preserving metadata which causes some challenges. Metadata seems to be very sensitive and thus can be manipulated even without such an intention. Through opening, copying, and moving a file, metadata can be easily changed. As a result of such changes, it would be difficult to determine the exact date of a document or related changes therein.[118]

Additionally, international arbitration would also be challenged by cultural differences between practitioners and members of the arbitral tribunal in the approach of evidentiary practices. The US and UK pertain to countries with well-established e-disclosure practices, whereas civil law countries are much more familiar with the inquisitorial tradition. In addition, some uncertainties concerning e-disclosure lead to varying expectations regarding the production of evidence in the course of arbitral proceedings. Given some approaches, if a party cannot produce material e-information, the arbitrator is deemed to make adverse interferences instead. Nonetheless, one must note that it seems unusual to penalize a party or even draw some negative consequence for the party concerned if they cannot satisfy expectations foreign to them. Consequently, during the arbitration process, on the one hand, arbitrators should properly balance the need to avoid unnecessary delays and expenses. On the other hand, they should also ensure that each party benefits from a fair chance to set forth its case and obtain not only a just but also enforceable award.[119]

The international arbitration community follows the approach adopted by the IBA Rules on the Taking of Evidence in International Commercial Arbitration. Therefore, such regulations aim at avoiding the disclosure of broad categories of information (e-disclosure and metadata). Experienced arbitration counsels and arbitrators seek to limit requests for expansive e-disclosure and metadata by representing rather a sceptical attitude.[120]

117 *Ibidem.*
118 S.R. Jagusch, *E-disclosure in international ...*, p. 41.
119 *Ibidem*, p. 44.
120 K. Larkin, J. Sherman, K. Renehan, A. Patel, *Using Technology and e-Disclosure ...*

International arbitral tribunals are flexible about the production of documents compared to domestic courts. The latter, by contrast, are largely limited by well-established evidentiary and procedural rules. Under Article 27(3) of the UNCITRAL Arbitration Rules[121], "At any time during the arbitral proceedings the arbitral tribunal may require the parties to produce documents, exhibits or other evidence within such a period as the arbitral tribunal shall determine". In addition, following the next paragraph, "the arbitral tribunal shall determine the admissibility, relevance, materiality and weight of the evidence offered" (Article 27(4).

According to Article 43 of the ICSID Convention, "[e]xcept as the parties otherwise agree, the Tribunal may, if it deems it necessary at any stage of the proceedings, ... call upon the parties to produce documents or other evidence". Similarly, Article 25(4) of the 2021 ICC Rules stipulates that "[a]t any time during the proceedings, the arbitral tribunal may summon any party to provide additional evidence".

Notably, arbitral tribunals have significant discretion over the use of technology and e-disclosure on a broad scale. However, it is noteworthy that document production takes place mostly after submitting the initial round of pleadings. This means that prior to document production in arbitration, parties have already set forth their main evidence to the arbitral tribunal.[122] Recently, the use of technology alongside the rise of ESI has led to substantial growth in the number of documents in international arbitration. Even though legal practitioners become more experienced with technological tools, it can result in emerging of the phenomenon, widely known as "mission creep". This means that the scope of document production can exceed its original purpose.[123]

Nonetheless, even if e-discovery and advanced review platforms become much more popular and thus result in more efficiencies in international arbitration, such technologies should not be interpreted as an invitation to make broader and extensive demands for electronic documents. Just like requests for paper-based document production, requests in the case of electronic documents should be limited in their scope and thus customized to fit the circumstances of a specific case.[124]

121 UNCITRAL Arbitration Rules, United Nations Commission on International Trade Law, https://uncitral.un.org/sites/uncitral.un.org/files/media-documents/uncitral/en/21-07996_expedited-arbitration-e-ebook.pdf, Accessed on 14.04.2023.

122 K. Larkin, J. Sherman, K. Renehan, A. Patel, *Using Technology and e-Disclosure ...*

123 *Ibidem.*

124 *Ibidem.*

The online depository of case data pertaining to the arbitral proceedings seems to be an interesting solution which allows for avoiding duplication of tasks. In addition, it also allows to enhance consistency across the board. It should be stressed, however, that there are different types of repositories. Therefore, a more advanced one provides the possibility to add up some tasks by the stakeholders. These possibilities go much beyond uploading, downloading and the simple storage of the relevant documents.

It is noteworthy that such new platforms could be very useful for parties, tribunals, and arbitral institutions. They could easily provide relatively efficient workflows along with better communication channels. Furthermore, such platforms could also provide analytics over case data and manage different stages of arbitral proceedings, including pleadings, evidence, hearing bundles and awards, among others. Such a solution could be a remedy for complex disputes which require a relatively huge amount of documentary evidence to be submitted.

3 Significance of AI in Arbitration

3.1 *Definition of AI*

The term "Artificial Intelligence" (AI) was introduced in 1956 by John McCarthy. As per McCarthy, AI is "the science and engineering of making intelligent machines, especially intelligent computer programs. It is related to the similar task of using computers to understand human intelligence".[125] In addition, he also stressed that AI cannot be limited merely to "biologically observable" methods. Further, Kathleen Paisley and Edna Sussman defined AI as a guideline for its operation. Therefore, according to Paisley and Sussman, AI is "a process where a large amount of data is combined with processing systems, allowing the software to learn automatically from patterns of features in the data" and "the term AI is often used loosely and encompasses many subjects including machine learning, and also natural language processing".[126] Finally, they also highlight that "AI is the software's ability to learn automatically from patterns or features in the data, thereby making it 'intelligent'".[127] It seems crucial to develop its own "thinking pattern" which would be of pivotal significance in

125 M. Waqar, *The Use of AI in Arbitral Proceedings*, "Ohio State Journal on Dispute Resolution" 2022, Vol. 37, no. 3, p. 346.

126 *Ibidem.*

127 *Ibidem.*

terms of developing more effective and enhanced arbitrations.[128] By contrast, European Union's High-Level Expert Group on AI outlined Ethics Guidelines for Trustworthy AI. Given this document, AI is described as:

> software (and possibly also hardware) systems designed by humans that, given a complex goal, act in the physical or digital dimension by perceiving their environment through data acquisition, interpreting the collected structured or unstructured data, reasoning on the knowledge, or processing the information, derived from this data and deciding the best action(s) to take to achieve the given goal.[129]

Indeed, AI is combined with two words such as "artificial" and "intelligence". The former refers to "human created", whereas the latter to "thinking power". Therefore, AI can be defined as "a man-made object with thinking power".[130] Nonetheless, one must note that intelligence is an intangible feature. As such, it can be summarized as "the ability of a system to calculate, reason, perceive relationships and analogies, learn from experience, store and retrieve information from memory, solve problems, comprehend complex ideas, use natural language fluently, classify, generalize, and adapt new situations".[131] In addition, thanks to AI, both machines and computers can perform intelligently. Yet, the availability of data is widely seen as a key element for the functioning of AI. Humans need devices or software to quickly process and handle large amounts of data. The entire procedure based on the processing and management of data refers to data science, which includes the scientific examination, storage, recording, and analysis of data for the benefit of society. This entails that "humans can learn faster and process certain things faster even with a limited amount of data, but AI-based systems need massive amounts of data to generate any useful inferences".[132]

Artificial intelligence (AI) develops rapidly in the last decades. AI is seen as a kind of innate challenge regarding the common belief about the superiority of human being. This entails a certain fear which is rooted in human consciousness. AI has currently a significant impact on the various branches of law. It also applies to international law. Given the historical perspective, the

128 *Ibidem.*

129 *Ethics guidelines for trustworthy AI*, "European Commission" 08.04.2019, https://digital-strategy.ec.europa.eu/en/library/ethics-guidelines-trustworthy-ai. Accessed on 12.06.2023.

130 P.K. Garg, *Overview of Artificial Intelligence* [in:] *Artificial Intelligence. Technologies, Applications, and Challenges*, ed. L. Sharma, P.K. Gard, Oxon 2022, p. 3.

131 *Ibidem.*

132 *Ibidem.*

concept of AI was centred around the human-versus-rational issue. This begs the question of whether either thought or behaviour could function separately. Such a distinction led to discussions about whether the AI could undertake human-like behaviour and thus make rational decisions. Therefore, it raises the question of whether the AI would be able to "think" and as a result "make the right decisions".

Lastly, it is worthwhile to note that AI programs are empowered with cognitive skills such as reasoning, learning, problem-solving, perception, and self-correction. Given the reasoning process, AI programs can easily select the most appropriate algorithm for the sake of obtaining the desired outcomes. This process is widely applied in the case of making judgments, decisions, and predictions. There are two types of reasoning processes such as inductive reasoning and deductive reasoning.[133]

The learning process is based on acquiring data and creating rules for the sake of extracting meaningful insights from that data. Such rules, aka algorithms, function in terms of sequences of instructions to carry out tasks through computational devices. This phase requires the acquisition of knowledge through studying, practising, and gaining experience.[134]

The problem-solving process is used to obtain the desired solution thanks to adopting an alternative approach in the current situation. Problem-solving phase very often involves decision-making which enables choosing the most appropriate option amongst several available alternatives.[135]

The perception stage refers to the selection, acquisition, interpretation, and analysis of information. Sensory organs support humans in perception, whereas AI mechanisms are empowered with perception mechanisms which appropriately integrate sensor data. Through the self-correction process, the algorithm is adjusted to produce the most precise and accurate outcomes.[136]

3.2 *AI in International Arbitration: General Approach*

One must note, however, that AI has not been in the purview of dispute-resolution mechanisms for a long time. Indeed, the international arbitral community was rather sceptical about the use of such new technologies in the proceedings. Therefore, there were too many features related to the public

133 *Ibidem*, p. 7.

134 *Ibidem*.

135 *Ibidem*.

136 *Ibidem*. See more: T.R. Dobry, T.M. Napoli, *Beyond E-Discovery: The Ethical & Legal Use of Machine Learning Technologies*, "Lexology" 09.03.2021, https://www.lexology.com/library/detail.aspx?g=cbbc81c3-c0cb-4999-8bc1-b86a85463d16. Accessed on 26.06.2023.

courts at the enforcement stage. Interestingly, Lucan Bento stresses that "the reason for this hesitance is the utilization of judgment in advocacy, which machines (previously) lacked".[137] In addition, such a stance seems to be updated if there is rather a pro-enforcement bias which even requires state courts to grant maximum effect to the arbitral award. As a result of the COVID-19 pandemic, the use of AI in arbitration[138] is worth analyzing given more virtualized and digital arbitral proceedings. As such, it is worth recalling David Gauke who said during the AI Summit in London in 2019 that "technological revolution is no longer on the horizon – it is here".[139]

At the outset, it is noteworthy that AI tools differ from other tools dedicated to automation and legal tech, mostly due to their ability to learn and adjust. There are twofold AI mechanisms thus far. The first one refers to rule-based learning and the second concerns the so-called machine learning (ML). The former is rather static, whereas the latter not only identifies some patterns based on the already-existing data and user feedback but also varies its algorithm. The ML mechanism is widely rooted in deep learning moderns (also known as artificial neural networks). Interestingly, this mechanism is inspired by the human brain. In addition, it is also able to identify features throughout the learning process based on heavy volumes of pre-existing data. It should be stressed that the entire process is conducted without the human being's intervention. This type of AI is widely considered the most effective in the case of unstructured data. Indeed, "AI tools today often make use of deep learning and natural language processing to perform tasks that require human intelligence and present them in the comprehensible form".[140]

Given the other classification, the classical machine learning (ML) models can make predictions based on probabilities. In practice, this model benefits from statistical methods in order to obtain the output. Therefore, the expression "tools of predictive justice" means that "historic and current facts are used

137 M. Waqar, *The Use of AI in Arbitral ...*, pp. 348–349.

138 See more: M. Scherer, *Artificial Intelligence and Legal Decision-Making: The Wide Open?*, "Journal of International Arbitration" 2019, Vol. 36, issue 5, pp. 539–573; K. Paisley, E. Sussman, *Artificial Intelligence Challenges and Opportunities for International Arbitration*, "Special Feature: Artificial Intelligence and New Arbitration Data Sources. NYSBA New York Dispute Resolution Lawyer" 2018, Vol. 11, no. 1; M. Gicquello., *Artificial Intelligence in International Arbitration* [in:] *The Oxford Handbook of International Arbitration*, ed. T. Schultz, F. Ortin, Oxford 2020.

139 See: D. Gauke, Lord Chancellor and Sec'y of State for Just., House of Commons, Statement at The Artificial Intelligence in Legal Services Summit (June 4, 2019).

140 A. Singh Chauhan, *Future of AI in Arbitration: The Fine Line Between Fiction and Reality*, "Wolters Kluwer" 26.09.2022, https://arbitrationblog.kluwerarbitration.com/2020/09/26/future-of-ai-in-arbitration-the-fine-line-between-fiction-and-reality/. Accessed on 12.03.2023.

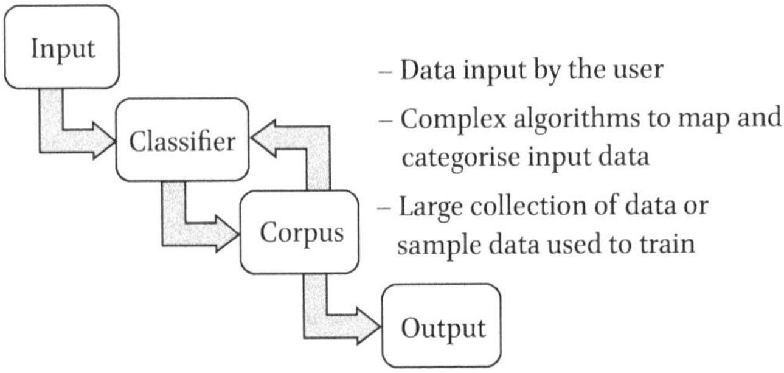

FIGURE 1 How machine learning works?
SOURCE: A. SINGH CHAUHAN, *FUTURE OF AI IN ARBITRATION: THE FINE LINE BETWEEN FICTION AND REALITY*, "WOLTERS KLUWER" 26.09.2022, HTTPS://ARBITRATIONBLOG.KLUWERARBITRATION.COM/2020/09/26/FUTURE-OF-AI-IN-ARBITRATION-THE-FINE-LINE-BETWEEN-FICTION-AND-REALITY/. ACCESSED ON 12.03.2023

to predict unknown future values or provide actionable insights".[141] Furthermore, it should be noted that the decision tree model is one of the most used models in the case of predictive analytics. This model can easily determine a course of action and further draw possible outcomes of a decision alongside its consequences.[142] Jacob Turner, in turn, differs AI and classifies them into two groups: autonomous and automated systems.

Therefore, the use of AI is based upon two universal assumptions which could be summarized as follows: the model performance can be improved merely in case of increasing available data for training and testing, and the trade-off will exist between the computational efficiency and interpretability. The latter refers to the situation where the process of automation is much more reliable in data analytics. Therefore, this process requires not only less human being's intervention but also domain knowledge usually contributed by the experts in the field. Therefore, while introducing the AI tools, their developers should opt for a "golden mean" which implies that they should strike the right

141 *Ibidem.*
142 See more on Decision Tree Model: *Value Your Legal Case with TreeAge Pro*, https://www.treeage.com/legal/. Accessed on 12.03.2023.

balance between the two.[143] Such an attitude is needed most in the case of the law.

This begs the question of which of the solutions related to AI could be used in international arbitration. Interestingly, the first- and second-level AI-supported tools are already applied in arbitration. In addition, third-level AI-supported tools are also allowed under the UNCITRAL Model Law, namely according to Articles 19(1) and 19(2). The use of translation and transcribing programs in international arbitration increases the efficiency of the arbitration proceedings. In addition, the so-called "text-mining" is widely used throughout the arbitral process to scan and process documents and to properly determine their contents. Throughout the adoption and application of new-innovation technologies based on AI tools, simple classification and clustering models are helpful to summarize heavy volumes of evidence.[144]

Notwithstanding the positive aspects of AI-supported tools, there are some doubts relating to their use in the decision-making process. Some scholars stress that the problems occur when the "technology is allowed to interfere excessively with the adjudication process".[145] The use of AI in case of arbitration may lead to violations of due process rights and public policy of the seat. Therefore, AI should not dominate the arbitral proceedings.

Overall, one could even say that AI represents "a set of techniques aimed at approximating some aspect of human or animal cognition using machines". Machine learning is one of the most significant categories within AI. This means that data scientists constantly seek to train machine learning systems by providing large amounts of data. As a result, the systems make use of their parameters which are important to enhance the reliability of the predictions. Following the features of machine learning, this tool widely spread not only in national security, but also in medicine, criminal justice, advertising, and self-driving cars, among others.

Interestingly, algorithmic capabilities can be useful in processing relatively large amounts of data quickly. In addition, these tools can also extract some patterns from the data which cannot be usually detected by human beings. They can even make some predictions. These tools could be widely used also by the foreign ministry lawyer who has not only a limited time but also some

143 A. Singh Chauhan, *Future of AI in Arbitration ...*

144 *Ibidem.*

145 *Ibidem.* Cf. C. Carrara, *Chapter IV: Science and Arbitration, The Impact of Cognitive Science and Artificial Intelligence on Arbitral Proceedings Ethical issues*, "Austrian Yearbook on International Arbitration" 2020, eds. K. Christian et al., p. 526.

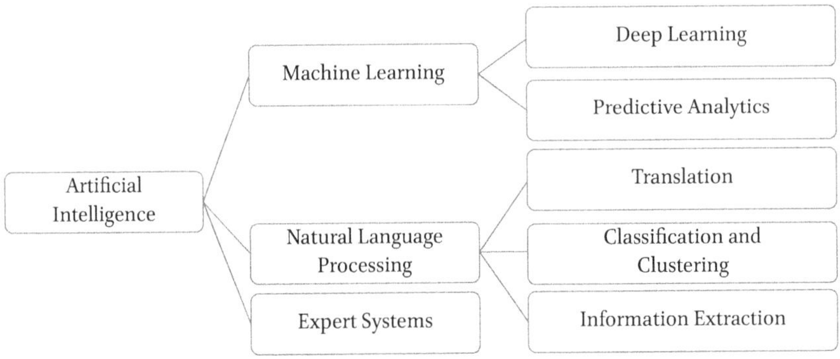

FIGURE 2 Overview of AI
SOURCE: A. SINGH CHAUHAN, *FUTURE OF AI IN ARBITRATION: THE FINE LINE BETWEEN FICTION AND REALITY*, "WOLTERS KLUWER" 26.09.2022, HTTPS://ARBITRATIONBLOG.KLUWERARBITRATION.COM/2020/09/26/FUTURE-OF-AI-IN-ARBITRATION-THE-FINE-LINE-BETWEEN-FICTION-AND-REALITY/. ACCESSED ON 12.03.2023

algorithmic tools that could easily help to extract some insights based on the data. Therefore, it would be much easier to enhance the negotiation posture and ensure better advice in terms of the possible outcome of the proceedings held in the arbitral tribunal.

AI techniques applied in the arbitral proceedings refer mostly to "machine learning" (ML). This means that there is no pre-code stage, instead, AI is based on the data. In addition, in the case of machine learning, "controlled learning" methods are used. To illustrate, the so-called "supervised learning" involves "a process that begins with a set of data labelled by people according to a measure of interest ("training data")".[146] Following this solution, the system can analyze the data set and then determine the appropriate outcome variable.

There are, in fact, threefold examples of the use of AI in arbitral proceedings for the sake of helping arbitrators to perform their daily work duties. They could be classified as follows: 1. in arbitral proceedings; 2. in the collection and analysis of the arbitral case and related facts; 3. in decision-making functions throughout the so-called predictive models. Firstly, although the platforms related to handling remote hearings do not require AI support, a machine with natural language processing (NLP) technology is widely used in the case of workload planning and scheduling. Therefore, such an AI tool could help

146 S. Gulyamov, M. Bakhramova, *Digitalization of International Arbitration and Dispute Resolution by Artificial Intelligence*, "World Bulletin of Management and Law" 2022, Vol. 9, pp. 79–80.

plan smart meetings. To illustrate, Instant Meeting Scheduling (X.AI) is widely recognized as an AI-powered tool introduced with the aim of scheduling and organizing meetings and hearings for parties and arbitrators. Interestingly, the X.AI can help parties to coordinate and plan their meetings simultaneously. As a result, human involvement is significantly limited.[147] Therefore, X.AI which works as a smart planning assistant, can "interact with people via email and machine learning models help virtual agents plan meetings with minimal human involvement receives the appropriate time, place and people to provide information".[148] This AI-supported tool was launched in 2014 for the sake of scheduling meetings effortlessly. Therefore, "With X.AI, you can automate the most tedious parts of schedule—things like finding compatible times to meet with large groups, sending follow-ups and reminders, as well as managing cancellations and rescheduling requests".[149]

Practically, it is noteworthy that this intelligent scheduling system is linked to users' calendars. In addition, this system is based on machine learning models. Therefore, the system can easily identify key components to search for the most appropriate time given the users' emails. This means that the system could choose the best parameters by considering the time, people, and location. In fact, given its functions, the system could find empty or busy slots and thus automatically book an appointment. Even though these types of applications are dedicated rather to the team manager than the arbitrator, they can significantly support the process of planning and conducting both business meetings and hearings. Nevertheless, this AI solution could be useful in the case of complex arbitrations with multiple parties stemming from different locations. Given this AI, the parties to the arbitration proceedings could easily schedule a meeting within the network, including the governing arbitration institutions.[150]

It is worthwhile to stress that AI-assisted arbitration does not violate the provisions of the New York Convention itself. This means that these innovation-driven solutions do not lead to any conceptual problems. Arbitral awards made thanks to AI-assisted tools are still human beings' products.[151] Therefore, they could be recognized merely as supporting tools.

Finally, it is worth mentioning a few examples of the current use of AI in dispute resolution. Firstly, Dispute Resolution Data is widely recognized as

147 A.S. Márquez, *Can Artificial Intelligence be used to appoint arbitrators?*¸"AVANI" 2020, no. 1, p. 264.

148 S. Gulyamov, M. Bakhramova, *Digitalization of International ...*, p. 80.

149 *Virtual Assistant*, https://www.virtualassistantassistant.com/x-ai/. Accessed on 12.03.2023.

150 S. Gulyamov, M. Bakhramova, *Digitalization of International ...*, p. 80.

151 *Ibidem*, p. 79.

an American start-up which focuses on building a global database on both international commercial arbitration and mediation. Given its features, this start-up collects information, including "industry type, claim amount, location, cost, duration, and outcomes i.e., whether the case is settled, withdrawn, or a final award is issued, etc.".[152] One must note that this start-up collects data from well-renown institutions (the International Chamber of Commerce, and the International Centre for Dispute Resolution, among others). Secondly, Arbitrator Intelligence functions as a non-profit initiative launched for the sake of increasing access to information concerning arbitrators themselves and their decision-making process. The latter refers to the post-award questionnaires which are sent to the participants of the arbitral proceedings. This initiative also grants confidentiality by functioning as a reliable body of data without the need to make arbitral awards published. Such examples of the use of AI are limited merely to collecting information.[153]

Indeed, the use of AI in international arbitration may result in many advantages. On the one hand, it could facilitate a return to legal formalism (aka "law in books") by addressing non-legal factors through the mechanical application of law to the facts of the disputed case. In addition, the appropriate use of AI can enhance the rule of law by focusing on both fairness and efficiency of the entire arbitral proceedings. The former refers to the requirements concerning the independence and impartiality of the arbitrator, whereas the latter pays attention to the reduction of costs and duration of the proceedings. Moreover, "it would dispense with the need for an appeal mechanism (concerned with the correctness of the decision) or a review mechanism (dealing with the integrity of the proceedings) that would compromise the finality of the arbitral award".[154]

There are many AI-supported tools widely used in international arbitration. To name a few, Ross offers navigation through many different legal documents, and submissions alongside the case law. One must note the advantage of this AI application. Indeed, it enables parties to compare their arguments with those outlined in previous cases.[155]

DISCO, in turn, is widely known as an AI-based alternative model offering solutions for better-organizing evidence, reviewing witnesses' videos and transcripts and searching for specific documents.[156]

152 M. Waqar, *The Use of AI in Arbitral ...*, p. 350.

153 *Ibidem*, p. 350.

154 M. Gicquello, *Artificial Intelligence in International Arbitration*, [in:] *The Oxford Handbook of International Arbitration*, ed. T. Schultz, F. Ortino, Oxford 2020, p. 7.

155 A.S. Márquez, *Can Artificial Intelligence ...*, p. 264.

156 *Ibidem*.

Kira as an AI app rapidly identifies, extracts, and analyzes text from different types of documents and contracts. Indeed, this AI provides advantages for arbitrators and parties due to its functions concerning the ability to review information on contracts for a specific case.[157]

Lastly, the so-called Arbilex has been launched specifically for international arbitration to improve the decision-making process by both law firms and litigation funds. Given its features, this AI application makes use of predictive data for the sake of quantifying uncertainties and maximizing favourable outcomes. As a result, the entire decision-making process is significantly enhanced.[158]

3.3 *AI Arbitrator's Selection Tools*

The innovation-driven technology may significantly help the selection of arbitrators by offering parties reliable information concerning their patterns, social, and professional networks. In addition, such technologies may also provide the previous and ongoing appointments as arbitrators and their performance. Even though such an AI tool would probably not solve all the problems regarding diversity in international arbitration, it could turn into an effective tool for selecting and assessing arbitrators in a stronger and more legitimate process. Nonetheless, one must note that this tool would not challenge the parties' autonomy in selecting arbitrators. Indeed, the parties, arbitral tribunal and other arbitrators would still have the power to make such a choice. On the other hand, the entire process would become more autonomized due to the emergence of new technologies. To illustrate, such a decision could be based on reliable data including both different aspects and qualities of the arbitrators themselves. Even though the idea itself seems to be interesting, there are already a few concerns relating to the solidity and correctness of analytics or data science. As such, "this is because, by being informed by datasets, artificial intelligence will necessarily reflect the society that produced such data and may inherit both social and particular (from those who fed it) bias. On data science, we are subject to encode, explicitly and intentionally or not, our prejudices and biases".[159] Such a trend has been already confirmed using algorithms within the US and Canadian Criminal Justice Systems.[160]

157 *Ibidem.*

158 *Ibidem.*

159 D. Becker, R.D. Marques, *Why the use of technology in arbitrators' selection process – although fostered – must still be handled carefully*, "Comitê Brasileiro de Arbitragem", https://cbar.org.br/site/why-the-use-of-technology-in-arbitrators-selection-process-although-fostered-must-still-be-handled-carefully/. Accessed on 06.06.2023.

160 *Ibidem.*

Although such algorithms could be potentially used for the sake of appointing arbitrators, they may cause many challenges. On the one hand, there is no objective definition of a suitable arbitrator. Therefore, given the AI, the well-ranked arbitrator could be classified as a person with good availability, namely rendering arbitral awards fast. In practice, this AI tool may prefer to appoint a man instead of a pregnant woman on temporary leave due to such reasons. This entails those female arbitrators may be lower scored and thus lower ranked amongst all arbitrators.[161]

As such, it is crucial to remember that innovation-driven technologies may provide more objective criteria in terms of appointing arbitrators, but they should be used carefully. Such tools are based on data input provided by human beings which means that they could be taught to act in a certain and biased way. In other words, even though proper data could be useful in terms of improving the entire process of selecting arbitrators, such automated AI decisions cannot be classified as completely "biased-free". By contrast, they should be properly addressed by the arbitration community. In addition, it is recommended to avoid information including gender, age, and ethnicity in such datasets to prevent and even decrease the possibility of unwanted outcomes stemming from such automated processes.[162]

To sum up, AI could potentially establish its own rules to appoint arbitrators based on criteria provided by human beings. Therefore, such a tool may easily determine the number of arbitrators, language requirements, specific field of expertise, and availability of the arbitrator with respect to the principles of international commercial arbitration (namely independence and impartiality). One must note that such an appointment of arbitrator thanks to the AI tools has the aim to generate a desired outcome by selecting the most suitable person given the disputed case. In addition, such a selection must comply with the parties' requirements. Nonetheless, the AI model should be fed properly with data to achieve reliable and accurate results.[163]

Overall, it seems inevitable that some AI tools would be incorporated into international arbitration. As such, the X.AI model may be useful in terms of verifying the availability of the potential arbitrators, whereas Arbilex may be employed to predict and identify the most appropriate arbitrator for a particular case. Although there are no obstacles in terms of international arbitration legal framework to apply such AI tools (mostly with regard to the principle of

161 *Ibidem.*
162 *Ibidem.*
163 A.S. Márquez, *Can Artificial Intelligence ...*, p. 263.

party's autonomy), two different aspects concerning AI-powered application should be first analyzed.

Firstly, it is necessary to determine whether an AI model can collect the required data and information to meet the criteria concerning the appointment of arbitrators. Indeed, this begs the question of how such an AI model can gather the necessary information to fulfil the requirements of appointing an arbitrator.

Secondly, it is crucial to examine the supplementary challenges of the AI model in terms of appointing arbitrators. Therefore, potential obstacles and limitations need to be addressed. Thereby, it is crucial to analyze the process of appointing an arbitrator given biases. Such biases can be reflected in many ways, including the influence of party-appointed arbitrators, repetitive appointments of the same arbitrator alongside a lack of sufficient information about the arbitrator.

One must note that the first two challenges can be easily overcome with the aid of AI-powered tools, mostly by composing the arbitrator panel. Nonetheless, the problem of insufficient information relates to data which are required by an AI-arbitrator appointer.[164] Many factors may lead to the existence of an information gap, most notably based on confidentiality and monopoly of the information stemming from law firms or arbitrators. In practice, it may cause many challenges concerning the implementation of such AI-powered technologies. It is crucial to remember that if an AI-arbitrator appointer lacks a set of rules, it may cause undesired outcomes. Therefore, the process of gathering complete information about the potential candidates is necessary in order to avoid the appointment process made by AI.[165]

3.4 *ChatGPT in International Arbitration: a Game-Changer?*

Legal visionaries have foreseen the ongoing changes and the transformation of the legal sector based on technological advancements. Nonetheless, one must note that such changes seem to be more gradual and progressive rather than revolutionary. The recent launch of ChatGPT by OpenAI on 30 November 2022 has already significantly marked the onset of a new era. Andrew Perlman even describes the introduction of this AI tool as the beginning of the revolution.[166]

164 *Ibidem*, p. 266.

165 *Ibidem*.

166 A. Perlman, *The Implications of OpenAi's Assistant for Legal Services and Society*, "The Practice. Harvard Law School" 2023, https://clp.law.harvard.edu/knowledge-hub/magazine/issues/generative-ai-in-the-legal-profession/the-implications-of-chatgpt-for-legal-services-and-society/. Accessed on 15.06.2023.

Recently, there is a new type of AI widely used in arbitration, namely ChatGPT which is an AI technology tool which can not only understand but also generate human language.[167] Although ChatGPT is considered a neural network, which is a computer system imitating the human brain, it can streamline arbitral proceedings in a significant way. Interestingly, this AI technology is widely based on deep learning. Therefore, given this specific mechanism, ChatGPT can process and analyze large amounts of data. Further, it can also assimilate such data and generate language. One must note that throughout being exposed to more data, the AI tool becomes better in the process of understanding and generating responses.[168]

ChatGPT may be widely used in international arbitration, most notably in the case of any activity concerning information processing such as researching, writing, or even predicting outcomes.[169] To name a few examples of potential uses, ChatGPT may enhance both legal research and analysis. Apparently, this AI tool can comprehend and handle excessive amounts of data and thus support arbitrators or involved parties in the course of legal investigations and evaluations. ChatGPT, by swiftly assessing the existing precedents, provisions, and many other resources, can easily enable arbitrators to issue decisions and arbitral awards promptly.[170] Secondly, ChatGPT through its proficiency in comprehending natural language may potentially lead to automation in the creation of legal documents and agreements, thereby decreasing both the time and resources needed to accomplish fully these tasks. Thanks to this advantage, the entire arbitration process may be streamlined and thus becomes more efficient. In addition, such an AI tool could also be used to swiftly generate procedural orders from the arbitral tribunal, summarize facts and even handle communications between the parties and the tribunal itself.[171]

Thirdly, ChatGPT may also play a crucial role in enhancing collaboration between parties and the arbitral tribunal. Given its features, this AI tool may help translate legal documents which facilitate the participation of parties

---

167 See more: H. Roos, *Arbitration Tech Toolbox: Let's Chat Some More about ChatGPT and Dispute Resolution*, "Kluwer Arbitration Blog" 08.04.2023, https://arbitrationblog.kluwerarbitration.com/2023/04/08/arbitration-tech-toolbox-lets-chat-some-more-about-chatgpt-and-dispute-resolution/. Accessed on 26.06.2023.

168 L.F. Souza-McMurtrie, *Arbitration Tech Toolbox: Will ChatGPT Change International Arbitration as We Know It?*, "Kluwer Arbitration Blog" 26.02.2023, https://arbitrationblog.kluwerarbitration.com/2023/02/26/arbitration-tech-toolbox-will-chatgpt-change-international-arbitration-as-we-know-it/. Accessed on 31.05.2023.

169 See more: S. Wade, *Practical implications of ChatGPT in the arbitration proceedings*, "LexisNexis" 02.02.2023, https://www.lexisnexis.co.uk/legal/news/practical-implications-of-chatgpt-in-the-arbitration-proceedings. Accessed on 25.06.2023.

170 L.F. Souza-McMurtrie, *Arbitration Tech Toolbox ...*

171 *Ibidem.*

stemming from different jurisdictions. In addition, it can also analyze memorials and distinguish between the facts of the disputed case and those that have been already agreed upon by the parties concerned. Indeed, ChatGPT can arrange such facts into tables. Besides, it has also the capacity of assessing its strength by analyzing both the relevant case law and statements from witnesses.[172]

Fourthly, ChatGPT is also empowered to predict the aftermath of the arbitral award. This entails that this AI tool may be employed for the sake of predictive analysis. Practically, this capability gives arbitrators the possibility to forecast the potential factual outcomes of the issued arbitral awards based on historical cases and jurisprudential data. Furthermore, given such a function, ChatGPT may also be useful to estimate the likelihood of an arbitral award that could be annulled, denied enforcement, or even complied with. One must note that such information provided by ChatGPT would allow the arbitrator to draft their arbitral awards to maximize their longevity.[173]

Fifthly, ChatGPT provides the so-called dialectical argumentation. This means that this tool can be used by a party for the sake of uncovering vulnerabilities in the legal strategy made by the opposing party or even provide some counterarguments to their reasoning. By uploading either transcripts or written documents that have been submitted by the opposing party into the system, ChatGPT may swiftly identify any inconsistencies, contradictions, or gaps that may exist therein. Indeed, this function of ChatGPT is useful to examine the opposing party's arguments.[174]

Briefly, some positive sides of using this AI tool could be summarized as follows. Indeed, it would not only increase the productivity and efficiency of the arbitral proceedings but also decrease the costs of arbitration itself. In addition, the appropriate use of ChatGPT may also be beneficial in terms of preventing unnecessary delays. Linda L. Beyea who is a Vice President of AAA-ICDR Innovation suggests that arbitrators should be eager to experiment with ChatGPT nowadays, most notably beyond the arbitral proceedings. This experience could be useful to enhance the arbitration proceedings with respect to the arbitrator's confidentiality duties stemming from the Code of Ethics for Arbitrators in Commercial Disputes and the AAA's rules.[175]

---

172 *Ibidem.*

173 *Ibidem.*

174 *Ibidem.*

175 L.L. Beyea, *The Rise of ChatGPT: Why Arbitrators Need to Take Notice: Potential Impact of ChatGPT in ADR*, "American Arbitration Association" 17.03.2023, https://www.adr.org/blog/The-Rise-of-ChatGPT-Why-Arbitrators-Need-to-Take-Notice. Accessed on 31.05.2023.

Aside from the positive sides, such an AI tool has also many limitations and can easily bring about some challenges. Firstly, ChatGPT may generate text which is neither legally accurate nor suitable. This entails that this AI tool often incorporates common statements stemming from online sources which seemingly random ideas. In addition, the outcome provided by ChatGPT can sometimes be not only wordy but also lacking in nuances or even coherence. One must note that ChatGPT does not provide similar outputs in other languages likewise in English. This is also one of the major disadvantages of this tool nowadays.[176] It seems obvious, however, that this tool will be improved constantly and would provide more outcomes in different languages in the foreseeable future.

Secondly, although the ChatGPT is an AI tool developed through training on data, such data may also contain some biases. Therefore, once the training data itself is biased, the decision made or provided by the system could also be biased. This may have a potential negative influence on the marginalized groups.[177] One must note that arbitrators are deemed to maintain impartiality. Such a duty result from many rules and provisions of international arbitration law, namely Article 12 of the UNCITRAL Model Law, Article 11 of the ICC Rules 2021, Rule 11 of the CIArb Code of Professional and Ethical Conduct, the IBA Guidelines on Conflict-of-Interest 2014, among others.[178] Impartiality is one of the key elements of the arbitration proceedings. It refers to the intellectual predisposition of the arbitrator towards the parties concerned or the subject matter under dispute. It also reflects the so-called "arbitrator's mindset". On the one hand, parties should have a certain confidence in a person handling their case which is crucial to prevent any challenges regarding unfavourable awards. On the other hand, a duty of being "impartial" is also rooted in codes to act fairly during the arbitral proceedings alongside treat parties equally and thus restrain from partiality towards matters unrelated to the legitimate merit of the arguments and evidence.[179]

Such unconscious biases can be classified into two chief groups, namely information processing biases and emotional biases. The former refers to some statistical and quantitative errors that occurred in the judgment. Indeed, such errors can be easily reduced or even resolved through the input of new

176 L.F. Souza-McMurtrie, *Arbitration Tech Toolbox ...*

177 *Ibidem.*

178 F. Singarajah, *Unconscious Bias in International Arbitration*, "Thomson Reuters. Practical Law Arbitration Blog" 21.06.2021, http://arbitrationblog.practicallaw.com/unconscious-bias-in-international-arbitration/#:~:text=This%20is%20a%20subtle%20bias,the%20arbitrator%20is%20accustomed%20to. Accessed on 01.06.2023.

179 *Ibidem.*

information. The latter, in turn, refers to attitudes and feelings either conscious or subconscious.[180]

Thirdly, ChatGPT could potentially influence the arbitral tribunal. Indeed, lawyers can manipulate the decision-making process by using ChatGPT. One must note that ChatGPT is classified as an AI language model which means that it can scrutinize not only previous judgments but also articles and viewpoints that have been expressed by the arbitrators. Based on such an analysis, ChatGPT identifies patterns in the reasoning and decision-making process of arbitrators. Interestingly:

> ChatGPT can be trained on the laws, legal precedents, and the facts of the case in question to generate possible arguments that the arbitrator might be more vulnerable to, not only in terms of their content, but also in terms of their style, by taking advantage of any unconscious biases the model may identify. This mechanism can be used at any stage of the procedure, from the appointment and challenge of arbitrators to the choice of experts, and lawyers can adjust their pleadings ever so slightly to favour their position before the tribunal.[181]

Fourthly, the use of ChatGPT may also result in unethical legal practices during arbitral proceedings. On the one hand, it can produce some deceptive and false statements or evidence both in arbitration and negotiation. In addition, it can also generate fraudulent documents or contracts to deceive the parties involved in the arbitral proceedings. ChatGPT can produce some persuasive or misleading arguments for the sake of influencing the decision-making process of the arbitrator.[182] Overall, the excessive and not enough cautious use of this AI tool can easily be harmful to the entire arbitral proceedings, including the process of rendering the arbitral award.

Fifthly, once an arbitrator makes use of ChatGPT while drafting an arbitral award, either entirely or partially, there is a risk that such an award may not be rendered fully independently. Additionally, an award generated by ChatGPT would not reflect the unbiased decision-making of the arbitrator himself. By contrast, such awards could be shaped by the biases resulting from the training data and the language model of the ChatGPT. On the other hand, too excessive reliance on ChatGPT may also challenge the arbitrator's level of knowledge on arbitration alongside comprehension of the case itself and expertise. Such

180 *Ibidem.*
181 L.F. Souza-McMurtrie, *Arbitration Tech Toolbox ...*
182 *Ibidem.*

concerns could potentially cast doubt upon the validity of the arbitral award rendered by the ChatGPt instead of a human arbitrator.[183]

Lastly, ChatGPT also provides the so-called "stylistic imitation". This entails that the users can easily change the style of the entire text through the function described as "style transfer". Given this technique, ChatGPT is trained based on the large dataset of text written by a certain individual. Therefore, it can acquire the unique writing style of a given person. This function available on ChatGPT can be used also by arbitrators to modify arbitral awards that have been prepared by secretaries and assistants. As such, they could overcome problems related to the stylistic analysis likewise in the case of Yukos.[184]

Briefly, such risks could be summarized as follows. On the one hand, ChatGPT is not error-proof which means that it can lead to many inherent biases in the datasets. This entails that the person making use of such AI should be responsible for verifying the accuracy of the final outcome. In addition, arbitrators are also deemed to abide by both Canon I of the Code of Ethics (referring to the integrity and fairness of the arbitration process) and Canon V (referring to no delegation of duty to decide and the importance of transparency). Linda Beyea suggests that arbitrators once using this AI tool during the arbitral proceedings should disclose to the parties this fact. Therefore, they would ensure not only the transparency of the entire process but also fulfil their duties stemming from the ethical code.[185]

3.5 *Risks of AI*

Through the unconscious use of AI, many concerns may arise, including discrimination, bias, oppression, exclusion, and even bad design. Such concerns are remarkably heightened in view of the vulnerable populations who may lack access to human rights laws or institutional remedies. One must note that the so-called risk assessment algorithms record is based on a multitude of personal attributes, basically including more than one hundred characteristics such as socioeconomic status, age, gender, geographical location, and employment status, among others.[186]

Even though the due process[187] clause raises significant concerns, it seems to be inadequate to fully address the challenges resulting from algorithmic

183 *Ibidem.*
184 *Ibidem.*
185 L.L. Beyea, *The Rise of ChatGPT …*
186 G.I. Zekos, *Advanced Artificial Intelligence and Robo-Justice*, Cham 2022, pp. 232–233.
187 See more: J. Serralda Hierro, *An Arbitration Center's Perspective: Due Process in Online Dispute Resolution* [in:] *Online Dispute Resolution. New Challenges*, ed. D. Moura Vicente, E. Dias Oliveira, J. Gomes de Almeida, Baden-Baden 2022.

risk assessments. There is a trend upholding that the use of such assessments should be rather limited to prevent technology from acting as judges. Nevertheless, regardless of this argument, both states and courts eagerly adopt risk assessment tools.[188]

It is noteworthy that there are two main sources to train data used for algorithms, namely third parties and the algorithm's architect. There is a significant concern once the training data is infected with unconscious biases. Detecting and addressing errors and biases within the algorithm's design seems to be easier compared to identifying and correcting them within the training data sets. Such biases, throughout the incorporation into the learning models during retraining, have the potential to both persist and undermine the reliability of the model itself. This leads to a real risk that undetected errors and biases in the data sets can become deeply entrenched. Therefore, they can develop their own significance and thus cause unintended alterations in the algorithm itself without the involvement of a human being.[189]

This begs the question of what solutions have been adopted to address these concerns. Even though there are some efforts undertaken to tackle these problems, the progress made thus far seems to be merely at the initial stage. Indeed, one must note various potential solutions. One approach considers requesting the developer of the data set and/or algorithm to undergo an audit of the internal processes prior to any deployment. Scrutinizing the internal mechanism of algorithms or the criterion for selecting data is deemed to reveal either errors or biases, it cannot be fully guaranteed. In addition, in practice, "there is a likelihood of resistance if the author is concerned about the trade secret value of the work. Some algorithms are open source".[190]

4 Conclusion

This chapter aimed to explore various new technologies widely applied in arbitration tribunals. Therefore, it focuses on finding answers to the following research questions: "what solutions within digitization and which new technologies have been adopted by arbitration tribunals? Which forms of IT tools and innovation-driven technologies are widely used in international arbitration? and what is the legal background of IT tools?".

188 G.I. Zekos, *Advanced Artificial Intelligence ...*, p. 233.

189 P.B. Marrow, M. Karol, S. Kuyan, *Artificial Intelligence and Arbitration: The Computer as an Arbitrator – Are We There Yet?*, "Dispute Resolution Journal" 2020, Vol. 74, no. 4, p. 60.

190 *Ibidem*, p. 62.

Notably, arbitral institutions make use of multifarious IT tools. The solutions adopted by the leading institutions globally, namely the American Arbitration Association, the International Chamber of Commerce in Paris, WIPO in Geneva, SCC in Stockholm, E-Arbitration-T as a European solution and ICSID differ significantly. These arbitration institutions have been chosen based on the level of their internationalization to outline different approaches how to benefit from innovativeness within the modern dispute resolution platforms. Through the adoption of these platforms, parties can not only easily file their cases online but also attach necessary documentation.

Further, the development of new technologies also allowed to handle remote hearings. Such analysis was based on the binding provisions of international arbitration law. Therefore, it was crucial to determine whether the provisions of the 1958 New York Convention and the UNCITRAL Model Law also allow for remote proceedings. Given this analysis, it is noteworthy to remember that international regulations provide merely a general framework and thus they do not explicitly forbid the use of new technologies while handling arbitration proceedings.

One must note, however, that changes have already been made at the level of arbitration institutions worldwide. Therefore, in the wake of technological development and changes, arbitral institutions have adjusted their rules to the new reality, albeit it also causes many new challenges ahead. One of the pressing topics is to ensure that fundamental principles of international arbitration are fulfilled. To address many concerns relating to remote hearings, the Seoul Protocol on Video Conferencing in International Arbitration was issued. It provides a set of practical solutions for conducting online proceedings. Likewise, the IBA also introduced its International Bar Association's Rules on the Taking of Evidence in International Arbitration, which focus on the production of documents in electronic form.

Lastly, this chapter deals with the new trend, namely the use of artificial intelligence in international arbitration. Notably, given the current status of technological development, artificial intelligence can be supportive in the daily work of both arbitral tribunals and arbitrators themselves. Indeed, the UNCITRAL Model Law together with other rules and guidelines of arbitral institutions explicitly do not cover the use of AI during arbitral proceedings. Nevertheless, there are no more detailed provisions to cover these issues. As such, international arbitration law also lacks regulations on the limits of the AI's use.

CHAPTER 3

Advantages of Digitalization in International Arbitration

1 Introduction

Digitalization provides many advantages compared to traditional dispute resolution mechanisms. As such, e-arbitration ensures that some procedures or even the entire proceedings are handled online, including the filing of a case, hearings, submission of documents, and evidence and rendering of an arbitral award. One could even say that there is no ideal framework for e-arbitration, but many international arbitral institutions seek to involve some innovation-driven technologies to make the entire process efficient, cost-effective, and expeditious.[1] Therefore, innovation-driven technologies are beneficial to render work processes in more effective, efficient, and convenient ways. This chapter aims to answer whether such innovation-driven technologies also comply with fundamental principles of handling arbitral proceedings specified in international law.

2 Rule of Law and Access to Justice

One must note that international arbitration is widely recognized as a close partner of the courts given its sustaining position to promote the rule of law. This is crucial mostly in terms of cross-border commerce.[2] Considering the rule of law[3] in international arbitration, it is important to analyze Article 18 of the UNCITRAL Model Law which reflects the requirements of due process. Therefore, according to this provision, parties should be treated with equality and each party should be given a full opportunity to set forth its case.[4]

1 H. Nasser Agil, *Electronic Arbitration: The new mechanism for dispute resolution*, "The Arbitrator & Mediator" December 2016, p. 71.

2 S. Menon, *Arbitration's Blade: International Arbitration and the Rule of Law*, "Journal of International Arbitration" 2021, Vol. 38, issue 1, p. 2.

3 See more: T. Dietz, *The Rule of Law Effects of Commercial Arbitration from a Socio-Legal Perspective* [in:] *The Oxford Handbook of International Arbitration*, ed. T. Schultz, F. Ortino, Oxford 2020.

4 *Ibidem*, p. 9.

DOI:10.1163/9789004700710_005

Sundaresh Menon stresses that „international arbitration can claim to support an attenuated model of the rule of law".[5] Interestingly, he explains his view based on the key features of the international arbitration itself that could be summarized as follows: consent-based limitations, the confidentiality of arbitral awards, party appointment of arbitrators and the general absence of a right to a right answer. Given the first feature, although the parties' agreement and thus willingness to submit any dispute to arbitration is rooted in contemporary international arbitration, there are also many constraints concerning the "arbitrator's ability to give full expression to the rule of law".[6]

"Access to justice" is widely considered a basic principle of the rule of law. Such a stance is presented by the United Nations (UN). The so-called "delivery of justice" is beyond any discrimination and should be accessible to all individuals, irrespective of their financial status or geographical location. This entails that the entire structure of the justice system should be easily reachable and open. Therefore, every person should have the right to be heard and to fully benefit from their rights in case of any infringement. Article 6 of the European Convention on Human Rights (ECHR) is widely recognized as a guarantee of the right to a fair and effective hearing. This means that every person should not only have access to an independent and unbiased tribunal but also should benefit from such a right within a reasonable time. In addition, every person should have an equal opportunity to set forth their case. This begs the question, however, of whether remote hearings truly support the "access to justice".[7]

Given the Special Counsel at the ICC Court in Paris, Mireze Philippe, "Everything is online except justice". Additionally, "justice is denied to millions of people who cannot afford going to courts, or who are disabled or in remote places with no access to justice to seek remedies, which ends up in a denial of justice".[8] Philippe even stressed that "Raising awareness and finding concrete tools that may help to overcome unequal access to information and justice is everyone's concern. After nearly 70 years of progress in technology and telecommunications, it is high time that both public and private justice offer access to justice around the globe that is fair and simple".[9]

5 *Ibidem*, p. 10.

6 *Ibidem*.

7 B. Hatami Alamdari, *The Question of Remote …*, p. 149.

8 *Three takeaways on how digital technologies are transforming arbitration*, "ICC" 30.08.2017, https://iccwbo.org/media-wall/news-speeches/three-takeaways-digital-technologies-transforming-arbitration/,. Accessed on 10.03.2023.

9 *Ibidem*.

Finally, it is noteworthy that ICC also supports and promotes access to justice through Jus Mundi system. Therefore, ICC has the aim to strengthen the global rule-based system by enhancing transparency in international arbitration. It is possible using Jus Mundi's advanced AI technology given which reliable arbitration content will be made available. Thanks to this collaboration between ICC and Jus Mundi, the public will have access to all arbitral awards rendered by the ICC International Court of Arbitration along with related documents since 1 January 2019.[10]

Indeed, such collaboration is based on the following key elements. First, according to the ICC Note to Parties and Arbitral Tribunals on the Conduct of the Arbitration, the Secretariat of the ICC International Court of Arbitration is deemed to inform parties that both arbitral awards and relevant documents pertaining to a specific case can be published. In addition, each party has the right to object to the publication of such an arbitral award at any stage. Second, such publication includes merely pre-approved information which means that all personal data are pseudonymized or anonymized, as deemed necessary. Therefore, given this procedure, only essential and pre-approved details along with names can be made available to the general public. Third, the ICC Court approves the digital version of the arbitral award based on previous pseudonymization or anonymization techniques. Afterwards, Jus Mundi transforms both the award and related documents into a digital format upon publication. Finally, after reviews and parties' approval, Jus Mundis makes the ICC award or relevant documents available on the ICC website. Such publications can be easily accessed in many languages. In addition, Jus Mundi's multilingual search engine along with other tools ensures that users can search, and access needed information efficiently.[11]

3 Transparency

The innovation-driven technologies introduced recently in the arbitration proceedings have the aim to ensure not only confidentiality but also transparency of such procedures. This means that "digital solutions have been implemented by arbitral institutions with the aim of increasing the transparency of arbitration as a dispute resolution process to assist in the accessibility and reliability

10 *Publication of ICC Arbitral Awards with JUS MUNDI*, "ICC", https://iccwbo.org/dispute-resolution/resources/publication-of-icc-arbitral-awards-jus-mundi-not-icc-publication/. Accessed on 10.06.2023.

11 *Ibidem.*

of arbitration, while protecting the confidentiality that is still favoured by parties across the globe".[12]

To increase the level of transparency of the arbitration proceedings, many institutions worldwide launched special platforms referring to the previously administered cases. To illustrate, the Arbitration and Mediation Center of the Lima Chamber of Commerce (CCL) introduced the platform "Faro de Transparencia" (Transparency Lighthouse) which covers the cases administered by this institution since 2012. Given this platform, it is possible to recognize the list of both national and international arbitrators, names of arbitrators who constituted arbitral tribunal, sanctions imposed on arbitrators, awards rejected by the judiciary, full texts of arbitral awards (concerning cases to which the Peruvian state was a party) alongside the anonymized summaries of commercial awards. It is noteworthy that the publishment of this information does not violate the principle of confidentiality in international commercial arbitration law. The other arbitral institutions also provide similar services. To name a few, the International Chamber of Commerce launched the so-called "case and arbitral tribunal directories". This platform provides information on the "arbitrator's name, nationality, role in the arbitral tribunal, how the arbitrator was appointed and the status of the case".[13] Additionally, since January 2020, this platform provides also details concerning the sector of the industry as well as the counsel who represented the parties in the disputed case. Likewise, the London Court of International Arbitration (LCIA) also introduced the so-called "database of the LCIA Court's decisions regarding challenges" which covers cases administered since 2010. This platform includes information regarding the anonymized summary of each case, the challenge (if applicable) and the court's decision. Interestingly, it should be stressed that "the LCIA considers that providing details of decisions on arbitrator challenges gives guidance in relation to acceptable standards of conduct and provides a greater understanding of the reasoning applied by the LCIA court in relation to such decisions".[14]

To sum up, digital platforms could be useful to provide better accessibility and reliability while maintaining the confidentiality of arbitral proceedings. Therefore, while entering the "age of arbitration", these digital solutions will be of key significance to the parties to facilitate the decision on how, when, and where to conduct arbitral proceedings and who select as an arbitrator.

12 L. Amado, D. Griffiths, *Improving transparency in international arbitration: digital solutions*, "Osborne Clarke" 19.05.2021, https://www.osborneclarke.com/insights/improving-transparency-international-arbitration-digital-solutions. Accessed on 12.03.2023.

13 *Ibidem.*

14 *Ibidem.*

This means that along with the more transparent process of the arbitration itself, more parties will recognize arbitration as a reliable method of handling disputes. These advancements in terms of technology, including the use of artificial intelligence are likely to assist arbitrators.

4 Efficiency, Flexibility, and Low Costs

Even though international arbitration was traditionally recognized as a more efficient and cost-effective mechanism of dispute resolution compared to litigation, it has also faced recent criticism for being too slow and expensive. Nonetheless, the widespread adoption of remote hearings in arbitral proceedings has the potential to overcome such criticism and enhance efficiency and lower costs.[15]

The IT tools are useful to reduce both costs and time, mostly with regard to travelling and document handling. The former is reduced due to online meetings that are conducted instead of traditional face-to-face meetings. Therefore, such cost savings consider lost working time related to the worst productivity, which is a result of jetlag, for instance. In addition, this solution allows that all travel-related costs, relating to all the parties concerned (arbitrators, parties, counsels, witnesses, and experts) can be easily avoided.[16] Indeed, both witnesses and experts are supposed to take part in the arbitral proceedings merely for a brief and uncertain period. Therefore, remote hearings would be beneficial to all parties. Additionally, remote hearings provide more flexibility to the parties to have merely some of the witnesses and experts in the course of the relevant stage of the arbitral proceedings. Hence, there is no need of requiring them to travel to the hearing venue. Likewise, counsels and arbitral tribunals can also manage different aspects of a particular case alongside the other responsibilities in private space, namely from their own chambers.[17]

---

15 K. Nagarajan, J.J. East, *Salient Considerations for Remote International Arbitration Hearings* [in:] *The Impact of Covid on International Disputes*, eds. S. Lalani, S.G. Shapiro, "International and Comparative Business Law and Public Policy" Vol. 2, Leiden-Boston 2022, p. 106. See more: C. Bull, *An Effective Platform for International Arbitration: Raising the Standards in Speed, Costs and Enforceability* [in:] *International Organizations and the Promotion of Effective Dispute Resolution. AIIB Yearbook of International Law 2019*, ed. P. Quayle, Gao Xuan, Leiden-Boston 2019, pp. 7–27.

16 G. Kaufmann-Kohler, T. Schulz, *The Use of Information* ..., p. 10.

17 R. Thirgood, *Remote hearings: storm clouds and silver linings*, "International Bar Association" 27.09.2022, https://www.ibanet.org/clint-september-2022-feature-5. Accessed 15.04.2023.

According to Patricia Shaughnessy's survey based on nineteen arbitral institutions, "the institutions have found the procedures for facilitating remote arbitration have worked well and meet the needs of clients for fair, efficient, and cost-effective arbitration".[18] This means that the widespread use of remote hearings platforms resulted in enhanced efficiency for participants in arbitral proceedings. Such benefits have been achieved without compromising the quality of arbitration itself. In addition, given the White&Case and Queen Mary (QM) School of International Arbitration Survey, 25% of respondents expressed their willingness to fully reject in-person hearings. As such, "the QM Survey points out, this statistic seems to reflect the newfound level of comfort with remote hearing platforms amongst stakeholder".[19] In addition, "If a hearing could no longer be held in person, 79% of respondents would choose to 'proceed at the scheduled time as a virtual hearing'. Only 16% would 'postpone the hearing until it could be held in person', while 4% would proceed with a documents-only award".[20]

Respondents even stress that:

> Recent (and, in many cases, new) experience of virtual hearings has offered an opportunity to gauge users' perception of this procedural adaptation. The 'potential for greater availability of dates for hearings' is seen as the greatest benefit of virtual hearings, followed closely by 'greater efficiency through use of technology' and 'greater procedural and logistical flexibility'. Aspects that gave respondents most cause for concern included the 'difficulty of accommodating multiple or disparate time zones', the impression that it is 'harder for counsel teams and clients to confer during hearing sessions' and concerns that it might be 'more difficult to control witnesses and assess their credibility'. The fallibility of technology and the phenomenon of 'screen fatigue' were also cited.[21]

Therefore, to fully benefit from remote hearings and digital transformation in arbitral proceedings, it is necessarsy to address the challenges ahead. Indeed, respondents even expressed their willingness to take part in "a mix of in-person and remote" hearings in all types of interactions, namely meetings and

---

18 K. Nagarajan, J.J. East, *Salient Considerations for Remote …*, p. 107.

19 *Ibidem.*

20 *2021 International Arbitration Survey: Adapting arbitration to a changing world*, "Queen Mary and White&Case" 2021, https://arbitration.qmul.ac.uk/media/arbitration/docs/LON0320037-QMUL-International-Arbitration-Survey-2021_19_WEB.pdf, p. 3.

21 *Ibidem.*

conferences. Nonetheless, they also stressed that the virtual format is much more appropriate in case of procedural hearings, whereas in-person hearings should prevail in case of substantive hearings.[22]

Secondly, the use of IT can also lead to the reduction of document handling costs. To illustrate, digital copies of documents are free, while the reproduction of documents on paper creates costs. This solution seems beneficial mostly in case of lengthy documents in more complicated arbitration disputes. Furthermore, the digital documents can be easily stored on any device. This means that there is no need to have storage space for paper-based documents. The shipment of documents is also less complicated. Transmission of electronic files could be made through email. Therefore, there is no need to send a courier around the globe with the paper documents.[23]

Thirdly, IT tools are useful in terms of time-saving concerning the realization of multifarious tasks during arbitral proceedings. To name a few, both remote hearings and the transfer of documents can be sped up while using appropriate technologies. Moreover, if the tasks are realized in a shorter time, the procedure of entire arbitral proceedings is also accelerated. This entails that there is no need to wait for shipping and delivery of documents. The use of IT ensures better workflows and thus increases productivity.[24]

Apparently, the shift towards remote hearings may be cost-effective, most importantly by shortening the duration of the hearings. Pursuant to the survey of arbitrators made by the Arbitration Institute of the Stockholm Chamber of Commerce (SCC), practitioners mentioned time, cost, convenience, and environmental impact to be advantages of remote hearings. It is also noteworthy that 75% of arbitrators stressed that timesaving is one of the significant benefits of remote proceedings. Additionally, the SCC mentioned in its report that:

> Because a virtual hearing does not require time-consuming travel, it can be scheduled for every other day or for shorter days, meaning that participants do not need to put all other work on hold during the hearing. According to the arbitrators surveyed, this makes it easier to find suitable hearing dates within a reasonable time frame, and awards can be rendered faster.[25]

22 *Ibidem.*
23 G. Kaufmann-Kohler, T. Schulz, *The Use of Information …*, p. 10.
24 *Ibidem.*
25 B. Sanderson, M. Scott, S. Croft, *Hearings in International Arbitration. What Has the Pandemic Taught Us about Virtual Hearings and What They Cn Offer in the Future?*, [in:] *The Impact of Covid on International Disputes*, eds. S. Lalani, S.G. Shapiro, "International and Comparative Business Law and Public Policy" Vol. 2, Leiden-Boston 2022, pp. 123–124; Cf.

Furthermore, the participants of the survey also highlighted that remote hearings may become more efficient in the case of being shorter and more focused. Indeed, such hearings are easier to organize logistically and there are fewer cancellations. Interestingly, one respondent in DLA Piper's survey noted that:

> The preparation for the virtual hearing seemed effortless. The virtual hearing was conducted seamlessly [...] the cross examination was clear, the recording/transcript was real time, the camera monitoring was completely captive. One wonders why we should ever have a physical hearing flying numerous parties across the world when technology can facilitate a hearing that is real time, face-to-face, much like the physical hearing in every sense that matters in an arbitration case.[26]

Through remote hearings technology, the resource gap can be significantly reduced. Therefore, parties would save both time and cost. Such development is advantageous, especially for cost-conscious and time-poor clients.[27] This suggests that the use of new technologies in international arbitration can contribute to an increased interest in this form of dispute resolution. As a result, it will become more accessible to parties and participants who have been excluded from the opportunity to make use of international arbitration thus far.

5 Effectiveness and Convenience

Aside from these positive aspects, IT could also lead to increased effectiveness of the arbitral procedure. To illustrate, even if witnesses or experts are not available for the hearing, they can easily be heard through videoconferencing. Given this solution, arbitral proceedings can be handled properly, mostly in the case of fast-track procedures. In addition, sometimes the IT tools can even be beneficial to increase the quality of different types of actions undertaken during the arbitral proceedings. As such, it is noteworthy that throughout the

---

SCC Virtual Hearing Survey," Arbitration Institute of the Stockholm Chamber of Commerce, October 2020, pp. 6–7, https://sccinstitute.com/media/1773182/scc-rapport_virtual_hearing-2.pdf.

26 B. Sanderson, M. Scott, S. Croft, *Hearings in International ...*, p. 124. Cf. J-P Douglas-Henry et al., *Virtual Hearings 2021: Virtual hearings*, "DLA Piper" 21.09.2021, p. 8, https://www.dlapiper.com/en/uk/insights/publications/2021/07/virtual-hearings-2021/ ("DLA September 2021 Report").

27 B. Sanderson, M. Scott, S. Croft, *Hearings in International ...*, p. 124.

videoconferencing, all the parties concerned could transfer richer information and a more detailed message compared to teleconferencing. It is crucial to satisfactory results in view of the arbitration procedure. Although videoconferencing is not equal to face-to-face meetings, this type of proceeding could be compared rather to teleconferencing. This entails that videoconferencing should be regarded as a midway between teleconferencing and face-to-face meetings. Therefore, one could even stress that videoconferencing may even replace very often teleconferencing by providing more advantages, mostly with regard to the quality of discussions. Some scholars even point out that "on those occasions where the level of details of the discussion does not matter so much, it may replace face-to-face meetings (a question of effectiveness) with advantages related to speed and costs (a matter of efficiency)".[28]

IT tools should also be analyzed through the lens of convenience. Aside from the cost- and time-effective factors, the use of IT in arbitral proceedings leads to making processes more convenient to the parties. To illustrate, it is much easier to search for specific wording in electronic documents compared to traditional ones. In addition, such electronic documents can be archived easily which is also very convenient while handling arbitral proceedings. Therefore, an enormous number of files can be stored without the need of having any physical place to archive them properly.[29]

Interestingly, online techniques based on the use of multi-media transcripts also apply during face-to-face hearings. On the one hand, such techniques allow participants to see and hear the evidence. On the other hand, participants can also see the written transcript of the case and follow it on the screen. Indeed, through the adoption of these technologies, all the parties involved can better comprehend the evidence itself. In addition, such a transcript can be easily searched and annotated directly on the screen. This technique also allows you to connect to the hearing remotely through a link.[30]

Lastly, it is worthwhile to remember that innovation-driven technologies should not be regarded as a goal, but only as processes needed to improve the arbitral proceedings. If they lead to the improvement of processes in terms of effectiveness (mostly with regard to the outcome) and efficiency (lower costs compared to traditional ways of handling disputes), they could not be recognized as a threat. Nevertheless, it should be stressed that the increased technological complexity also needs time to acquaint with these changes and realize

28 G. Kaufmann-Kohler, T. Schulz, *The Use of Information ...*, p. 11.

29 *Ibidem*, p. 11.

30 J. Hörnle, *Online Dispute Resolution ...*, p. 31.

how to benefit from these solutions in a daily work routine.[31] Therefore, it is recommended to follow the rule "first master it, then use it". This entails that the IT tools should be first tried and mastered before being used in serious situations such as arbitral proceedings, for instance.[32]

6 Enhanced Diversity in International Arbitration

The ongoing adoption of remote hearings is likely to advance the diversity in international arbitration. Patricia Shaughnessy stresses that "[t]here is a great need for greater diversity and more inclusiveness in arbitration" because it "will improve arbitration performance and legitimacy".[33]

One must note that diversity includes many factors such as race, gender, culture, socioeconomic status, sexual orientation, geographical background, and disability-related aspects. Such a comprehensive and sustained approach is recommended for the sake of promoting diversity. By contrast, remote hearings provide a practical pathway towards fostering inclusivity within international arbitration.[34]

Remote hearings may be useful in terms of enhanced diversity. To illustrate, through remote hearings, counsels stemming from either underrepresented groups or geographical regions may benefit from international arbitration. As a result, they could even gain practical experience and knowledge in this field, and thus become arbitrators in the future. One of the advantages of remote hearings refers to reduced time and expenses related typically to arbitral proceedings.[35]

Secondly, thanks to remote hearings, legal counsels may benefit from more flexible schedules. As such, they could also attract potential clients. Such flexibility may boost the representation of minority groups or individuals, most notably women and men with young families. These groups face challenges while dealing with in-person events or long travel schedules. Through innovation-driven technologies, international arbitration promotes and supports gender diversity. Indeed, such a new remote paradigm plays a crucial role in enhancing more flexible arrangements in the case of women with families.

31 G. Kaufmann-Kohler, T. Schulz, *The Use of Information* ..., pp. 12–13.
32 *Ibidem*, p. 13.
33 K. Nagarajan, J.J. East, *Salient Considerations for Remote* ..., p. 110.
34 *Ibidem*.
35 *Ibidem*.

Therefore, women could more easily perform their duties despite previously existing difficulties.[36]

Third, remote hearings also provide better access to justice. It is crucial for individuals or small businesses who can also benefit from arbitration. This entails that by eliminating expenses related to in-person hearings, all parties concerned may fully present and litigate their case instead of seeking solutions at the early stage of proceedings.[37]

7 Conclusion

This chapter deals with the benefits of digitalization and the use of new technologies in the field of international arbitration. Therefore, such an analysis was necessary to answer, "whether the process of digitization and the introduction of new technological solutions is beneficial from the perspective of international arbitration". Furthermore, "In what way do new technologies guarantee fundamental rights arising from international conventions and international arbitration law?".

Indeed, such innovation-driven tools can significantly increase the efficiency and flexibility of the entire arbitral proceedings. Such solutions based on innovation-driven technologies are also cost-effective. In addition, one must note that remote hearings can be useful to enhance diversity in international arbitration. Through remote hearings, many women that normally could be exempted from arbitral proceedings, could actively take part therein. In addition, although there are no specific regulations on such technologies in international arbitration at international level, the interpretation of binding provisions, most notably in terms of fundamental principles and rights lead us to the conclusion that such innovations comply with international standards. As such, they provide better access to justice.

---

36 *Ibidem*, pp. 111–112.

37 *Ibidem*, p. 112.

CHAPTER 4

Challenges Related to Digitalization in International Arbitration

1 Introduction

This chapter explores many challenges arising from the digitalization of international dispute resolution and the use of new technologies in international arbitration. To name a few, practical challenges relate to the effectiveness of arbitration agreement in electronic form, the seat of arbitration in case of online proceedings, procedural issues, e-proceedings, e-evidence, digital arbitral award, cybersecurity, and data protection issues, as well as an inability to observe parties' demeanour and credibility, among others.

Innovation-driven technologies in international arbitration could lead to many challenges and troubles of some kind. To illustrate, key legal instruments could be denied legal recognition when it comes to international arbitration. Indeed, both arbitration agreements and arbitral awards are widely considered to be subject to specific requirements. As such, arbitration agreements are mostly concluded in written form. Likewise, the arbitral awards are also rendered in writing and signed by the arbitrators. Requirements related to the form of arbitration agreement date to the times of telegrams which were the most advanced technology.[1] Article II (2) of the New York Convention stipulates that "The term 'agreement in writing' shall include an arbitral clause in a contract or an arbitration agreement, signed by the parties or contained in an exchange of letters or telegrams". Nonetheless, this begs the question of whether the old provisions provided by the 1958 New York Convention evolve simultaneously with the technology or if they efficiently challenge the use of digital technologies while concluding the arbitration agreements and rendering arbitral awards.

1 R. Wolff, *E-Arbitration Agreements and E-Awards: Arbitration Agreements Concluded in an Electronic Environment and Digital Arbitral Awards*, [in:] *Arbitration in the Digital Age: The Brave New World of Arbitration*, eds. M. Piers, C. Aschauer, Cambridge 2018, p. 151.

 | DOI:10.1163/9789004700710_006

2 Electronic Arbitration Agreement: An Overview

Many international arbitral institutions offer e-arbitration services, for instance, the International Chamber of Commerce, the Chartered Institute of Arbitrators, American Arbitration Association, among others. There are still some major challenges related to the requirement in writing to be fulfilled. Interestingly, some countries require such an arbitration agreement in writing merely as evidence, whereas others recognize it as a formality.[2]

2.1 *Electronic Consent to Arbitration*

Digital arbitration agreements seem to be one of the pressing topics in times of evolving technology. This raises a question relating to both the form and other prerequisites for the validity of the arbitration agreement. One could even say that there are twofold difficulties in concluding such a contract through electronic means. The former refers to the party's responsibility for drafting the electronic contract. On the one hand, it is not obvious neither to what extent the party ensures the accessibility of the arbitral clause nor how the electronic contractual process should be organized. The latter, in turn, refers to the acceptance of the electronic offer. The so-called communication protocol is based on a navigation tool which allows one to switch from one file to another through hypertext links. This means that the electronic documents in the majority of cases are not outlined in sequence. In turn, the user must take the initiative by switching from one file to another. This procedure is widely recognized as "incorporation by reference".[3]

The incorporation by reference should be understood as a technique which does not lengthen the principal contract. Therefore, the parties are allowed to access the contract from elsewhere. This entails that "the general conditions are not included in the contract but are available simply on request".[4] It is noteworthy that the "incorporation by reference" is currently allowed under international arbitration law. To illustrate, the French Court of Cassation even opts for a fully consensual approach. In addition, this court stresses that such a reference should not be even made "in writing". Given this Court, "whereas in matters of international arbitration, an arbitral clause is valid when incorporated by reference to a document mentioning it, as long as the party against

2 H. Nasser Agil, *Electronic Arbitration: The new mechanism for dispute resolution*, "The Arbitrator & Mediator" December 2016, p. 71.

3 *Dispute Settlement. International Commercial Arbitration: Electronic Arbitration*, "United Nations Conference on Trade and Development" 2003, pp. 15–16.

4 *Ibidem*, p. 16.

which it is invoked was aware of it at the moment the contract was concluded and, even if through its silence, accepted this reference".[5]

Considering the electronic conclusion of the arbitration agreement, it can be achieved either through email or a web application (such as a declaration of conduct). In this case, such declarations made through a web application refer to the "click-wrap" declarations. This means that the user merely clicks on a specific place such as the "ok" or "agree" button. Such a web application does not allow us to go further without such a click. Aside from this type, there are also web-based declarations which recognize the "browse-wrap" declarations. Therefore, the user does not need to click anything, but directly downloads a file or access a certain website according to the terms displayed thereon.[6]

2.2 *Accessibility of the Arbitration Agreement*

The aforementioned "incorporation by reference" should also be analyzed in terms of the accessibility of the arbitral clause. This means that the co-contractor should have had access to the external information, otherwise, he could not give his consent. Hence, the general conditions are very often unavailable due to technical reasons such as problems with hypertext links, for instance. To avoid this kind of situation, there is a universal legislative trend opting for the explicit requirement to have access to the general conditions in electronic contracts. For example, according to Article 10.3 of the Directive on Electronic Commerce, "contract terms and general conditions provided to the recipient must be made available in a way that allows him to store and reproduce them".[7]

One must note that the traditional incorporation by reference is applied with the aim of not lengthening the principal contract. Instead of repeating the already existing documents, based on this method, parties may refer to a document which can be accessed from different locations. Therefore, although the general terms are not included in the contract, they could be easily obtained upon request. It is also worth adding that the practice of incorporation by reference is commonly acceptable under international trade law.[8]

---

5 Cass. 1st civ., December 20, 2000, Prodexport II, unpublished, cf. judgement Prodexport I, Cass. 1st civ, June 3, 1997, Revue de l'arbitrage [Arbitration Journal] 1998, p. 537, note Xavier Boucobza in which the Court of Cassation still required «a written reference to the document» containing the clause.

6 R. Wolff, *E-Arbitration Agreements and E-Awards ...*, p. 152.

7 Directive 2000/31/EC on Certain Legal Aspects of Information Society Services, in Particular Electronic Commerce, in the Internal Market, OLEC, July 17, 2000, L 178/1, Dalloz 2000, leg., p. 133.

8 *Dispute Settlement. International ...*, p. 16.

2.3 *Electronic Form of the Arbitration Agreement*

The COVID-19 pandemic affected simultaneously contracts which do not include the physical signatures of all parties concerned. Therefore, it has also an impact on arbitration, most notably on the conclusion of the effective arbitration agreement.

According to Article 2 of the New York Convention, an arbitration agreement should be defined as "an agreement [...] under which the parties are committed to submit to arbitration all or any differences which have arisen, or which may arise between them in respect of a defined legal relationship, whether contractual or not". This provision together with paragraph 2 was slightly changed into Article 7(1) of the UNCITRAL Model Law. Under this Article, arbitration agreement means "an agreement of the parties to submit to arbitration all or certain disputes which have arisen, or which may arise between them in respect of a defined legal relationship, whether contractual or not".

Under Article 7(2) of the UNCITRAL Model Law, the effective arbitration agreement should be concluded in writing. Such an agreement should be understood as "an arbitral clause in a contract or an arbitration agreement, signed by the parties or contained in an exchange of letters or telegrams". It is noteworthy, however, that electronic communication allows to exchange information between the contracting parties via electronic data. Simultaneously, according to Article II (2) of the New York Convention, it is also possible to include an arbitration agreement in "an exchange of letters or telegrams". Based on the explicit wording of Article II (2) of the 1958 New York Convention, one could even say that there are merely two ways to conclude a binding arbitration agreement, namely handwritten or contained in letters or telegrams. Nonetheless, it is noteworthy that the 1958 New York Convention was adopted prior to introducing innovation-driven technologies. Therefore, many solutions which are commonly available to the parties have not even existed at the time of the adoption of this Convention. For that reason, it is simply natural to interpret Article II (2) of the 1958 New York Convention in light of Articles 7(2) to (4) of the UNCITRAL Model Law. Given such a stance, the 1958 New York Convention should be recognized as including an exhaustive list of options to conclude an effective arbitration clause. As follows, the conclusion of the arbitration agreement could be also possible through electronic means of communication. Such an interpretation complies not only with the UNCITRAL Model Law itself but also with the UNCITRAL report concerning the session from 19 June until 7 July 2006. Furthermore, it is worth stressing that Article II (2) of the New York Convention has been repeated by Article I(2) of the European Convention on International Commercial Arbitration. According to this Convention, the arbitration agreement is effective while signed by the parties, contained in an exchange of letters, telegrams or in a communication by teleprinter.[9]

At the outset, it is noteworthy to indicate two different types of arbitration agreements concluded "in writing". The former refers to the traditional arbitration agreement included physically, namely a physical "wet-ink" signature. The latter, in turn, requires that the arbitration clause has been signed with a special "qualified electronic signature". Interestingly, such a signature is based upon a certificate that has been issued by qualified trust service providers (both private and public).[10]

To illustrate, according to Polish law (Article 1162 of the Polish Code of Civil Procedure), the arbitration clause should be in writing. Nonetheless, it is also possible to include such a clause in letters which have been exchanged between the parties through the means of remote communication, if such content has been successfully recorded.[11] The Polish law is rather liberal towards the requirements concerning the "in writing" form of the arbitration agreement. Given the Polish perspective, "means of remote communication" should be understood as simple electronic forms (which do not require the parties' signatures), including telefax, telegram, email, or even short text messages. Such a perspective complies with the 1958 New York Convention. In addition, it should be stressed that the Polish Supreme Court even ruled that there is no need for an electronic signature in case of an exchange of electronic correspondence. This entails that a valid arbitration clause could also be concluded in a "simple" electronic form. As a result, a secure electronic signature is not needed (see: Polish Supreme Court III CSK 406/16, 28 November 2018).[12]

Despite these positive sides, two exceptions should be mentioned. Firstly, Article 1162(2) of the Polish Code of Civil Procedure cannot be applied in the case of an arbitration agreement concluded with consumers. Therefore, this means that arbitration clauses concerning disputes stemming from contracts

9 L. Ryšavý, *Form of Arbitration Agreement in a Comparative Perspective*, "ICLR" 2020, Vol. 20, no. 2, pp. 49–50.

10 J. Kisielińska-Garncarek, Ł. Ostas, *Concluding an Arbitration Agreement via Means of Remote Communication under Polish Law: A Short Guide for Practitioners*, "Kluwer Arbitration Blog" 13.11.2022, https://arbitrationblog.kluwerarbitration.com/2022/11/13/concluding-an-arbitration-agreement-via-means-of-remote-communication-under-polish-law-a-short-guide-for-practitioners/. Accessed on 17.02.2023. See more: A.W. Wiśniewski, *Międzynarodowy arbitraż handlowy w Polsce. Status prawny arbitrażu i arbitrów*, Warszawa 2011.

11 J. Kisielińska-Garncarek, Ł. Ostas, *Concluding an Arbitration ...*

12 Postanowienie Sądu Najwyższego z dnia 28 listopada 2018 r., sygn. akt III CSK 406/16, https://www.sn.pl/sites/orzecznictwo/Orzeczenia3/III%20CSK%20406-16-1.pdf. Accessed on 17.02.2023.

where a consumer is one of the parties must be concluded in writing (namely either with a traditional "wet-in" signature or qualified electronic signature).

Secondly, arbitration agreements covering the so-called "arbitration clauses by reference" cannot be concluded via remote communication. Under Article 1162(2) of the Polish CCP, such a reference to comply with the requirements of the form of an arbitration clause should be made "in writing". Given the actual Polish legal scholars' perspective, the requirement of the "arbitration clauses by reference" to be "in writing" is understood either as a handwritten signature or a qualified electronic signature. In practice, following this stance, it is not possible to conclude any arbitration agreement by reference throughout the remote communication.[13]

Additionally, it is possible to submit an arbitration agreement in an electronic form while using the aforementioned "qualified electronic signature".[14] According to Article 781§1 of the Civil Code, "in order to maintain the electronic form of a legal transaction, it is sufficient to submit a declaration of will in an electronic form and affix a qualified electronic signature to it".[15]

One could even ask how to prove the conclusion of the arbitration agreement through remote communication. This is a practical question in the case of the party's petition to obtain recognition and/or enforcement of the arbitral award. The arbitration agreement which has been originally concluded through the means of telegram or email cannot be presented in original. The Polish Supreme Court even stressed that "in the event the arbitration agreement is concluded via email, there is no 'original' thereof within the meaning of Article IV(1)(b) of 1958 New York Arbitration Convention; in such a case, supplying the court with written confirmation of the agreement (e.g., print-out of emails) is sufficient".[16]

Interestingly, there are different approaches to the use of new technologies in international arbitration.[17] Some legislations ever require proving the existence of electronic agreements in arbitration. To illustrate, to prove such an agreement, the Egyptian Law No. 15 of 2004 on electronic signature provides that "the system should be based on the technology of the code of the public

13 J. Kisielińska-Garncarek, Ł. Ostas, *Concluding an Arbitration* ...

14 P. Polański, J. Gołaczyński, *Online Dispute Resolution* ..., p. 231.

15 It is noteworthy that by 2016, instead of "qualified electronic signature", the Polish lawmaker used the notion of "secure electronic signature verified with a valid qualified certificate".

16 J. Kisielińska-Garncarek, Ł. Ostas, *Concluding an Arbitration* ... See: Postanowienie Sądu Najwyższego z dnia 13 września 2012 r., sygn. akt V CSK 323/11, https://www.sn.pl/sites/orzecznictwo/Orzeczenia2a/V%20CSK%20323-11-1.pdf. Accessed on 17.02.2023.

17 See more: M. Piers, C. Aschauer, eds. *Arbitration in the Digital Age: The Brave New World of Arbitration*, Cambridge University Press 2018.

and private keys" (Article 3). Therefore, there is a "need for specific technology and a neutral third party that can be resorted to ensure that the electronic signature belongs to the signer and that the signer still controls its signature".[18] Indeed, this technology is based on encryption via the two keys, namely the private and public keys. The former refers to the key with the encryption which is carried out and merely the owner knows it. The latter, in turn, has the aim to decrypt the encryption of the private key. In addition, these keys are introduced by the so-called "electronic certification bodies" which act as third-party entities. These bodies are responsible for generating electronic signatures for individuals seeking their own e-signatures. This entails that such authorities affix an electronic certification to e-signature.[19]

Indeed, the 1958 New York Convention represents an old piece of international legislation on arbitration. At the time of its adoption, no one could foresee and predict the development of innovation-driven technologies as a means of communication. Even though some arbitrators and legal practitioners opt for its modernization to comply with the "new normal", it seems rather challenging to modify an international convention. On the other hand, it is noteworthy that both new national laws on international commercial arbitration and arbitral institutions' rules have already introduced more softened requirements on the written form of the arbitration agreement. Therefore, they directly refer to the modern means of communication. This means that such provisions already validate the technological equivalent for the old requirement on written form.[20]

To illustrate, Article II of the New York Convention may easily be adapted to electronic exchanges achieved through multifarious ways. In the case of the conclusion of the contract via electronic emails, Article II could also be interpreted by analogy. Specifically, there is even no need for the parties' signature in the case of an agreement that "is contained in an exchange of letters or telegrams".[21]

---

18 M.N. Al Dalaien, Z. Al Enizi, A. Al Dalaien, *Problems of Proving the Electronic Arbitration Agreement in Applicable International Laws and Agreements*, "Journal of Applied Security Research" 2021, Vol. 18, issue 3, p. 10.

19 *Ibidem*, p. 11.

20 L. Biukovic, *International Commercial Arbitration in Cyberspace: Recent Developments*, "Northwestern Journal of International Law & Business" 2002, Vol. 22, p. 246–246.

21 *Dispute Settlement. International* ..., p. 20.

3 Seat of Arbitration

The seat of arbitration is widely considered a key issue in determining the legal framework in the case of international arbitral proceedings. This entails that the courts of the seat are empowered to supervise the arbitral process. Therefore, they can remove an arbitrator due to a lack of independence or impartiality, among others.[22]

Based on the principle of party autonomy, the parties can select the seat of arbitration in their agreement. It seems to be of significant value to determine one of the countries rather than another to be a seat of arbitral proceedings. Nonetheless, in practice, many "pathological" arbitration clauses exist. Therefore, a national court has the power to decide where the seat of arbitration is. It is also noteworthy that the term "seat of arbitration" is widely interchanged with the "place of arbitration". This means that the two terms are considered synonyms.[23]

Overall, it is noteworthy that international arbitration does not have a (national) forum. This begs the question, however, of whether such international arbitration has any forum. Considering different jurisdictions, the venue of international arbitration plays a crucial role, mostly with regard to the application of mandatory rules and principles of the so-called *lex fori*. Therefore, it concerns such issues as arbitrability and validity of arbitration agreements. Given the enforcement of arbitral awards according to national arbitration laws, the seat of arbitration is widely seen as a determinative element to decide whether such an award is national or foreign. This means that there are some practical problems with the seat of arbitration in the case of online proceedings. How should it be determined? Given the situation that the arbitral proceedings are handled completely online, that is without a meeting of arbitrators in a certain place, such an arbitration "would not be pertaining to any particular geographical territory".[24]

Practically, the aforementioned situation should be considered in terms of "delocalized arbitration". Nonetheless, such "delocalized arbitration" leads to many legal problems. To illustrate, "as UNCTAD points out, the seat of arbitration overcomes the problem of multiple locations of procedural acts and more

22 J. Hill, *Determining the Seat of an International Arbitration: Party Autonomy and the Interpretation of Arbitration Agreements*, "International & Comparative Law Quarterly" 2014, Vol. 63, pp. 517–518.

23 *Ibidem*, pp. 518–519.

24 S. Halla, *Arbitration going online* ..., p. 218. Cf. J. Hörnle, *Online Dispute Resolution – More Than The Emperor's New Clothes*, "Proceedings of the UNECE Forum on ODR" 2003, p. 9.

importantly, it still has essential character with regards to the law applicable to the procedure, the competence of national courts and ensuring the lawfulness of any rendered award".[25]

The seat of arbitration plays a crucial role in international commercial arbitration law nowadays. According to the UNCITRAL Model Law, the place of arbitration determines the application of this law according to Article 1(2). It is also a key element while determining whether the arbitration is international. Therefore, under Article 1(3) of the UNCITRAL Model Law, it should fulfil one of the following conditions:

> (a) the parties to an arbitration agreement have, at the time of the conclusion of that agreement, their places of business in different States; or (b) one of the following places is situated outside the State in which the parties have their places of business: (i) the place of arbitration if determined in, or pursuant to, the arbitration agreement; (ii) any place where a substantial part of the obligations of the commercial relationship is to be performed or the place with which the subject-matter of the dispute is most closely connected; or (c) the parties have expressly agreed that the subject matter of the arbitration agreement relates to more than one country.

Further, the place of arbitration is also important to determine where the arbitral award was issued. According to Article 31(3), "The award shall state its date and the place of arbitration as determined in accordance with article 20(1). The award shall be deemed to have been made at that place". In addition, the place of arbitration indicates the basic rules of procedure in the case where parties have not reached any agreement. Therefore, under Article 36(1)a(IV): "the composition of the arbitral tribunal or the arbitral procedure was not in accordance with the agreement of the parties or, failing such agreement, was not in accordance with the law of the country where the arbitration took place". Finally, the place of arbitration has also influence on "the award [that] has not yet become binding on the parties or has been set aside or suspended by a court of the country in which, or under the law of which, that award was made" (Article 36(1)a(v)).

The European Convention on International Commercial Arbitration considers the seat of arbitration as a determinative element to appoint arbitrators

---

25 *Ibidem*, p. 219. Cf. *Course on Dispute Settlement: International Commercial Arbitration*, UN Conference on Trade and Development, New York and Geneva, UNCTAD/EDM/Misc.232/Add.20, p. 47.

in *ad hoc* arbitration. Likewise, the Inter-American Convention on International Commercial Arbitration and the 1958 New York Convention include the same regulations.[26]

Following the practice of international commercial arbitration law, the parties are allowed to determine the seat of arbitration. If they cannot reach a consensus, the rules of the institution determine such a place, mostly the seat of the arbitral institution itself or in the case of jurisdictions following the UNCITRAL Model Law solutions, the arbitrators are deemed to designate such a place.[27]

4 Procedural Challenges

As a result of technological developments in arbitral proceedings, a few questions arise concerning due process (already mentioned in the context of remote hearings), equality of the parties and contradiction. As per Mohamed S. Abdel and Ethan Katsh,

> unequal access to technology and/or e-platforms hosting the proceedings could undermine the procedural integrity of the proceedings and compromise the sacrosanct principles of due process, equality, and contradiction, as a party would have procedural and technological leverage over the other, which might prejudice the ability of the party who is technologically disadvantaged to presents its case reasonably and adequately.[28]

These principles are of significant value while handling arbitral proceedings. They ensure not only fairness and integrity of the entire proceedings but also the decision-making process. Given these principles, parties should have a chance to set forth their case given equal grounds and present their evidence and counterclaims. Indeed, they should also be informed about the party's submissions. As such, it is crucial to determine whether all the parties involved in the arbitral proceedings have expressed their consent and willingness to conduct the arbitral proceedings wholly or partially online. In addition, simultaneously it is important to ascertain if they have equal access to technology and thus necessary equipment which allows them to make use of both audio

26 S. Halla, *Arbitration going online ...*, p. 219.
27 *Ibidem*, p. 220.
28 M.S. Abdel Wahab, E. Katsh, *Revolutionizing Technologies and the Use ...*, p. 44.

and visual ICT applications. Such solutions aim to avoid any leverage or prejudice to the parties concerned.[29]

5 E-proceedings

Arbitral proceedings which are held either online or electronically are cost-effective compared to traditional ways of handling disputes. In the case of online arbitration, parties must deal with the so-called e-proceedings. This means that the entire process from e-request for arbitration is a first step, further followed by the e-hearings (including audio and/or videoconferencing), e-submissions and e-production of documents as well as evidence. The next step requires that the parties take part in e-deliberations, and/or e-communication. The latter, in turn, could be handled either inter-parties, inter-tribunal or even party-tribunal. The entire arbitral proceedings end with the issuance of an e-award.[30]

Based on already practices in international arbitration, emails have become the common means of communication nowadays. Therefore, the parties can not only swiftly and efficiently communicate through emails but also add some written texts or audio or video files, if necessary. Although this solution is widely used in arbitration, it also causes some inconveniences mostly with regard to email capacity which is very often limited and is subject to certain constraints.[31] Aside from the positive sides of handling e-proceedings (including online platforms, chatrooms and videoconferencing, among others), some challenges need to be addressed. The International commercial arbitration law advocates for two chief legal principles to be fulfilled. As such, it is worth analyzing the principle of procedural autonomy and the principle of neutrality in view of the e-proceedings. The former gives the party a chance to organize arbitral proceedings according to their will and in such a manner that would be adjusted to the digital world. The latter, in turn, pays attention to the use of e-communications and the Internet itself which is recognized as a "stateless" tool. Therefore, these tools provide a neutral space which can be commonly used by the parties to communicate and interact. From this perspective, it is also worthwhile to remember that the ICT tools are considered neutral and thus they do not have any impact on the outcome of the disputed case. Nonetheless,

29 *Ibidem*, p. 44.
30 *Ibidem*, p. 37.
31 *Ibidem*.

> given the possible transformation of the process as a result of the utilization of ICTs, it may not be inconceivable that more data and information could be submitted, processed, and ascertained in a much easier way. This may ultimately impact the decision-making process, in a manner that could distinctively differ from what would have likely ensued in a more conventional procedure.[32]

On the one hand, there is no doubt that the use of electronic files documents instead of paper-based facilitated the process of transferring and analyzing data. It has also a significant influence on both the taking of evidence and document production. On the other hand, once the parties and the arbitral tribunal make use of such cutting-edge technologies, mostly concerning the exchange of communications, documents along with information, they would pay less attention to the oral evidence. Therefore, displacement could be one of the results of this new trend. Throughout the development and further proliferation of ICTs tools, reconstruction of both factual and historical events would be much easier. In addition, any legal gaps along with the contradictions could be easily identified thanks to the use of artificial intelligence therein. Interestingly, the ICT tools could also be beneficial in case of hearings of witnesses. The human beings' memory is not able to remember all details concerning relevant factual events. To address such problems, the so-called system- or even program-generated cross-examination questions could be helpful to decrease the number of lacunas and contradictions in the case of witness testimony. Even though ICT has become interesting compared to traditional means of settling disputes, the efficiency of such e-proceedings would vary depending on the quality of the tools.[33]

Even though these solutions are cost-effective and very often speed up the arbitral proceedings, there are many concerns which are worth discussing.

Firstly, all arbitrators taking part in the proceedings must express their consent to this digital format and thus allow to make use of electronic means for deliberation. This entails that one of the key issues is to provide for conveniently available, accessible, and welcoming format to handle proceedings. By way of explanation, once there is an opt-in agreement, the e-proceedings could apply, otherwise, the traditional one is handled. It is worth stressing, however, that probably the near future will bring us an opt-out agreement that would apply if someone would be against electronic deliberations. As such, throughout the proliferation of ICTs tools, the "conventional" proceedings would be

32 *Ibidem.*
33 *Ibidem*, p. 38.

understood as "electronic ones" instead of "physical face-to-face meetings" in the foreseeable future.[34]

Secondly, some practical problems arise as a result of granting the parties power to decide whether to handle e-proceedings or not. Both the deliberations themselves alongside their format should be determined by the arbitral tribunal, instead of the parties' willingness.[35]

Finally, there is also a need to address the procedural legality of such e-proceedings. "This requires due consideration of any mandatory requirements under the *lex loci arbitri*; absent such overriding mandatory requirements, the arbitral tribunal retains the discretion to deliberate in the format it so prefers and desires".[36]

It is also worthwhile to note that according to modern arbitration laws and rules, there are no provisions for electronic deliberations that could be handled among the arbitrators. On the contrary, such deliberations can take place by email, telephone, or videoconferencing. In addition, different solutions apply depending on the national arbitration laws in countries.

As such, given the Italian law, the deliberation conducted via videoconferencing is allowed. The Swill law went even further providing that arbitrators are not supposed to meet in person. In turn, they could handle deliberations through any type of electronic means (i.e. email), if they ensure some precautions that satisfy four conditions. Therefore, all arbitrators should express their consent to use this kind of electronic means and actively take part in a discussion, unless there are obvious reasons to be absent, including illness or even inability to perform their duties as an arbitrator or a total refusal to take part in any deliberation (regardless of its form in-person or remote one). Arbitrators can benefit from these remote deliberations unless they have already excluded such an option. Lastly, the possibility of such electronic deliberations should also be well-documented based on the parties' agreement or in a procedural order, for instance.[37]

6 E-evidence in Arbitration

6.1 *Definition of Electronic Evidence*

"Electronic evidence", aka e-evidence is a broad term which includes twofold categories of evidence such as "analogue evidence" and "digital evidence".

---

34 *Ibidem*, p. 41.
35 *Ibidem*.
36 *Ibidem*.
37 *Ibidem*, p. 40.

The former refers to the concept of a machine generating output which was straightforward to comprehend. To illustrate, "analogue evidence" encompasses vinyl records, audio tapes, photographic fil, and telephone calls that have been made over the public switched telephone network. Indeed, such analogue systems or products may generate data which can be easily preserved in a lasting form. A camera could produce both primary evidence such as a negative transparency or plate and secondary evidence in the form of photographs developed from the film itself.[38]

There is a distinction between "analogue evidence" and "digital evidence". Apparently, the "analogue evidence" is mostly stored on physical carriers such as paper or photographic film. In addition, it can even not be recorded sometimes. Instead, it can merely be represented by continuous readings, namely radar systems. This type of evidence can be manipulated. Even though modifying the negative of a photographic film requires certain skills, such changes can still be detected. Nonetheless, by contrast, "digital evidence" can be changed with ease. Such digital data refers to "anything that has been created or stored on a computer or is made available by way of the Internet, including CD s, DVD s, MP3s, and digital broadcast radio. The essential point about digital evidence, which is not readily understood by many judges and lawyers, is the complexity of the topic and the nature of the characteristics of digital evidence".[39]

One must note that the term "electronic evidence" is commonly used, whereas mostly it refers to "digital evidence" which is rather a generative term. Therefore, it includes all possible forms of data regardless of being generated by an analogue device or existing in digital format.[40]

Overall, Mason defines "electronic evidence" as "data (comprising the output of analogue devices or data in digital format) that is created, manipulated, stored, or communicated by any device, computer or computer system or transmitted over a communication system, that is relevant to the process of adjudication".[41]

It seems crucial to remember that there is widespread use of digital devices. This entails that much electronic evidence can be captured, investigated, and disclosed during legal proceedings.[42] To illustrate, digital devices can easily provide data classified as electronic evidence. In this context, the so-called system clocks play a crucial role in time stamping events. As such, the operating

38 S. Mason, *Introduction* [in:] *International Electronic Evidence*, ed. S. Mason, London 2008, p. XXXV.

39 *Ibidem.*

40 *Ibidem*, p. XXXVI.

41 *Ibidem*, p. XXXV.

42 G.R.S. Weir, S. Mason, *The sources of electronic evidence*, [in:] *Electronic evidence*, ed. S. Mason, D. Seng, London 2017, p. 17.

system makes use of the date and time settings to properly mark its record of events like file creation or modification. Such information, widely known as file "metadata" describes or interprets the base data or linked to the file itself but cannot be classified neither as part of the data contained within the file nor data directly controlled by the user. System events, including user logins, and password changes along with the sensor-recorded events like step counts taken by the wearer are also assigned time stamps. This means that both the specific dates and times linked to such events are well documented within the system log files, aka event logs. These logs hold significant values given the sequence of evidence and thus can shed light on the suspected user actions.[43]

Lastly, one must stress the difference between electronic evidence and the so-called videolinked evidence. The latter refers to the situation "if both parties are represented or if a member of the tribunal is present at either end of the link. However, this might not always be possible. Alternatively, a trusted third party such as a law firm, an arbitral institution, a notary, or a court could be used".[44] This means that the evidence is merely presented through innovation-driven technologies.

Likewise, the cross-examination of witnesses could be used via written synchronous online technology, namely online chat. Through such technology, parties can communicate with each other in real-time by both writing and answering questions online. In practice, it may impose many challenges to assess the credibility of such witness examination based on online chat. Indeed, online chat cannot simply replace either oral or visual hearing.[45]

6.2 *Definition of Blockchain*

Blockchain technology has been primarily used in the case of Bitcoin and other types of cryptocurrencies. Afterwards, the potential of blockchain has been noticed and nowadays this technology is widely used in other areas.[46]

43 *Ibidem*, p. 3.

44 J. Hörne, *Online Dispute Resolution: The Emperor's New Clothes? Benefits and Pitfalls of Online Dispute Resolution and its Application to Commercial Arbitration*, "International Review of Law Computers & Technology" 2003, Vol. 17, no. 1, p. 31.

45 *Ibidem*.

46 J. Barnett, P. Treleaven, *Algorithmic Dispute Resolution – The Automation of Professional Dispute Resolution Using AI and Blockchain Technologies*, "The British Computer Society" 2017, p. 402. See more: W. Pfadt, *Blockchain*, [in:] *Leksykon prawa nowych technologii. 100 podstawowych pojęć*, ed. A. Krasulski, Warszawa 2021, pp. 17–18; P. Ortolani, *The Judicialization of Blockchain* [in:] *Regulating Blockchain: Techno-Social and Legal Challenges*, ed. P. Hacker et al., Oxford 2019, pp. 289; P. Tasca, R. Piselli, *The Blockchain Paradox* [in:] *Regulating Blockchain: Techno-Social and Legal Challenges*, ed. P. Hacker et al., Oxford 2019, p. 27.

Blockchain is widely defined as "a distributed database or ledger that is shared among the nodes of a computer network".[47] This means that blockchain functioning as a database can store information electronically in digital format. One of the key features of blockchain technology is ensuring not only fidelity but also the security of a record of data. For that reason, blockchain technology is trusty and there is no need for a trusted third party. In the case of blockchain, data is well structures, and all the information is collected in groups, the so-called "blocks". Each of the blocks has some storage capacity. This means that once a block has already been filed with data, such a block is closed and strictly associated with the previous one. As such, many blocks create a chain of data which is widely known as the blockchain. In addition, "All new information that follows that freshly added block is compiled into a newly formed block that will then also be added to the chain once filled".[48]

The blocks are linked together through cryptography. Interestingly, it is noteworthy that such decentralized blockchains[49] are widely considered immutable. Given that, once data entered a blockchain, it cannot be reversed. Therefore, digital information which has been recorded becomes permanent.[50]

Indeed, one of the advantages of blockchain technology is that data is marked with a timestamp. Therefore, it provides not only permanence but also resistance to tampering and changes. Furthermore, by adding data to the blockchain, any attempt to modify the content would necessitate changes in all subsequent blocks. It is possible merely based on the consensus of the network majority.[51] Such a mechanism is widely recognized as "harsh cryptography". Therefore, each block storing information which is included in the blockchain has been assigned a unique "hash" value. One must note that such value is generated by a mathematical algorithm which encodes the original data. Interestingly,

47 A. Hayes, *Blockchain Facts: What Is It, How It Works, and How It Can Be Used?*, "Investopedia" 27.09.2022, https://www.investopedia.com/terms/b/blockchain.asp. Accessed on 20.03.2023.

48 *Ibidem.*

49 See more: Y. Aouidef, F. Ast, B. Deffains, *Decentralized Justice: A Comparactive Analysis of Blockchain Online Dispute Resolution Projects*, "Frontiers in Blockchain" 2021, Vol. 4, pp. 1–8.

50 O. Puertas Álvarez, O. Valentí i Vidal, L. Díaz Vallespinós, *Unlocking Blockchain Evidence in International Arbitration*, "Spain Arbitration Review, Revista del Club Español del Arbitraje", Wolters Kluwer España 2022, Vol. 2022, issue 43, https://www.cuatrecasas.com/resources/unlocking-blockchain-evidence-in-international-arbitration-636a8db7a3d02887902120.pdf?v1.42.2.20230126, p. 16.

51 *Ibidem.*

> The next block on the chain must contain the hash number of the previous block. Therefore, if someone wanted to modify the information on the chain, the hash produced by even a slight change would essentially be different, and the hashes of the subsequent blocks would no longer match. Since every node includes a duplicate of the chain history, any attempt to modify a node that makes it inconsistent with the chain history will automatically be disregarded and not be recorded in the chain.[52]

Blockchain has already impacted the dispute resolution landscape in the following ways. Firstly, blockchain has become a subject of legal disputes because of the growing adoption of this technology. Given that, there is an increasing number of litigations related to its proper implementation and use.[53]

Secondly, blockchain has led to the establishment of specialized forums dedicated to resolving disputes. Through the increasing number of blockchain-related disputes, many national courts decided to launch specialized courts to handle such cases. To illustrate, China[54] makes use of such a solution to provide a court responsible for litigation arising between companies using blockchain. Indeed, the submission of blockchain records seems to be crucial in terms of proving their cases. Aside from national courts, specialized arbitral tribunals have also emerged for the sake of addressing blockchain-related disputes, namely the Arbitration Court of the Blockchain and the New Technologies of the Chamber of Commerce in Poland. Furthermore, many blockchain platforms, including Confideal or JuryOnline have already decided to incorporate special dispute resolution mechanisms within their systems. Such a trend has already confirmed the specificity of blockchain-related disputes that need to be addressed by specialized venues.[55]

Thirdly, blockchain itself also functions as a platform for dispute resolution. For instance, a "digital court" operates using a blockchain system in Japan. Given this technology, the consensus of the nodes determines whether a party has breached their agreement with another party. Similarly, China's Internet Courts also established their blockchain platforms in 2019. In addition, they could settle more than three million litigation cases in 2019 thanks to the use of this platform. There is much more acceptance towards the adoption

52 *Ibidem.*

53 *Ibidem.*

54 See more: 《国际商事仲裁》刘晓红、袁发强主编，北京2015年 [*Guójì shāngshì zhòngcái*, Liú Xiǎohóng, Yuán Fāqiáng zhǔbiān, Běijīng 2015].

55 *Ibidem*, p. 17.

of blockchain technology within the international dispute resolution landscape, despite some sceptical approaches to digitalization itself and ongoing transformation. Nonetheless, one must note that blockchain platforms such as Kleros have already emerged (discussed below).[56]

Finally, blockchain technology is widely used to ensure better security of information, most notably in terms of storage and management of evidence. Interestingly, the Ministry of Justice in the United Kingdom launched a special pilot program for the sake of managing digital evidence through blockchain technology in 2018. Indeed, Estonian solutions were an inspiration. This country makes use of blockchain to safeguard sensitive data such as citizens' health records.[57]

6.3 *Collecting of E-evidence*

At the outset, it is noteworthy to name two main guidelines applied in international arbitration to take evidence, namely the International Bar Association "IBA Rules on the Taking of Evidence in International Arbitration" and the "Rules on the Efficient Conduct of Proceedings in International Arbitration (Prague Rules)" from 2018. When the parties express their willingness to follow these rules, the arbitral tribunal is deemed to apply these parameters "on how the arbitrators must conduct the proceedings when it comes to evidence and the way to assess the evidence".[58] The former guidelines are considered as reflecting procedures used in various legal systems, therefore they are useful in case of parties coming from different legal cultures". One could even say that these rules have been designed to serve as a kind of bridge between the common and civil law jurisdictions.[59] Indeed, the common law jurisdictions prefer to follow the IBA Rules, whereas the civil law jurisdictions prefer to follow the Prague Rules. As such, "the IBA Rules have an adversarial approach, whereas the Prague Rules advocate an inquisitorial approach, which leaves room for a proactive role of the tribunal in fact-finding".[60]

It is noteworthy that parties involved in arbitration have the right to decide whether fully or partially use IBA Rules or treat IBA Rules merely as

56 *Ibidem.*

57 *Ibidem*, p. 18.

58 D.B. Ferreira, E.A. Gromova, *Electronic evidence in arbitration proceedings: empirical analysis and recommendations*, "Digital Evidence and Electronic Signature Law Review" 2023, Vol. 20, p. 31.

59 See: Note from the Working Group, Draft Prague Rules of 1 September 2018, https://praguerules.com/upload/medialibrary/b2e/b2e26123ac310b644b26d4cd11dc67d8.pdf. Accessed on 10.06.2023.

60 D.B. Ferreira, E.A. Gromova, *Electronic evidence in arbitration* ..., pp. 31–32.

a framework to create their own customized procedure. Likewise, the Prague Rules have been introduced in December 2018 for the sake of offering direction for the effective management of international arbitration proceedings. As such, these Rules also refer to issues of evidence. In addition, similar to IBA Rules, the Prague Rules are adopted to complement institutional rules. This entails that they can be applied either as binding principles or as guidelines.[61]

Indeed, the Prague Rules had the aim to overcome the perception that the IBA Rules are focused on the common law system. By contrast, the Prague Rules address twofold concerns, namely the excessive amount of document production within the adversarial systems and the inefficiencies linked to oral testimony and witness examination. Hence, the Prague Rules provide a less adversarial approach given the document production, fact witnesses and party-appointed experts.[62]

6.4 *E-evidence before an Arbitral Tribunal*

6.4.1 Admissibility of E-evidence

The UNCITRAL Model Law stipulates the evidence in Article 27. According to this provision, "The arbitral tribunal or a party with the approval of the arbitral tribunal may request from a competent court of this State assistance in taking evidence. The court may execute the request within its competence and according to its rules on taking evidence". One must note, however, that this provision does not explicitly apply to electronic evidence. Even though there is no explicit rule provided by the UNICTRAL Model Law on this topic, Article 19(2) could be interpreted to allow the proper assessment of e-evidence during arbitral proceedings. Under Article 19(2), "failing such agreement, the arbitral tribunal may, subject to the provisions of this Law, conduct the arbitration in such manner as it considers appropriate. The power conferred upon the arbitral tribunal includes the power to determine the admissibility, relevance, materiality, and weight of any evidence". Indeed, given this provision, the arbitral tribunal is empowered to assess this type of evidence. In addition, the arbitral tribunal must be flexible and thus adjust the procedure to the specific features of a given case. This entails that each procedure would differ.

The 2021 ICC Rules of Arbitration also does not refer to electronic evidence. Likewise, the 2020 LCIA Rules do not provide specific regulations on electronic

61 J. El Ahdab, P. Berenguer, M. Chik, J. Choo, J. Jaeger, N. Peacock, L. Pitts, G. Zuo, *Approaches to Evidence across Legal Cultures*, [in:] *The Guide to Evidence in International Arbitration*, ed. A.C. Kläsener, M. Magál, J.E. Neuhaus, London 2021, p. 16.

62 *Ibidem*, p. 17.

evidence, even though they allow to have an arbitral award signed electronically (under Article 26.2). Lastly, the American Arbitration Association – 2021 International Centre for Dispute Resolution Rules (AAA-ICDR) address the e-evidence. According to Article 24(6) of these Rules,

> When documents to be exchanged are maintained in electronic form, the party in possession of such documents may make them available in the form (which may be paper copies) most convenient and economical for it, unless the tribunal determines, on application, that there is a compelling need for access to the documents in a different form. Requests for documents maintained in electronic form should be narrowly focused and structured to make searching for them as economical as possible. The tribunal may direct testing or other means of focusing and limiting any search.[63]

The arbitral tribunal could also follow the IBA Rules on the Taking of Evidence in International Arbitration which provides some criteria concerning the admissibility of evidence. Nonetheless, it is noteworthy that these criteria are neither exhaustive nor they do not address certain jurisdiction-specific issues, namely limitations and exclusions on evidence admissibility. In addition, there are practical challenges regarding illegally obtained evidence which could lead to unjustifiable and even unreasonable conclusions, thereby threatening due process and resulting in future challenges to the arbitral award itself. The IBA Rules seek to address these issues in Article 9(2) which stipulates that:

> The Arbitral Tribunal shall, at the request of a Party or on its own motion, exclude from evidence or production any Document, statement, oral testimony or inspection, in whole or in part, for any of the following reasons: (a) lack of sufficient relevance to the case or materiality to its outcome; (b) legal impediment or privilege under the legal or ethical rules determined by the Arbitral Tribunal to be applicable; (c) unreasonable burden to produce the requested evidence; (d) loss or destruction of the Document that has been shown with reasonable likelihood to have occurred; (e) grounds of commercial or technical confidentiality that the Arbitral Tribunal determines to be compelling; (f) grounds of special political

63 Article 24(6) of the 2021 International Dispute Resolution Procedures (Including Mediation and Arbitration Rules), https://www.icdr.org/sites/default/files/document_repository/ICDR_Rules_1.pdf?utm_source=icdr-website&utm_medium=rules-page&utm_campaign=rules-intl-update-1mar. Accessed on 06.06.2023.

> or institutional sensitivity (including evidence that has been classified as secret by a government or a public international institution) that the Arbitral Tribunal determines to be compelling; or (g) considerations of procedural economy, proportionality, fairness or equality of the Parties that the Arbitral Tribunal determines to be compelling.[64]

As such, it is also crucial to address the illegally obtained or "hacked" evidence and its admissibility during arbitral proceedings.

6.4.2 Illegally Obtained or "Hacked" Evidence

It is crucial to remember that the significance of evidence prevails over the legality of its source, for instance in the case of obtaining evidence through unauthorized access to computer systems or data. This begs the question of how the arbitral tribunal can admit and even make use of such unlawfully obtained evidence. Although at first glance, it seems that evidence acquired through the unlawful breach contradicts the principles of justice, certain exceptional circumstances may necessitate and thus allow to admit such evidence in the pursuit of justice.[65]

Another example refers to the use of so-called "hacked evidence". This term means information which is acquired through unauthorized access to electronic systems (regardless of being obtained directly or with the help of a third party). Indeed, "hacked evidence" mostly encompasses different types of digital content, including "emails, digital documents, electronically stored audio and video recordings, instant messages and logs, or financial transaction records".[66] Arbitration rules grant tribunals a relatively significant discretion in determining and assessing the admissibility of unlawfully obtained evidence. As such, it seems crucial to properly balance two factors. On the one hand, both the process and context of acquitting materials, including also assessing its consistency with principles of good faith, and procedural fairness alongside

64 2021 IBA Rules on the Taking of Evidence in International Arbitration adopted by a resolution of the IBA Council, 17 December 2020, International Bar Association, https://www.ibanet.org/MediaHandler?id=def0807b-9fec-43ef-b624-f2cb2af7cf7b. Accessed on 07.06.2023.

65 N. Jain, *Can an Arbitral Tribunal Admit Evidence Obtained through a Cyber-Attack?*, "Kluwer Arbitration Blog" 27.01.2019, https://arbitrationblog.kluwerarbitration.com/2019/01/27/can-an-arbitral-tribunal-admit-evidence-obtained-through-a-cyber-attack/. Accessed on 06.06.2023.

66 G. García-Perrote, *Admissibility of 'Hacked Evidence' in International Arbitration*, "Kluwer Arbitration Blog" 07.07.2021, https://arbitrationblog.kluwerarbitration.com/2021/07/07/admissibility-of-hacked-evidence-in-international-arbitration/. Accessed on 07.06.2023.

equality of the parties. On the other hand, the so-called probative values of the evidence touch upon its privilege and relevance.[67]

It is worth mentioning that the international community realized the problem of obtaining "hacked evidence" and decided to address these issues. The 2020 IBA Rules even directly refer to such illegally acquired evidence. Under Article 9.3, "Tribunal may, at the request of a Party or on its own motion, exclude evidence obtained illegally". This provision is widely considered as reinforcing the discretion of arbitral tribunal to rule on evidence that has been obtained in an illegal way. Prior to the revision of IBA Rules in 2020, certain arbitral tribunals have already implemented their own procedures on the admissibility of "hacked evidence" due to the lack of a specific rule that explicitly permitted its exclusion.[68]

Firstly, the arbitral tribunal must assess whether a party of the arbitral proceedings was in some kind involved in the illegal activity. Therefore, the so-called doctrine of "clean hands" plays a significant role in determining the admissibility of evidence. As such, once a party introduces evidence with "clean hands", even the potentially unlawful manner of obtaining such evidence cannot be used against them. In addition, "Evidence originally obtained through unlawful conduct should be considered *prima facie* admissible if it has found its way to the tribunal through the hands of a third disinterested party".[69] Therefore, such evidence is deemed to be *prima facie* of superior credibility. Nonetheless, if a party lacks "clean hands" and thus seeks to benefit from unlawfully obtained evidence, such evidence is inadmissible. Apparently, in practice, the wrongdoings should be egregious to be classified as inadmissible. In other words, the arbitral tribunal could be less willing to admit the evidence acquired through illegal means if it concerns a particularly grave situation.[70]

Secondly, the arbitral tribunal must ensure the parties' right to be heard, including the rights of fair trial and due process which once violated could lead to the annulment of the arbitral award. The right to be heard requires that a party may submit evidence on pertinent facts. This entails that dismissal of evidence which is essential to the case undermines the party's right to a fair trial. During the arbitral proceedings, a party should have the opportunity to present its case, also including evidence. It is worth adding, however, that

---

67 *Ibidem.*
68 *Ibidem.*
69 N. Jain, *Can an Arbitral Tribunal ...*
70 *Ibidem.*

arbitral tribunal may admit even illegally obtained evidence in case of no other evidence to prove a necessary aspect of the case.[71]

Thirdly, if the arbitral tribunal rejects the admissibility of illegally obtained evidence, it may lead to rendering a factually wrong award. As such, both the relevance and materiality of evidence presented during arbitral proceedings play a fundamental role. Indeed, the evidence is deemed to be relevant once it supports, challenges, or undermines any claim or fact in the proceedings or fulfils its burden of proof. While assessing the admissibility of evidence, the arbitral tribunal should first consider its materiality. Such evidence is useful to determine the truthfulness of factual allegations and thus uphold the rendering of the arbitral award. In addition, "uncovering the truth outweigh the unlawfulness in which submitted evidence was obtained".[72]

To address these challenges, the Draft Convention on Electronic Evidence was outlined. Given its features, this Draft Convention has the aim to deal with the status of electronic evidence in both civil and criminal cases, investigate and examine the significance of such evidence and recognize and admit e-evidence from foreign jurisdictions.[73]

According to the preamble, this Draft Convention has been prepared to address risks that electronic evidence can be misunderstood and misinterpreted. It focuses also on "recognizing that evidence in electronic form has unique characteristics that are significantly different to paper and other objects, which raise complex questions about the integrity and reliability of data in electronic form"[74], among others.

Finally, trust in electronic evidence plays a crucial role. Eoghan Casey even stresses that a lack of such trust may lead to many grave consequences, including mishandling, misinterpretation, concealment and misexplanation. Furthermore, Stephen Mason and Timothy Reiniger pay attention to the distrust of machines which have been controlled by software.[75] Nonetheless, one must note that there are no institutional arbitration rules, guidelines or domestic laws which authenticate evidence.[76]

---

71 *Ibidem.*

72 *Ibidem.*

73 Draft Convention on Electronic Evidence, https://www.google.com/url?sa=i&rct=j&q=&esrc=s&source=web&cd=&ved=0CAIQw7AJahcKEwjI3r3m67r_AhUAAAAAHQAAAAAQAg&url=https%3A%2F%2Fjournals.sas.ac.uk%2Fdeeslr%2Farticle%2Fdownload%2F2321%2F2245%2F0&psig=AOvVaw310dubAlYP-321nVKGGiKU&ust=1686559757235749. Accessed on 07.06.2023.

74 Preamble of the Draft Convention on Electronic Evidence.

75 D.B. Ferreira, E.A. Gromova, *Electronic evidence in arbitration* ..., p. 34.

76 *Ibidem*, p. 35.

6.4.3 Blockchain as Evidence

There are twofold approaches concerning the admissibility of blockchain evidence during arbitral proceedings. Some scholars believe that it is crucial to its overall avail, whereas "others find it 'virtually useless' if unreliable in court".[77] Notwithstanding such discrepancies, blockchain evidence seems to be undisputable given its immutability, encryption along with time-stamping features. Indeed, the evidentiary significance of blockchain systems can be classified into two groups.

Firstly, blockchain can serve as evidence in case of transactions which have been overseen within the system. As such, through a blockchain receipt, it is possible to track, validate, record, and timestamp a transaction in the chain based on a hash. Once approved in the legal proceedings, blockchain may serve as authenticated evidence concerning both the timing, location, and type of the transaction itself.[78]

Secondly, blockchain systems can be useful in view of verifying information which comes from outside the blockchain. Information stored on a blockchain, which works as a tamper-proof and time-stamped database, significantly impacts the pre-establishment of evidence itself. To illustrate, a design that has been uploaded on a blockchain platform may be classified as proof of existence at a specific time. This is crucial in terms of determining its ownership, for instance. In addition, some argue that the blockchain itself provides a solution to the challenging problem of the uncertainty of the digital data compared to the original document, most importantly in terms of its source, integrity, and authenticity. Throughout the comparison of the original external document with the one stored on a blockchain, it is possible to determine whether they are exact copies.[79]

Even though the so-called technical experts widely recognize the immutability of blockchain, both lawmakers and the judiciary are sceptical about its reliability for substantive and procedural law. In addition, it is crucial to understand the value of blockchain itself which is unaffected despite not being officially acknowledged or used within the court system.[80] In practice, practitioners have also some doubts about how properly submit blockchain evidence in the arbitral tribunal. Nonetheless, one must note that there will be an increasing number of companies using blockchain technology. Therefore, it

77 O. Puertas Álvarez, O. Valentí i Vidal, L. Díaz Vallespinós, *Unlocking Blockchain Evidence …*, p. 17.

78 *Ibidem*, p. 18.

79 *Ibidem*, p. 19.

80 *Ibidem*.

will also impact the use of blockchain evidence in the foreseeable future. One of the advantages of such evidence is time efficiency. The submission of such evidence can accelerate the probative process due to its valuable features, such as being tamper-proof, time-stamped, and authentic. As such, there would be no need for lengthy witness hearings or presentation of documentary evidence. Through the selection of arbitrators already experienced with blockchain technology, the entire arbitral proceedings would be shortened.[81]

Notably, if blockchain technology were widely recognized as admissible in international arbitration, it would speed up the digital transformation in this dispute resolution mechanism. Such a relationship between new technologies and arbitration has been discussed in recent years. Much of the discourse focused on "whether fully automated arbitration platforms are a viable option, whether an award stored on a blockchain would fulfil the requirements for recognition and enforcement under the New York Convention, the use of smart contracts in arbitration, and whether artificial intelligence could supersede the role of arbitrators".[82]

Even if the international community is willing to benefit from the advantages of blockchain technology in arbitral proceedings, there is still a lack of more specific regulations covering these issues, most notably in terms of the admissibility of blockchain evidence. Nonetheless, one must note four reasons that a binding arbitral framework already allows such evidence.

Firstly, arbitration is one of the most flexible dispute resolution mechanisms which not only allows parties to agree on procedural aspects of the proceedings but also grants arbitrators the right to apply such procedural rules. As such, once parties agreed to apply rules which do not prohibit the admissibility of blockchain evidence, the arbitral tribunal may allow such submission of evidence. Article 1.5 of the IBA Rules on the Taking of Evidence in International Arbitration, Article 19 of the ICC Rules, and Article 17.1 of the UNCITRAL Arbitration Rules express the same principle of leaving unregulated matters to the discretion of the arbitral tribunal.[83] These provisions already leave a room for more open approach in terms of using new technologies in international arbitration.

Secondly, there is no explicit provision neither in the main rules nor in the guidelines prohibiting the admission of blockchain evidence. By contrast, their wording could be even interpreted as allowing such practices.

81 *Ibidem*, p. 24.
82 *Ibidem*, p. 25.
83 *Ibidem*, p. 26.

To illustrate, according to the IBA Rules, "document" given the evidence submission is understood as "a writing, communication, picture, drawing, program or data of any kind, whether recorded or maintained on paper or by electronic, audio, visual or any other means". Commentators point out that such a broad description allows the recognition of blockchain data in arbitral proceedings.

Thirdly, the Prague Rules is a soft law instrument for taking evidence in international arbitration. Even though, there is no definition of "document" therein, digital evidence is allowed under Article 4.7. Notwithstanding some uncertainties on whether the wording of the Prague Rules permits the admissibility of electronic evidence, a pro-innovation interpretation of these Rules suggests such a solution. Following the concept of e-discovery recognized by the Prague Rules, the request or search for ESI, including blockchain records seems to be admissible. A similar solution was adopted by the ICC which acknowledged the admissibility of electronic documents and metadata. This entails that blockchain records should also be deemed admissible in arbitral proceedings.[84]

Lastly, there is still little guidance concerning the admissibility of blockchain evidence. Therefore, it is mostly based on the arbitrator's discretion. One must note, however, that arbitrators are rather sceptical about rejecting such evidence due to possible challenges to the arbitral award in case of unjustified refusal. This factor may be a basis that the blockchain records will be admitted as evidence during the arbitral proceedings.[85]

6.4.3.1 *People's Republic of China*

Chinese Hangzhou Internet Court was the first one to accept blockchain evidence. Such a breakthrough took place in June 2018 in the case of Hangzhou Huatai Media Culture Media Co., Ltd. v. Shenzhen Daotong Technology Development Co., Ltd.[86] Therefore, this Court recognized the advantages regarding the use of blockchain technology, including distributed storage, tamper-proof

84 *Ibidem*, p. 27.

85 *Ibidem*.

86 See: Hangzhou Internet Court Province of Zhejiang People's Republic of China (Judgment), https://go.dennemeyer.com/hubfs/blog/pdf/Blockchain%2020180726/20180726_Blog Post_Chinese%20Court%20is%20first%20to%20accept%20Blockchain_Judgment_EN _Translation.pdf. Accessed on 27.06.2023.

mechanisms, traceability, and the possibility of extracting electronic evidence, among others.[87]

It is worth adding that:

> The technologies like blockchain should not be dismissed or the standard of determination thereof should not be raised because they are novel and complex technical means at present, nor should the standard of determination thereof be lowered because it is difficult to tamper with or delete the technology.[88]

In addition, the admissibility of blockchain evidence was also confirmed by the Supreme People's Court (SPC) in September 2018. As such, the SPC issued Provisions on Several Issues Concerning the Trial of Cases by Internet Courts.[89] These provisions recognized the evidence, which is authenticated through electronic signatures, time stamps, hash value verification, blockchain, and many other tamper-proof verification ways. Likewise, these provisions were a landmark in using blockchain evidence in the case of Beijing Weibo Shijie Technology Co., Ltd. v Baidu Network Technology (Beijing) Co., Ltd. In this case, the Beijing Internet Court made use of e-evidence that has been preserved thanks to third-party blockchain service providers. Interestingly, this e-evidence stemmed from two popular short video streaming platforms.[90]

In the wake of these provisions, the Online Litigations Rules for People's Court[91] came into force on 1 August 2021. These Rules apply in both Supreme People's Court and lower courts across mainland China. Therefore, given these regulations, electronic evidence stored on the blockchain can be accepted if it meets two conditions, namely the technical verification of consistency and the absence of contrary evidence.[92]

87 V. Chan, A.M. Koo, *Blockchain Evidence in Internet Courts in China: The Fast Track Evidence Collection for Online Disputes*, "Lexology" 15.07.2020, https://www.lexology.com/library/detail.aspx?g=1631e87b-155a-40b4-a6aa-5260a2e4b9bb. Accessed on 25.06.2023.

88 O. Puertas Álvarez, O. Valentí i Vidal, L. Díaz Vallespinós, *Unlocking Blockchain Evidence ...*, p. 20.

89 最高人民法院关于互联网法院审理案件若干问题的规定, "The Supreme People's Court of the People's Republic of China", https://www.court.gov.cn/zixun-xiangqing-116981.html. Accessed on 25.06.2023.

90 V. Chan, A.M. Koo, *Blockchain Evidence in Internet ...*

91 Online Litigation Rules of the People's Courts, https://cicc.court.gov.cn/html/1/219/199/201/2208.html. Accessed on 26.06.2023.

92 O. Puertas Álvarez, O. Valentí i Vidal, L. Díaz Vallespinós, *Unlocking Blockchain Evidence ...*, p. 20.

Finally, it is worth adding that once the authenticity of the evidence is challenged by the parties involved, there are twofold situations that could potentially happen. Therefore, the rules make a difference between tampering before and after the storage of such evidence on the blockchain. Nonetheless, one must note that the authenticity of evidence before being uploaded to the blockchain must undergo more rigorous scrutiny. This entails that once party would like to benefit from such evidence, it will be necessary to provide some additional information, including documents, testimonies along with other corroborating evidence, if needed.[93]

6.4.3.2 *United States of America*

Under the US Federal Rules of Evidence (FRE) 803(6), a record can be recognized as admissible if it fulfils certain conditions. The first one refers to the evidence if it is maintained as a part of the regular activities of a business, organization, occupation, or profession. The second concerns creating such records which are a standard practice within that activity. Therefore, one must note that the so-called blockchain ledgers, when used for business transactions, are likely to meet such requirements. Nonetheless, the key issue is to establish a proper foundation to prove such evidence. It can be achieved either by setting forth the testimony or written declarations from a custodian of records or any other witnesses. Such a person is deemed to provide necessary factual information about the creation of the documents and the circumstances infolding them.[94]

To address practical challenges regarding the admissibility of blockchain evidence, several states in the US have already taken some measures. To illustrate, Vermont adopted a law providing that blockchain receipts, once accompanied by a written declaration from an individual verifying the transaction details, can be admissible as evidence. In addition, according to the 12 V.S.A. §1913, blockchain receipts are presumed to be authentic given the Vermont Rules of Evidence. Likewise, Arizona also enacted its own law (HB 2417), amending the Arizona Electronic Transaction Act to include provisions regarding blockchain records, signatures, and smart contracts. Such amendment had the aim to clarify that these blockchain-based elements should not be denied legal effect, validity, or enforceability. Similar law entered into force in Ohio in 2018, accepting the legal validity of blockchain records, signatures,

93 *Ibidem.*

94 *The Admissibility of Blockchain as Digital Evidence*, "Concord Law School" 23.03.2019, https://www.purduegloballawschool.edu/blog/news/admissibility-blockchain-digital-evidence. Accessed on 26.06.2023.

and smart contracts.[95] Finally, the Illinois Blockchain Technology Act provides that blockchain data can be used in terms of evidence during legal proceedings, once it is well authenticated. This approach complies with the Illinois Rules of Evidence. Given this act, such authentication can be made by presenting electronic data together with an affidavit from a qualified individual. Indeed, such provisions have already confirmed that Illinois is a supportive environment for practitioners of blockchain technology.[96]

7 Digital Arbitral Award

7.1 *Form of the Digital Arbitral Award*

The Convention on the Recognition and Enforcement of Foreign Arbitral Awards (the so-called 1958 New York Convention) was adopted far before the digital era. As such, at the time of its enactment, the Internet has not been invented and thus many long-distance communication means have not even existed. Although the 1958 New York Convention recognizes merely telegraph, international arbitration is very flexible in adjusting to a new normal. Therefore, it recognizes many recent innovation-driven technologies which allow for managing long-distance communications. It is noteworthy, however, that such a trend of being open to innovations is visible among the arbitrators and international community, whereas the backbone is almost the same.[97]

Interestingly, the New York Convention does not provide any specific form requirements for arbitral awards. Nonetheless, one must note that such requirements can play a significant role in two stages. Firstly, they may already have been incorporated in the definition of an arbitral award. Hence, if the required form is not met, the provisions of the New York Convention would be inapplicable under Article I (1). Secondly, the form of an arbitral award may

95 *Ibidem*. See more: Chen Lei, *Regulating Smart Contracts and Digital Platforms: A Chinese Perspective* [in:] *The Cambridge Handbook of Smart Courts, Blockchain Technology and Digital Platforms*, ed. L.A. DiMatteo, M. Cannarsa, C. Poncibò, Cambridge 2019, pp. 183–210; Wang Jia, Chen Lei, *Will Innovative Technology Result in Innovative Legal Frameworks? – Smart Contracts in China*, "European Review of Private Law" 2018, Vol. 26, issue 6, pp. 921–942; Tao Jingzhou, M. Zhang, *Resolving Disputes in China: New and Sometimes Unpredictable Development* [in:] *International Organizations and the Promotion of Effective Dispute Resolution. AIIB Yearbook of International Law 2019*, ed. P. Quayle, Gao Xuan, Leiden-Boston 2019, pp. 56–76.

96 O. Puertas Álvarez, O. Valentí i Vidal, L. Díaz Vallespinós, *Unlocking Blockchain Evidence …*, p. 21.

97 S. Halla, *Arbitration going online …*, p. 221.

also lead to non-binding results for the parties involved. This entails that a lack of the appropriate form may result in the rejection of recognition and enforcement of the arbitral award under Article V(1)(e) of the New York Convention.[98]

It is noteworthy that the notion of an arbitral award under Article I(1) of the New York Convention is lively discussed. Within the ongoing debate, there are three main positions to be distinguished. On the one hand, some argue that the New York Convention acknowledges an independent definition of the arbitral award. On the other hand, others believe that the notion of an arbitral award is determined by national law through an autonomous conflict of law rule or under *lex arbitri* or the *lex fori*. Lastly, some opt for a combination of these standards to be applied alternatively or cumulatively. Indeed, given the enforcement and recognition of foreign arbitral awards, the third option combining an independent standard and the *lex fori* seems to be more appropriate. Apparently, this approach also extends the recognition-friendly minimum standard of Article VII (1) of the New York Convention to its applicability. As a result, it also favours a relaxed independent standard in terms of the form requirements of the arbitral award.[99]

One must note that the New York Convention demonstrates a certain willingness to hold modern technologies, including electronic form. As such, even form requirements have evolved to permit digital awards.[100] In addition:

> It would run counter to these developments if the Convention's autonomous standard for awards stayed behind the form standard recognized by UNCITRAL's harmonizing instruments. Therefore, an autonomous interpretation results in the same standard as under the UNCITRAL Model Law on International Commercial Arbitration.[101]

The emergence of electronic signatures (e-signatures) may significantly influence the enforceability of arbitral awards. Currently, many jurisdictions

98 R. Wolff, *E-arbitration agreements and e-awards – arbitration agreements concluded in an electronic environment and digital arbitral awards* [in:] *Arbitration in the Digital Age: The Brave New World of Arbitration*, ed. M. Piers, C. Aschauer, Cambridge 2018, pp. 151–181.

99 *Ibidem*.

100 See more: B. Gessel-Kalinowska vel Kalisz, *Wyrok arbitrażowy w czasie pandemii – dopuszczalność współczesnych form elektronicznych (skrót artykułu opublikowanego w „Przeglądzie Prawa Handlowego")*, "Biuletyn Arbitrażowy. Nowe technologie w arbitrażu instytucjonalnym" 2020, no. 26.

101 R. Wolff, *E-arbitration agreements and e-awards* ..., pp. 151–181.

worldwide follow Article 31(1) of the UNCITRAL Model Law[102] and require that arbitral awards must be in writing and have the signatures of the arbitrators. One must note, however, that the degree of risk linked to using an e-signature for the sake of authenticating an arbitral award varies based on the applicable law at the place of enforcement of such an award (the so-called *lex fori*) or by the laws of the arbitral seat.[103]

Under Article IV(1)(a) of the New York Convention, the party seeking for recognition and enforcement of an arbitral award is required to provide to the court at the time of such application, the "duly authenticated original award or a duly certified copy thereof". Notwithstanding, one must note that the New York Convention does not specify requirements concerning such authentication or certification to be valid. In addition, NYC is also silent on the applicable laws according to which such requirements should be determined.[104]

Authentication is understood as a formality necessary to determine whether the signature on the original document is genuine. Certification, by contrast, means the formality to verify whether a copy of the document is a true copy of the original. Nevertheless, it is noteworthy that specific requirements for such formalities (both authentication and certification) differ from one jurisdiction to another. Likewise, the requirements concerning who may legalize the attestation of the arbitral award also are different depending on the jurisdiction.[105]

One must note, however, that an arbitral award once signed electronically possesses a comparable degree of trustworthiness to a wet-ink signed award given its genuineness and reliability in most legal jurisdictions. Such an e-signature refers to information which is presented in an electronic format and linked to a data message. Through such a linkage, it is possible to identify a signing person about the data message. Therefore, it is much easier to demonstrate the signer's agreement with the information included in the data message as provided in Article 2(2) of the UNCITRAL Model Law on Electronic Signatures with Guide to Enactment (MLES).[106] This Convention aims

102 "The award shall be made in writing and shall be signed by the arbitrator or arbitrators. In arbitral proceedings with more than one arbitrator, the signatures of the majority of all members of the arbitral tribunal shall suffice, provided that the reason for any omitted signature is stated".

103 F.V. Soley, *Signing the Arbitral Award in Wet Ink: Resistance to Technological Change or A Reasonable Precaution?*, "Kluwer Arbitration Blog" 06.11.2020, https://arbitrationblog.kluwerarbitration.com/2020/11/06/signing-the-arbitral-award-in-wet-ink-resistance-to-technological-change-or-a-reasonable-precaution/. Accessed on 12.05.2024.

104 *Ibidem.*

105 *Ibidem.*

106 *Ibidem.*

to promote and simplify the adoption of electronic signatures. To achieve this goal, it sets forth standards for technical dependability that ensure the equivalence of electronic signatures with handwritten signatures. In addition, the MLES may contribute to creating a contemporary, consistent, and equitable legal framework that effectively addresses the legal recognition of electronic signatures. As such, it provides certainty to their status.[107]

It is worthwhile to note that the New York Convention is silent on the use of electronic signatures in arbitral awards. Nonetheless, given the New York Convention's pro-enforcement approach, such silence should be regarded in favour of technology. One must stress a new trend in international arbitration. Courts tend to be lenient while accepting the authentication and certification of an arbitral award provided that the award itself is authentic. Considering e-signatures, different jurisdictions may apply different standards with regard to the authentication and certification of the arbitral award according to applicable law.[108]

The growing significance of electronic authentication methods as alternatives to handwritten signatures and traditional patterns of authentication has already proved that there is a need for a dedicated legal framework to address these issues. Within this framework, it seems crucial to mitigate uncertainties concerning the legal consequences of making use of such electronic means. Given these concerns, the MLES builds upon the core principle provided in Article 7 of the UNCITRAL Model Law on Electronic Commerce.[109] This principle stresses the fulfilment of the signature function in an electronic environment. One must note, however, that the MLES represents a technology-neutral approach. Therefore, it avoids bias towards any specific technology or process. Such an approach entails that legislation based on the MLES can recognize both digital signatures involving cryptography (namely public key infrastructure, aka PKI) along with electronic signatures based on other technologies.[110]

The appropriate authentication of the e-award is needed prior to the enforcement and recognition thereof. To make it possible, it is worth referring to an apostille which is widely recognized as an additional authentication. This apostille is useful in terms of notarized documents. Therefore, the so-called

107 UNCITRAL Model Law on Electronic Signatures with Guide to Enactment 2001, https://uncitral.un.org/sites/uncitral.un.org/files/media-documents/uncitral/en/ml-elecsig-e.pdf. Accessed on 12.05.2024.

108 F.V. Soley, *Signing the Arbitral ...*

109 See: UNICTRAL Model Law on Electronic Signatures...

110 *Ibidem.*

e-Apostille Pilot Program (e-APP) could be helpful to facilitate cross-border recognition of foreign e-awards.[111]

7.2 *Enforcement of the Digital Arbitral Award*

The enforcement of the arbitral award is stipulated by the 1958 New York Convention. Nonetheless, while adopting this Convention, no one could even consider the possibility of rendering a digital arbitral award. This begs the question of whether the binding provisions of the 1958 New York Convention allow to fully recognize and enforce such an arbitral award. It seems that there are threefold aspects to be considered.

Firstly, under Article V(1)(b) of the New York Convention, "the party against whom the award is invoked was not given proper notice of the appointment of the arbitrator or of the arbitration proceedings or was otherwise unable to present his case". Therefore, this provision refers to the violation of the basic right, namely the right to be heard. The aforementioned Article allows refusal of the enforcement of the arbitral award based on the violation of due process by the arbitral tribunal. It is noteworthy that "the right to be heard" is one of the key elements of due process. Although Article V(1)(b) allows the refusal of enforcement of the arbitral award, merely very serious irregularities should happen to make it possible. Interestingly, given the actual development of new technologies, one could even say that such serious irregularities could be the result of making use of case management websites (platforms), videoconferencing and virtual workspaces. To illustrate, if the arbitral tribunal has chosen a technology to handle a case that enables the party to allege facts, and submit documents or evidence on time.[112] Another problem occurs alongside the absence of both a videoconferencing and in-person meeting. Given this situation, the right to be heard orally was violated. Nonetheless, if a videoconferencing session was held successfully, there is no violations. Therefore, remote hearing made throughout the videoconferencing is valid. One must note that some technical issues could appear, mostly with regard to disruption of sound and image transmission in the course of arbitral proceedings. Finally, the use of certain platforms for remote hearing could also lead to gross inequalities.[113]

---

111 M.S. Abdel Wahab, E. Katsh, *Revolutionizing Technologies and the Use* ..., p. 51.

112 G. Kaufmann-Kohler, T. Schulz, *The Use of Information* ..., p. 38.

113 *Ibidem.*

8 Cybersecurity

To start with, cybersecurity is considered one of the primary obstacles and challenges in the transition process to online platforms. Indeed, such concern is sensitive in view of arbitration. In the case of complex international disputes, which are handled via arbitral proceedings, the use of digital documents become a new normal to some extent. Such documents very often encompass sensitive data along with classified information and trade secrets. In addition, arbitral proceedings are private by nature. Confidentiality is one of the key issues and differs from the notion of privacy.[114] Confidentiality[115] denotes either information about or revealed in the arbitral proceedings. Even though both notions (confidentiality and privacy) are closely connected, this begs the question of whether "privacy entails confidentiality". Even though there is a prevailing opinion that arbitral proceedings are not fully confidential unless parties explicitly agree to it, there is a common standpoint that "the concept of privacy would have no meaning if participants were required to arbitrate privately by day while being free to pontificate publicly by night".[116]

Given confidentiality,[117] the entire arbitral proceedings should be handled in such a way as to provide that the identities of the involved parties remain undiscovered. One must note, however, that the so-called interconnectedness of participants based on digital means can easily become a target for hackers or spies. Therefore, they may seek to manipulate the highly sensitive data related to confidential matters of the disputed case. Indeed, multinational disputes involving parties from different countries result in benefiting from information exchange through electronic storage. Nonetheless, the use of

114 See more: R. Torres Vouga, *A Judge's Perspective: Privacy and Confidentiality in Voluntary Commercial Arbitration* [in:] *Online Dispute Resolution. New Challenges*, ed. D. Moura Vicente, E. Dias Oliveira, J. Gomes de Almeida, Baden-Baden 2022, pp. 159–180.

115 See more: M. Henry, *An Arbitrator's Perspective: Confidentiality – Privacy – Security in the Eye of the Arbitrators or the Story of the Arbitrator who Became a Bee* [in:] *Online Dispute Resolution. New Challenges*, ed. D. Moura Vicente, E. Dias Oliveira, J. Gomes de Almeida, Baden-Baden 2022, pp. 181–204.

116 A. Zwolankiewicz, A. Sachan, *Big Data, Bigger Disruption: In Institutional Arbitration Ready?*, "Biuletyn Arbitrażowy. Nowe technologie w arbitrażu instytucjonalnym" 2020, no. 26, p. 14; Y. Fortier, *The Occasionally Unwarranted Assumption of Confidentiality*, "Arbitraion International" 1999, no. 15, p. 132. For further details see G. Born, *International Commercial Arbitration*, "Kluwer Law International" 2014, pp. 2780–2783.

117 See more: S. Ribeiro Mendes, *A Lawyer's Perspective: Confidentiality, Privacy and Security in Arbitration in Times of Covid* [in:] *Online Dispute Resolution. New Challenges*, ed. D. Moura Vicente, E. Dias Oliveira, J. Gomes de Almeida, Baden-Baden 2022, pp. 205–232.

such electronic tools exposes the data to vulnerabilities such as cyberattacks.[118] Therefore, such cyberattacks may result in disclosing, manipulating, or even changing crucial evidence in the entire arbitral proceedings. This entails that such intrusions significantly undermine the core elements of the arbitral proceedings. As such, they violate contractual obligations and expose participants and parties involved to an overall risk.[119]

International arbitration is widely recognized as a neutral forum to handle disputes in the commercial and investment sectors, involving high-profile targets of cyberattacks. To name a few, they involve multinational corporations' governments, state entities, public figures, and NGOs, among others. Even though both the level and extent of confidentiality may be different, arbitration as means of dispute resolution provides the chance to solve conflicts in a private setting. As such, disputes that are subject to international arbitration very often require evidence of facts which could have an impact on politics and financial markets. Indeed, international arbitration also involves parties stemming from diverse jurisdictions who work in different environments. Therefore, large, and cross-border teams are popular in international arbitration. Consequently, all the parties concerned, including arbitrators, in-house attorneys, and legal counsels travel frequently and work from multifarious locations (i.e. hotels, airport lounges, private residences). These factors may also increase the likelihood of being hacked in the virtual world and thus be subject to both social engineering and theft of physical data.[120]

Arbitrators, like judges, are independent practitioners but they can work in a context with different levels of cybersecurity, involving law firms and universities or they may work independently without any affiliation instead. The former requires that arbitrators must abide by data security protocols and policies that are beyond their control. Indeed, it may not be appropriate for their role as arbitrators. The latter, in turn, ensures a higher level of freedom and flexibility to arbitrators who may not have access to any sophisticated IT support.[121]

Nonetheless, one must note that the use of technology in international arbitration is a kind of double-edged sword. Many innovation-driven technologies

118 See more: J. Chaisse, C. Bauer, *Cybersecurity and the Protection of Digital Assets: Assessing the Role of International Investment Law and Arbitration*, "Vanderbilt Journal of Entertainment and Technology Law" 2020, Vol. 21, pp. 549–589.

119 A. Zwolankiewicz, A. Sachan, *Big Data, Bigger Disruption* ..., p. 14.

120 C. Morel de Westgaver, *Cybersecurity in International Arbitration – A Necessity And An Opportunity For Arbitral Institutions*, "Wolters Kluwer" 06.10.2017, https://arbitrationblog.kluwerarbitration.com/2017/10/06/cyber-security/. Accessed 07.04.2023.

121 *Ibidem*.

and IT tools provide the possibility of long-distance communication. Such innovations not only facilitate the transmission of evidence but also reduce the costs of the entire arbitral proceedings. On the other hand, the use of technology also results in many new risks, most notably in terms of privacy and confidentiality. Therefore, the risk of information leakage is highly developed in contemporary international arbitration. This entails that a matter of "if" a security breach will occur is no longer actual. By contrast, this begs rather a question of "when" such a breach will happen. Apparently, cyberattacks are taking place in everyday life and international arbitration is not resistant to such threats.[122]

In the context of the digital age, the concept of confidentiality has transformed and expanded. Therefore, it is not considered in terms of interpersonal confidentiality but rather as technological confidentiality. Hence, both arbitral institutions and arbitrators themselves should recognize potential risks related to being involved in cyberspaces.[123] In addition, they should also take steps for the sake of implementing measures to safeguard the privacy of the parties involved in the arbitral proceedings.[124]

According to most rules and legal systems, arbitrators together with arbitral tribunals have the authority to issue necessary orders for the sake of protecting confidential information alongside documents. Indeed, it should be noted that arbitrators' broad procedural powers concern the ability to issue orders regarding the storage, use and transfer of data created and produced during arbitral proceedings. On the one hand, both protocols and recommendations concerning cybersecurity risks for the parties and arbitral tribunals are widely acknowledged as a positive development. Therefore, they should be embraced by the international arbitration community. On the other hand, if implemented by the arbitral tribunal, such measures would have limited scope and enforceability. Given that, it is noteworthy to remember that some arbitrators may have extended knowledge of cybersecurity issues, whereas others cannot be named as IT experts. Consequently, relying on such arbitrators with the aim of enhancing cybersecurity may not lead to sustainable and sufficient results.[125]

Online arbitration also may cause some problems related to transparency, enjoyment of third-party rights and cybersecurity issues. Although the arbitral institutions adjusted their rules to comply with the new trends arising from the

122 A. Zwolankiewicz, A. Sachan, *Big Data, Bigger Disruption ...*, p. 15.

123 See more: L. Biukovic, *International Commercial Arbitration in Cyberspace: Recent Developments*, "Northwestern Journal of International Law & Business" 2002, Vol. 22, issue 3, pp. 319–352.

124 A. Zwolankiewicz, A. Sachan, *Big Data, Bigger Disruption ...*, p. 15.

125 C. Morel de Westgaver, *Cybersecurity in International ...*

COVID-19 pandemic (mostly regarding online submissions, access to the relevant documents and remote hearings), many new challenges require attention. Confidentiality is one of the pressing topics in international arbitration. The other problem refers to electronic data breaches or even cyberattacks that could happen in the case of remote proceedings. As a result, such incidents could significantly impact not only the security and privacy of the parties involved but also industrial secrets and case information.[126]

In the case of e-arbitration, much documentary evidence is in digital format. In addition, such evidence is processed electronically by both sides, namely clients and lawyers. Likewise, communication itself, involving arbitrators and parties, is also made digitally, regardless of printing some files out on paper. Consequently, such information is transferred through digital means instead of traditional, physical storage methods. One must note that digital records (documents) can be modified online in an easy way. Therefore, it seems difficult to track all the changes and even verify whether a digital record is truly authentic. Notably, there is a potential cyber risk to identify the authenticity of digital evidence submitted electronically. This means that it is even more difficult to detect and prove any tampering with data or falsifying data during transit. Once any party contests the authenticity or integrity of data, the examination process begins based on the usual procedural means, including a computer forensic expert.[127]

Protective cybersecurity measures are introduced for the sake of maintaining the accuracy and authenticity of data alongside preventing unauthorized manipulation of data by other parties. In addition, such measures aim to limit physical access to the hardware including digital evidence. This goal is achieved through the establishment of a user rights management system which is entitled to determine what legitimate users can do with the data concerned (i.e. read, write, delete, copy). Therefore, a "legitimate user" is properly defined to grant access to the digital system merely to these users who are admitted. Given that, only a real person can access the system by using a username, password and a one-time security code which is sent through SMS, mobile app, or email. To ensure the highest level of cybersecurity, regular backups of data are made regularly. Such backups are encrypted and time-stamped. It is worth adding that:

126 B.O. Giupponi, *"Virtual" Dispute Resolution ...*, p. 72.

127 E.G.W. Schäfer, *Managing Data Privacy and Cybersecurity Issues*, "Global Arbitration Review" 03.09.2021, https://globalarbitrationreview.com/guide/the-guide-evidence-in-international-arbitration/2nd-edition/article/managing-data-privacy-and-cybersecurity-issues. Accessed on 07.04.2023.

> Since in nearly all cases any digital information (documents) will automatically be stored as identical copies within the same system, or on other systems to which it was intentionally transmitted, and the meta data will normally at least allow to date some copies, there is a relatively good degree of likelihood that covert manipulations of documents can be detected by a computer forensic, provided the described procedures are implemented, the system is backed up frequently and there are sufficiently long retention periods.[128]

A certain level of security is also needed in the case of e-arbitration not only to satisfy the legal requirements in this regard but also to ensure that parties' correspondence is well preserved and confidential. This entails that all the information communicated or exchanged in the course of arbitral proceedings must be properly protected from being illegally stored or hacked. Aside from confidentiality requirements therein, it is crucial to ensure information security, including data integrity, and availability alongside other requirements.[129] Data integrity should be understood as providing no unauthorized changes to the files such as data-in-transit (which concerns the flow of data from one PC to another one) and data-at-rest (which refers to stored data, i.e. hard disk or even cloud storage). Recently, the latter became even more popular due to their accessibility through the Internet regardless of location. The requirements concerning both confidentiality and data integrity are linked to authenticity. Hence, "a recipient of an electronic communication [must] be certain of the identity of the originator of the particular communication".[130]

The availability, in turn, should ensure that data are accessible to all authorized parties once needed. This requirement faces many dangers including not only hardware failure but also targeted attacks (the so-called 'denial of service', DoS). This kind of attack could lead to much damage, most importantly when the document must be submitted at a certain deadline.[131]

Finally, compliance with other legal requirements is also one of the key elements of ensuring the security of data. Importantly, such compliance could concern the requirement of auditability understood as access to specific

128 *Ibidem.*

129 P. Schaumann, M. Burger-Scheidlin, *The Security and Reliability of Electronic Communication With a Critical Note on the Human Factor*, [in:] *Arbitration in the Digital Age: The Brave New World of Arbitration*, ed. M. Piers, C. Aschauer, Cambridge University Press 2018, p. 56.

130 *Ibidem*, p. 57.

131 *Ibidem.*

aspects of data. Indeed, "such requirements can also arise from the need to deliver a proof that is accepted as evidence in the jurisdictions concerned".[132]

Apparently, arbitral institutions are vulnerable to cybersecurity risks based on their role as the depository of sensitive data. To ensure the cybersecurity of data during arbitral proceedings, threat assessment could be used. On the one hand, this methodology is helpful to determine the level of security which is needed. On the other hand, it outlines the specific security measures that should be undertaken. To properly benefit from the threat assessment, it is crucial to evaluate the credibility, seriousness, and likelihood of potential threats. As such, "to do this, first a list of the potential adversaries needs to be compiled. In the next step, the likelihood of their attack is to be evaluated based on the value that an attack could bring for adversaries".[133]

There are twofold threats: amateur hackers and hacktivists as well as professional adversaries. The latter refers to hackers "for rent" working for one of the parties or government intelligence for the sake of aiding "their" businesses. To properly assess the situation, the following questions should be addressed: why a certain IT setup has been attacked? What are the benefits of attacking such an IT system? What level of proficiency is needed to attack such a system? Who is interested in obtaining such data? The answer to these questions varies based on the type of cases being conducted and the number of disputed cases. One could even say that in the case of two large international companies which are handling a dispute over hundreds of millions of euros/dollars, a few hundred thousand euros/dollars paid to the professional hacker is not a bad solution. In addition, such practices appear mostly in the case of arbitration proceedings of strategic significance for a certain country. Therefore, when similar situations arise, the government intelligence services may be involved. Global organizations benefit from their power to control and monitor the Internet traffic in various regions around the world as "global attackers". Protecting data from global attackers seems to be challenging.[134]

It is worth noting that cyberattacks have already happened in international arbitration. To illustrate, the Permanent Court of Arbitration's (PCA's) website became a target of hackers in the course of a maritime border dispute between the People's Republic of China and the Philippines. Given this case, PCA's website has been infected with malware which also resulted in the infection of visitors' computers. The latter could lead to data theft. The said example confirms that international arbitration is threatened by cyberattacks.

132 *Ibidem.*
133 *Ibidem.*
134 *Ibidem*, p. 58.

Although it is commonly acknowledged that arbitration provides confidentiality, sometimes parties must disclose sensitive information or materials during the proceedings to prove certain facts. To address such challenges concerning cyberattacks, the International Council for Commercial Arbitration together with the New York City Bar Association and the International Institute for Conflict Prevention and Resolution issued a draft Cybersecurity Protocol for International Arbitration in 2018. This protocol was published for the sake of introducing security measures for the case and could apply because of the parties' agreement or decision of the arbitral tribunal. Such measures should consider the following aspects: 1. the transmission of materials; 2. communication between the arbitrators; 3. the storage of submitted data and information; 4. data security.[135]

Currently, an updated version of this protocol (2022) is binding. This version was published with the assistance of the Permanent Court of Arbitration (PCA) in the Hague. This protocol provides 14 principles to apply in the e-arbitration proceedings to ensure the appropriate level of protection with regard to cybersecurity issues. As such, the principles are divided into the following groups: scope and applicability, standard, determining reasonable cybersecurity measures and process to establish reasonable cybersecurity measures.[136]

According to the first Principle, "the Cybersecurity Protocol provides a recommended framework to guide tribunals, parties, and administering institutions in their consideration of what information security measures are reasonable to apply to a particular arbitration matter". This Protocol should be recognized as a general framework to be considered in view of security measures applied to the information processed. It also defines "processing" which should be understood as:

> anything that is done to, or with, arbitration-related information. It includes automated and non-automated operations, such as collection, recording, organization, storage, adaptation or alteration, retrieval,

135 P. Bienvenu, B. Grant, *Data protection and cyber-risk issues in arbitration: regulation, cyberattacks and hacked evidence*, "Lexology" 17.10.2019, https://www.lexology.com/commentary/arbitration-adr/international/norton-rose-fulbright/data-protection-and-cyber-risk-issues-in-arbitration-regulation-cyberattacks-and-hacked-evidence#cyberattacks. Accessed on 03.04.2023.

136 ICCA-NYC Bar-CPR Protocol on Cybersecurity in International Arbitration (2022 Edition) with the assistance of the Permanent Court of Arbitration, Peace Palace, the Hague, "ICCA Reports" 2022, no. 6, https://static.cpradr.org/docs/Cybersecurity%20ICCA-NYC%20Bar-CPR-protocol-international-arbitration-2022.pdf. Accessed on 04.04.2023.

consultation, use, disclosure by transmission, dissemination, alignment or combination, restriction, erasure, or destruction.[137]

One must note that the Protocol does not provide a uniform solution for information security. This entails that reasonable security measures should be implemented individually, that is given the specific features of arbitral proceedings. Therefore, what is deemed reasonable depends on the unique facts and circumstances of each case alongside the evolving nature of technology and potential risks. Consequently, parties and arbitral tribunals who opt for using this Protocol may freely refer to its provisions to determine which of the information security measures would be appropriate in their specific situation.[138]

By "information security", the Protocol means all types of forms of electronic and non-electronic information which covers commercial and personal data. Interestingly, the Protocol outlines examples of negative consequences in the case of not paying enough attention to information security. To name a new, it could lead to the economic loss experienced by individuals due to the exposure of their commercial information or personal data; loss of integrity of data or damage to trustworthiness and correctness of data as a result of cybersecurity breach; inaccessibility of data, networks, platforms, websites caused by the disruption; legal liability under relevant laws and regulations (i.e. applicable data protection regulations); damages to the parties, arbitrators, third-parties and administrating arbitral institutions and the entire arbitration systems.[139]

Modern international arbitrations rely on digital and innovation-driven technologies. The Protocol introduces cybersecurity measures intending to ensure better protection of key features of arbitration proceedings such as confidentiality, integrity, and availability of digital information. Indeed, the Protocol applies to all information security measures which means that it covers not only cybersecurity but also physical security. Indeed, currently, many disputes are resolved through digital means and thus the appropriate level of security for the information exchanged in the arbitral proceedings is needed. Such security included not only the confidentiality of the information but also its integrity and availability.[140]

The second principle introduces the notion of "baseline security" which should be understood as the implementation of reasonable information

137 *Ibidem*, p. 7.

138 *Ibidem*.

139 *Ibidem*, p. 7–9.

140 *Ibidem*.

security measures by all persons who have access to information on arbitration. Through the excessive exchange of information between parties, tribunals, and administering institutions, strong digital independence is created. By any security breach concerning arbitral information by one party concerned, all other participants of the arbitral proceedings could be affected. This entails that the protection of information in the course of arbitral proceedings relies on the actions and decisions undertaken by all the parties involved. Importantly, many security incidents result in individuals' behaviour instead of a breach of systems or infrastructure.[141] To avoid this kind of situation, the appropriate education process should be implemented to familiarize all the parties involved in the arbitral proceedings that they must abide by information security measures (Principle 3).[142]

It is noteworthy to stress that this Protocol merely provides guidelines for cybersecurity. This entails that it may be superseded by other binding legal obligations. Therefore, such obligations can determine or even affect the aforementioned information security measures in particular arbitration (principle 4). Fully up to date, there are more than 100 data protection laws, regulations, and industry standards worldwide. These provisions apply to both personal data and data of public importance. To name a few examples of such laws, one must note GDPR in Europe, the California Consumer Privacy Act in the United States,[143] and Personal Information Protection Law (PIPL) in the People's Republic of China, among others. Data protection laws may differ importantly based on the jurisdiction by including multifarious definitions of "personal data". On the one hand, non-compliance with such regulations may lead to significant penalties and/or litigation risks. On the other hand, both enforcement and legal risks linked to data protection may not be consistent in different jurisdictions. Therefore, it can pose challenges to transnational information exchanges, most notably in terms of international arbitration proceedings. It is worth adding that these rules and regulations are evolving constantly to comply with the changing environment. As a result of such changes, all parties involved in the arbitration proceedings, also including arbitrators, and administering institutions must fulfil their legal obligations concerning the processing of data.[144]

In the case of institutional arbitration, parties, and their legal representatives have to co-work with the arbitral institution to ensure the appropriate

141 *Ibidem*, p. 9–10.
142 *Ibidem*, p. 11.
143 *Ibidem*, p. 12.
144 *Ibidem*, p. 13.

level of information security measures. As such, they could align with and be implemented pursuant to the arbitral institutions' rules, practices, technical capabilities, and legal obligations, among others. Given the specific institution's obligations stemming from the data protection laws, certain information security measures may be adopted by both the parties and the arbitral tribunal in the ongoing proceedings.[145]

The Protocol also sets forth that the specific information security measures should apply in the following cases: "(a) asset management; (b) access controls; (c) encryption; (d) communications security; (e) physical and environmental security; (f) operations security; and (g) security incident management, including breach notification expectations and procedures" (Principle 7). There are circumstances where it may be appropriate to adjust the information security measures to address the risks revealed in multifarious aspects of the arbitration. Such risks may be linked to the following situations: "(a) information exchanges and transmission of arbitration-related information; (b) storage of arbitration-related information; (c) travel; (d) hearings and conferences whether in-person or fully or partially remote; and/or (e) post-arbitration retention and destruction policies" (Principle 8). This entails those various types of information security measures enumerated in principle 7 may be understood differently depending on the different aspects of the arbitration proceedings.[146]

Considering the principles outlined in the Cybersecurity Protocol, the parties should express their willingness to adopt rational measures for information security since the first instance. Indeed, party autonomy is crucial in information security alongside other aspects of arbitral proceedings. This entails that the parties and their legal representatives will decide on the appropriate information security measures to be used throughout the arbitration. In addition, such measures on information security should be addressed at the outset of the arbitration proceedings. Therefore, according to principle 10, it is highly recommended to discuss with the parties and administering institution, the aforementioned information security rules at the initial case management conference or procedural hearing. In addition, one must note that the arbitral tribunal is deemed to uphold any mutual agreement reached by the parties on information security measures unless such an agreement overrides legal or other obligations and there are important countervailing considerations.[147]

145 *Ibidem.*
146 *Ibidem*, p. 15–19.
147 *Ibidem*, p. 21–22.

Another example of cyber hack concerns the Sao Paulo tribunal which stopped the implementation of a partial award that was in favour of the claimant in a multibillion-dollar ICC dispute. The case concerned the sale of a pulp manufacturer. The implementation was paused based on the allegation that the arbitration proceedings were corrupted by cyber hacking. As a result, the defendant contested the award by assuming that the claimant hacked into its servers for the sake of accessing confidential information, i.e. more than 70 000 emails sent in the course of arbitral proceedings. Even though the claimant denied undertaking such actions, the state Sao Paulo police found illegal spyware on a few defendants' email accounts. Two hackers have confessed to entering illegally the defendant's IT system; however, they have not confirmed to have any connection to the claimant.[148]

Irrespective of the person who was responsible for handling the cyber-attack, the confidential information may have been breached. Given that, there are justified doubts concerning both the fairness and impartiality of the arbitral tribunal's conduct. Additionally, the police have arrested people in relation to the cyber-attack allegations.[149]

This case already demonstrates how cybersecurity risks are not merely theoretical issues in arbitral proceedings but importantly they can transform into real problems for the arbitral tribunal. The key question, thus, would likely be whether and to what extent the tribunal might have been impacted by any compromised evidence which affected its decision-making process while rendering an award. Although the arbitral tribunal is deemed to evaluate the presented facts and evidence, the ramifications of using tainted evidence could lead to far-reaching consequences. Therefore, in the case of a successful challenge of an arbitral tribunal based on tainted evidence, the entire arbitral proceedings may be re-set and start from the beginning.[150]

Although it seems impossible to fully eliminate the risk of cyber-attacks while handling remote proceedings given the evolving types of tactics undertaken by cyber attackers, the parties concerned may wish to benefit from measures for the sake of mitigating possible risks and ensuring smooth proceedings. Hence, multifarious types of measures could be deployed based on the nature of the arbitration proceedings, risk profile and proportionality considerations, among others. Practically, the following measures may be undertaken with the

148 K. Baetens, *Cyber hack challenges ...*

149 *Ibidem.*

150 K. Baetens, J. Suschinski, *Cyber hack challenges in international arbitration – Part 2*, "Linklaters" 13.05.2021, https://www.lexology.com/library/detail.aspx?g=b350fa18-ad82-4828-a21e-e5aed590512f. Accessed 07.04.2023.

aim of ensuring cybersecurity in the arbitral proceedings. To name few, firstly, it seems important to develop a comprehensive protocol involving both cybersecurity and data protection measures. Secondly, a cyber incident response plan is needed alongside a protocol which specifies procedures to apply in the case of a security breach. Indeed, any party concerned should report such a breach and cooperate in good faith to fully investigate the case. Thirdly, technical security measures, including encryption, access control, and secure online platforms for storage and case management should be established. Fourthly, "Informed selection of arbitrators; in case of a higher susceptibility of the arbitration for a potential cyber hack preferably relies on tech-savvy, and cyber-risk and data protection conscious arbitrators".[151] Fifthly, an agreement concerning penalties that the arbitral tribunal can enforce in the case of non-compliance with cybersecurity measures should be reached. Sixthly, parties should also decide on the admissibility of hacked information in terms of evidence, possibly by coming to a consensus that excludes the use of any data obtained through a security breach. Simultaneously, so-called backup plans and alternative communication tools are needed, most notably in the case of unexpected technical failures and difficulties. Finally, it is also crucial to make arrangements concerning a sufficiently secure IT environment. To realize such an environment, there is a need to consider both the scope and effectiveness of different security measures to stay updated with emerging security threats and solutions.[152]

International arbitral institutions become much more aware of cybersecurity issues that need to be addressed. As a result, the ICC International Court of Arbitration outlined the so-called "Checklist for a Protocol on Virtual Hearings" (Annex I) and "Suggested Clauses for Cyber-protocols and Procedural Orders dealing with the Organisation of Virtual Hearings" (Annex II).[153]

It is noteworthy that these Annexes were previously included in the ICC Guidance Note on Possible Measures Aimed at Mitigating the Effects of the COVID-19 Pandemic (issued on 9 April 2020). Currently, these provisions belong to the ICC Rules of Arbitration (see: section VIIc of the Note to the Parties and Arbitral Tribunals on the Conduct of the Arbitration). These provisions are effective as of 1 January 2021.

---

151 *Ibidem.*

152 *Ibidem.*

153 ICC Checklist for a Protocol on Virtual Hearings and Suggested Clauses for Cyber-Protocols and Procedural Orders Dealing with the Organisation of Virtual Hearings, https://iccwbo.org/publication/icc-checklist-for-a-protocol-on-virtual-hearings-and-suggested-clauses-for-cyber-protocols-and-procedural-orders-dealing-with-the-organisation-of-virtual-hearings/. Accessed on 21.01.2023.

To sum up, one could note that notwithstanding this modern threat and related risks, many arbitral institutions worldwide still make use of relatively insecure storage and communication systems. Additionally, institutional rules very often keep silent and do not properly address cybersecurity concerns. Thus, they allow electronic communication and data transfer through any remote means. Notably, the majority of arbitral institutions still do not pay enough attention to cybersecurity issues by using commercially available cloud data repositories and unencrypted email.[154]

The 2021 Queen Mary and White&Case Survey on International Arbitration even confirm such a statement. In this survey, "Only around a quarter of respondents said they have 'frequently' or 'always' seen cybersecurity measures being put in place in their international arbitrations. The majority (57%) encountered such measures in less than half of their cases".[155]

To address such threats and challenges, arbitral institutions could update their arbitration rules and policies to properly apply cybersecurity measures. Therefore, they could require the parties to use a secure Internet-based platform while filing a case and communicating with each other, instead of external drives, hard copies ad emails including sensitive attachments. This online platform could provide separate areas allowing members of the arbitral tribunal to have access to store and share draft awards. Additionally, such a platform could include multi-factor authentication and special tools to prevent any editing, printing, downloading, or emailing of certain types of documents. One must note that such tools are already available on the market, but they are currently used merely on *ad hoc* basis.[156]

Finally, it is noteworthy to mention one of the prevailing reasons why parties prefer institutional arbitration over *ad hoc* one. Such reason refers to procedural security concerning all aspects of the arbitral proceedings. In addition, there are already many concerns raised in the literature in view of the technological proficiency of the older generation of arbitrators. To illustrate, according to statistical data, the average age of arbitrators that have been appointed in the ICC arbitrations in 2018 was equal to 56 years. In addition, merely 35% of arbitrators were below the age of 50. Indeed, without the necessary support and technical assistance from the arbitral institutions, elder arbitrators may face some challenges to technology-based solutions. As such, the COVID-19 pandemic is widely considered a catalyst in the process of going online and

154 C. Morel de Westgaver, *Cybersecurity in International ...*

155 *2021 International Arbitration Survey ...*, p. 3.

156 C. Morel de Westgaver, *Cybersecurity in International ...*

thus encourages many young arbitrators to be involved in the arbitration practice and adopt these technological advancements.[157]

9 Data Protection

At the outset, it is noteworthy that the processing of data plays a significant role in international arbitration.[158] Such processing results from globalization itself and advancements in technology. The former leads to an increased demand for international commercial arbitration, whereas the latter is crucial in supporting and facilitating the entire arbitration process. Even though the parties involved in international commercial arbitration must abide by their contractual agreements and the confidentiality of the proceedings, the processing of data in case of cross-border disputes requires compliance with data protection and privacy laws.[159]

Therefore, cybersecurity threats are linked to data protection issues. The former concerns mostly cases of infiltrating a system to gather information which cannot be obtained according to legal means. In the majority of cases, this kind of threat refers to legally protected, confidential, or proprietary information, technical know-how, the so-called privileged information in the common law sense (that is information which is excluded from being disclosed based on the request) or the information of confidentiality protected by applicable laws or other regulations. The latter involves the sharing of information among members of the arbitral tribunal with the aim of rendering awards (concerning the secrecy of the deliberations). Gaining access to this kind of information requires having access to the directory structure of the target system. In addition, the right to read and copy information is also needed at a minimum.[160]

Indeed, an intruder would have to obtain and use the rights of a user to enter such a system, most notably an administrator with broad access to the system. One must note that all computer systems are connected to the Internet. This entails that the improper configuration of the protocols (including the access to communication ports or software flaws such as exploits) could lead to the negligent penetration of the system. As such, malicious software may be installed allowing an unauthorized person to have access rights and

157 A. Zwolankiewicz, A. Sachan, *Big Data, Bigger Disruption* ..., p. 19.

158 See more: Huang Jie, *Conflicts and Tentative Solutions to Protecting Personal Data in Investment Arbitration*, "The European Journal of International Law" 2021, Vol. 32, no. 4, pp. 1191–1220.

159 A. Zwolankiewicz, A. Sachan, *Big Data, Bigger Disruption* ..., p. 19.

160 E.G.W. Schäfer, *Managing Data Privacy* ...

thus to extract desired information from the system without being detected. Nonetheless, in the majority of cases, a human being error such as clicking on a hyperlink results in revealing sensitive information. Likewise, once a human being accessed a website which pushes malicious code, unauthorized infiltration easily could happen.[161]

Although all the protective cybersecurity measures do not ensure full protection against this kind of risk, their effectiveness depends on the quality of implemented measures. Notably, such measures may prevent an illicit attempt to access the computer system. One must note that data shared in arbitration cases is neither excessively large nor contain a significant amount of personal information. Such data is related to individuals involved in the disputed case or those who are connected to one of the parties in the ongoing arbitration. The persons are very often aware that their data have been used through the arbitration proceedings. As arbitration is confidential in nature, the likelihood of sharing such personal information is relatively low.[162]

Apparently, both the General Data Protection Regulation (GDPR) alongside other data protection laws aim to fill the gap related to rapid technological developments and so-called globalization. At the outset, it seems crucial to recall the Recitals to the GDPR, that is "the processing of personal data should be designed to serve mankind". In addition, there is no doubt that data protection has become part and even parcel of new technologies. One must even stress that such data protection will increase in relevance due to more involvement of digital tools during legal practice.[163]

Interestingly, international arbitration lawyers realized the need to focus on data protection while dealing with arbitral proceedings. As a result, they seek to cover these issues. To illustrate, the ICCA-IBA Joint Task Force on Data Protection in International Arbitration has even issued a special "Roadmap to Data Protection in International Arbitration". In addition, it is also worth analyzing provisions of the European GDPR which functions as a "model law" of data protection. GDPR has even become a prototype for adopting similar standards in other jurisdictions worldwide. Nonetheless, other jurisdictions provide their own regulations on data protection that may differ significantly from the European GDPR. Therefore, such ambiguities may also influence the ongoing arbitral proceedings by being either equal or even more strict compared to the GDPR.[164]

161 *Ibidem.*

162 *Ibidem.*

163 E. Hay, *Data protection and international arbitration: never the twain shall meet?*, [in:] *International Arbitration and Technology*, ed. P. Ortolani, A. Janssen, P. Wolters, Kluwer Law International 2022, Chapter 7.

164 *Ibidem.*

Data protection issues appear during both the conduct and management of arbitral proceedings. Therefore, the ICCA-IBA Roadmap introduced the term "arbitral participants", including parties, legal counsels, the arbitral tribunal, and arbitrators. In addition, data protection obligations also cover many other participants involved in the arbitral proceedings such as tribunal secretaries, experts, and service providers, among others.[165]

Considering arbitration, under Article 3 GDPR applies in twofold situations such as:

> a) the processing of personal data in the context of the activities of an establishment of a controller or a processor in the Union, regardless of whether the processing takes place in the Union or not; b) the processing of personal data of data subjects who are in the Union by a controller or processor not established in the Union, where the processing activities are related to the offering of goods and services, whether for free or not, or for monitoring the behaviour of data subjects.[166]

One must note that GDPR refers to all activities related to the handling of personal data within the framework of arbitral proceedings. The term "processing" is understood broadly and encompasses multifarious operations concerning personal data. According to the definition of "processing" included in the GDPR, this term should be understood as:

> any operation or set of operations which is performed on personal data or sets of personal data, whether or not by automated means, such as collection, recording, organization, structuring, storage, adaptation or alteration, retrieval, consultation, use, disclosure by transmission, dissemination or otherwise making available, alignment or combination, restriction, erasure or destruction.[167]

Likewise, any activities on data retention, review, correspondence with the parties along with disclosure of information and gaining access to material information would also fall within the scope of GDPR.[168]

165 *Ibidem.*
166 European General Data Protection Regulation, Article 3, https://gdpr-info.eu/. Accessed on 12.05.2024.
167 GDPR Recital 52, Art. 4(2), p. 33
168 A. Zwolankiewicz, A. Sachan, *Big Data, Bigger Disruption* ..., p. 20.

The European GDPR provides acquiring, storing, and processing of personal data for the sake of proving the facts of the case without the consent in majority of situations according to Article 5 of the GDPR paragraphs (1) and 6(1), subparagraphs (b), (c), (e) and (f). Nonetheless, this provision cannot be recognized as an exemption from the parties' duties to inform, correct, and allow for objections under Articles 14, 15, 16, and 21 of the GDPR. Indeed, once the arbitral award is rendered and the entire arbitral proceedings completed, the personal data must be deleted within the specified time limit under Article 5(1)(e). It is worth noting that the subsequent use of personal data for other purpose than arbitration is not allowed unless it complies with Article 6(1) of the GDPR.[169] Under this provision:

> Processing shall be lawful only if and to the extent that at least one of the following applies:
>
> 1. the data subject has given consent to the processing of his or her personal data for one or more specific purposes;
> 2. processing is necessary for the performance of a contract to which the data subject is party or in order to take steps at the request of the data subject prior to entering into a contract;
> 3. processing is necessary for compliance with a legal obligation to which the controller is subject;
> 4. processing is necessary in order to protect the vital interests of the data subject or of another natural person;
> 5. processing is necessary for the performance of a task carried out in the public interest or in the exercise of official authority vested in the controller;
> 6. processing is necessary for the purposes of the legitimate interests pursued by the controller or by a third party, except where such interests are overridden by the interests or fundamental rights and freedoms of the data subject which require protection of personal data, in particular where the data subject is a child.

Some issues may occur in the case of introducing personal data into the arbitration case which is not important for processing due to its irrelevance to the outcome of the case. Indeed, it is a challenge to properly identify this information among the large amount of data produced and transferred in the course of early fact-finding in arbitration proceedings. Nevertheless, such an

---

169 E.G.W. Schäfer, *Managing Data Privacy ...*

identification should be made based on customer lists of natural end users and similar names through their relevance to the disputed case.[170]

To ensure data protection, it is recommended to use merely necessary personal data during the arbitration proceedings. In addition, the parties and their legal representatives are required to minimize the introduction of personal data into the proceedings. As such, they should also verify whether such data require consent or whether necessary consent has already been acquired. An alternative solution is to anonymize personal data in documents.[171]

According to the 2021 Queen Mary and White&Case Survey on International Arbitration, respondents stress that:

> Even though users generally acknowledge data protection issues and regulations may have an impact on the conduct of arbitrations, the extent and full implications of that impact are not understood by all. 34% of respondents predicted that data protection issues and regulations have 'limited impact at present but [this is] likely to increase'.[172]

10 Inability to Observe Parties' Demeanour and Credibility

The possibility of seeing parties' responses in person in the course of physical hearing is of significance. On the one hand, videoconferencing features can offer high-quality magnification of the parties' faces on the screens of the arbitral tribunal. Therefore, they allow closer scrutiny of the witness's demeanour compared to traditional in-person hearings. On the other hand, merely relying on a witness's demeanour that could be a basis for decision-making can result in many inherent dangers. One must note that there is a relatively high danger of misinterpreting "body language", namely recognizing nervousness as uncertainty or insincerity, as well as shyness and hesitation as doubt.[173]

The possibility that a witness may be influenced or guided by someone in the course of remote hearings is much higher than in a physical hearing where someone can simply sit with them and suggest answers to questions. To properly minimize such a risk, both arbitrators and parties can take certain measures, including impartial individuals in the room with a witness or recording

170 *Ibidem.*

171 *Ibidem.*

172 *2021 International Arbitration Survey ...*, p. 3.

173 R. Thirgood, *Remote hearings: storm ...*

such a place in 360-degree video to avoid the possibility if any "coaching" of the witness.[174]

11 Conclusion

This analysis led us to the conclusion that the 1958 New York Convention, which serves as an aged international arbitration legislation, did not foresee the emergence of innovation-driven technologies in terms of long-distance communication. Even though some arbitrators and legal professionals advocate for its adjustment to the "new normal", indeed, amending an international convention sets forth significant challenges. Nonetheless, one must also note that recent national laws on international commercial arbitration and rules established by arbitral institutions worldwide have already paved the way for more flexible criteria concerning the written form of arbitration agreements. Therefore, such provisions explicitly recognize the equivalence of modern communication methods. Given that, they even validate technology as an acceptable alternative to the previously written form requirement.

It is significant to acknowledge the absence of a unified international legal framework addressing the new arising technologies in arbitration. As a result, the decision regarding whether a hearing should be conducted traditionally, with all parties physically present, or if a "remote presence" suffices, is determined by the procedural rules of the arbitration venue and the specific guidelines of the arbitral institution itself. As such, this creates a potential risk of future challenges to the arbitration award if a physical presence is required but the hearing is conducted remotely via videoconference, for instance.

In addition, the unequal access to technology or e-platforms established by arbitral institutions may result in a violation of procedural fairness of the proceedings and the fundamental principles of due process, equality, and the right to be heard. Therefore, such a situation may lead to imbalances where one party has an advantage in both procedural and technological aspects, whereas the other fail to benefit from these technologies. Given that, it is a possible outcome that impedes the ability of the technologically disadvantaged party to present its case reasonably and adequately.

Likewise, there are many practical challenges regarding the admissibility of e-evidence by arbitral tribunals. Interestingly, American Arbitration Association – 2021 International Centre for Dispute Resolution Rules (AAA-ICDR) – is

174 *Ibidem.*

the only institution worldwide which directly refers to the e-evidence within its arbitral rules. Nevertheless, it is also noteworthy that the international community joins its efforts in addressing challenges concerning e-evidence. Therefore, the Draft Convention on Electronic Evidence was drawn around. With its specific characteristics, this proposed Convention intends to address the admissibility of electronic evidence in both civil and criminal cases. Its purpose is to investigate and assess the importance of such evidence, as well as acknowledge and accept electronic evidence originating from foreign jurisdictions. Although it refers merely to civil and criminal cases, it could serve as guidelines in future works on similar pieces of legislation in international arbitration law.

Notably, another problem refers to the use and widespread acceptance of blockchain technology in international arbitration. Indeed, such technology would significantly impact and even accelerate the entire process of digitalization in the context of the dispute resolution process. It is noteworthy, however, that the relationship between new innovation-driven technologies and international arbitration has been a subject of discussion in recent years. Many of these discussions touched upon topics, including the feasibility of fully automated arbitration platforms alongside the compliance of blockchain-stored awards with recognition and enforcement requirements under the 1958 New York Convention. Likewise, many debates focus on the use of smart contracts in arbitration, and the potential for artificial intelligence to replace the role of arbitrators. Despite many pro-arbitration stances, there is currently limited guidance concerning the admissibility of blockchain evidence, and it primarily relies on the arbitrator's discretion. It is worth noting, however, that arbitrators are generally sceptical about rejecting such evidence. Indeed, such an unwarranted refusal could lead to challenges against the arbitral award.

It is also worth remembering that the rise of electronic signatures, or e-signatures, has the potential to significantly impact the enforceability of arbitral awards. At present, various jurisdictions globally follow Article 31(1) of the UNCITRAL Model Law, which provides that arbitral awards must be in written form and include the signatures of the arbitrators. Nonetheless, it is important to realize that the extent of risk linked to the use of an e-signature for the sake of validating an arbitral award may differ following governing law at the enforcement location (aka *lex fori*) or the laws applicable to the arbitral seat.

Finally, the so-called authentication plays a crucial role in contemporary international arbitration. Authentication is widely considered a process of confirming the authenticity of a signature on an original document, while certification refers to the process of verifying if a copy of the document is a faithful reproduction of the original one. Nonetheless, specific requirements for such formalities concerning both authentication and certification differ significantly across jurisdictions. Likewise, the criteria for who can legalize the proof of an arbitral award vary based on the jurisdiction.

Overall, some disadvantages could be summarized as follows: advocacy style and the need to adapt cross-examination to the new arbitral environment, namely the online one. One of the drawbacks of these new solutions considers the risks of technological failure while conducting remote arbitral proceedings. In addition, despite some guidelines on cybersecurity, there are still some concerns in this regard. These questions are also linked to confidentiality which is one of the most important features of arbitral proceedings. One could even say that confidentiality is a key point in choosing arbitration instead of traditional court litigation. Throughout protocols, it is possible to protect not only remote hearings, but also access to data stored online, including different types of documents, videos, and transcripts. In addition, such protocols are widely recognized as a kind of guarantee of the proper protection of data.[175]

175 B.O. Giupponi, *"Virtual" Dispute Resolution …*, p. 77.

CHAPTER 5

Future of International Arbitration

1 Introduction

This chapter discusses digitization and the use of new technologies in international arbitration within the framework of the UN Sustainable Development Goals. In addition, it also analyzes recent trends, including green arbitration, AI-arbitrators, and blockchain-based arbitration. Therefore, it seeks to find answer "whether there are legal solutions in the field of green arbitration, AI-arbitrators, and blockchain-based arbitration" and "How does technological progress in international arbitration relate to the achievement of sustainable development goals?"

2 Digitalization of International Arbitration in View of the UN Sustainable Development Goals

2.1 *Definition of the UN Sustainable Development Goals*

The concept of sustainable development dates to early treaties from the nineteenth century. Nonetheless, it has been fully developed at the international level due to efforts of the United Nations through the adoption of non-binding instruments in the past five decades. Therefore, the UN's works on the adoption of the 2030 Agenda can be classified into three different phases.[1]

The first phase, from 1970 to 1992, reflects significant milestones in sustainable development, including the Stockholm Conference in 1972, the establishment of the UN Environmental Program, and the release of the so-called "Our Common Future Report" in 1987. Indeed, these landmarks laid the groundwork for addressing sustainable development issues.[2]

The second phrase is recognized by the adoption of Agenda 21 in 1992. This document provides a comprehensive framework in terms of global cooperation. In addition, it also represents national guidelines in view of promoting sustainable development practices.[3]

1 Z. Meskic, M. Albakjaji, N. Jevremovic, E. Omerovic, J. Adams, *Digitalization and Innovation in Achieving SDGs – Impacts on Legislation and Practice*, "IOP Conference Series: Earth and Environmental Science" 2022, p. 2.

2 *Ibidem.*

3 *Ibidem.*

 | DOI:10.1163/9789004700710_007

The last phase lasting from 1992 to 1994 resulted in many milestones such as the Oslo Symposium in 1994, the Johannesburg World Summit in 2002, and the Rio Declaration in 2012. These events are considered to plating significant roles in advancing the discourse on sustainable development. Indeed, they have also an impact on the global agenda.[4]

Briefly, it is worth noting that although sustainable development is rooted in early treaties, it gained prominence thanks to the UN's work, most notably given the adoption of soft-law instruments over fifty years.

The 2030 Agenda, adopted in 2015,[5] has the aim to build upon the achievements of the Millennium Development Goals.[6] It is also widely regarded as a key instrument given human rights and international law. The 2030 Agenda represents 17 Sustainable Development Goals (SDGs) alongside 169 specific targets. Compared to the former UN's initiatives, the 2030 Agenda represents greater ambition. Therefore, it outlines a comprehensive set of goals and targets that can be achieved universally in both developed and developing countries.[7]

Notably, the 2030 Agenda is based on an interdisciplinary approach for the sake of accomplishing the SDGs. It also recognizes the need for diverse stakeholders to contribute effectively to achieve such goals within the specified timeframe. It acknowledges the significance of private investment, and private business activities alongside innovation which are crucial to inclusive economic growth. This entails that involvement of these stakeholders is necessary to foster sustainable development.[8]

"The 2030 Agenda for Sustainable Development: Transforming Our World" is widely regarded as the UN's blueprint for the sake of promoting sustainable development. The previous UN Secretary-General Ban Ki-moon stressed that

---

4 *Ibidem.*

5 C. L. Carpentier, H. Braun, *Agenda 2030 for Sustainable Development: A powerful global framework*, "Journal of the International Council for Small Business" 2020, Vol. 1, no. 1, pp. 14–23.

6 See: F. Stewart, *The Sustainable Development Goals: a comment*, "Journal of Global Ethics" 2015, Vol. 11, no. 3, pp. 288–293; R.B. Swain, F. Yang-Wallentin, *Achieving sustainable development goals: predicaments and strategies*, "International Journal of Sustainable Development & World Ecology" 2020, Vol. 27, issue 2, pp. 96–106; L. Camacho, *Sustainable Development Goals: kinds, connections and expectations*, "Journal of Global Ethics" 2015, Vol. 11, no. 1, pp. 18–23; K.A. Reinert, *From Sustainable Development Goals to Basic Development Goals*, "Ethics & International Affairs" 2020, Vol. 34, no. 2, pp. 125–137.

7 Z. Meskic, M. Albakjaji, N. Jevremovic, E. Omerovic, J. Adams, *Digitalization and Innovation* ..., p. 2.

8 *Ibidem.*

"the seventeen Sustainable Development Goals (SDGs) are our shared vision of humanity and a social contract between the world's leaders and the people".[9]

In addition, the SDGs represent a voluntary agreement instead of a mandatory treaty. Indeed, this has also some disadvantages as some states may not fully commit their obligations. On the other hand, states may be more inclined to embrace an agenda with broader scope and vision, most notably while there are no legally binding responsibilities therein.[10]

This Agenda encompasses a Declaration and a collection of the SDGs. The former outlines the significance of information and communications technology (ICT) because of advancing sustainable development.[11] This means that the Declaration pays attention to the immense potential stemming from the widespread availability of ICT in the context of accelerating human progress through digital transformation.[12]

2.2 *Digitalization and 16th SDGs*

The COVID-19 pandemic could be recognized as evidence that sustainable access to the Internet is currently a priority. In addition, such access is an indispensable element to fully participate not only in society but also in democracy and the economy. Given the SDGs, each human being should benefit from safe and affordable Internet connectivity till 2030. This means that every person could have the possibility to freely use digitally enabled services. Currently, there is still a lack of access to such services for everyone. Therefore, one could even say that the necessary prerequisite for ensuring social welfare should be based upon universal connectivity. To achieve such a goal, it seems crucial to pay attention to a more human-centric and holistic approach with regard to digital equity. Practically, the so-called digital inclusion should focus on combining affordable, robust services with Internet-enabled devices, digital skills, and equity, among others.[13]

---

9 *Sustainable Development Goals kick off with start of new year*, "United Nations" 30.12.2015, https://news.un.org/en/story/2015/12/519172. Accessed on 11.06.2023.

10 T. Pogge, M. Sengupta, *The Sustainable Development Goals: a plan for building a better world?*, "Journal of Global Ethics" 2015, Vol. 11, no. 1, p. 56.

11 See: F-F. Rothe, L.V. Audenhove, J. Loisen, *ICT for development and the novel principles of the Sustainable Development Goals*, "Third World Quarterly" 2022, Vol. 43, issue 6, pp. 1495–1514; F-F. Rothe, *Rethinking positive and negative impacts of 'ICT for development' through the holistic lens of the sustainable development goals*, "Information Technology for Development" 2020, Vol. 26, issue 4, pp. 653–669.

12 M. van der Velden, *Digitalisation and the UN Sustainable Development Goals: What role for design*, "Interaction Design and Architectures(s) Journal" 2018, no. 37, p. 162.

13 K. Szubert, *The Future is Digital*, [in:] *Internet and New Technologies Law. Perspectives and Challenges*, eds. D. Szostek, M. Załucki, Nomos 2021, p. 17. See more: Soares Francisco Uribarr, *New Technologies and Arbitration*, "Indian Journal of Arbitration Law" 2018, Vol. 7.

FIGURE 3 United Nations' Sustainable Development Goals
SOURCE: HTTPS://WWW.UN.ORG/SUSTAINABLEDEVELOPMENT/. THE CONTENT OF THIS PUBLICATION HAS NOT BEEN APPROVED BY THE UNITED NATIONS AND DOES NOT REFLECT THE VIEWS OF THE UNITED NATIONS OR ITS OFFICIALS OR MEMBER STATES.

Digital transformation is widely seen as a key element in achieving SDGs. Besides, advanced technologies, including Artificial Intelligence (AI) can analyze datasets, identify patterns alongside generate insights in terms of decision-making and service delivery. Thanks to the development of Internet of Things (IoT) devices, both real-time and multi-source data can be easily collected and then transmitted efficiently. Through blockchain ledgers, it is more secure to share and make use of tamper-proof data. In turn, cloud computing can be useful in terms of facilitating data storage and processing within public sector organizations. In addition, augmented and virtual reality technologies are innovative ways of visualizing information in the public sector.[14]

The state of data is of crucial importance in the context of the SDGs. Through the rapid advancement of emerging technologies such as AI, IoT, and Blockchain, there are also new risk factors. Given the effective use of emerging technologies, access to high-quality data is needed. Therefore, it involves many different actions such as the collection, storage, processing, and sharing of data, among others. Such digital transformation and integration of emerging technologies result in a need of taking adaptive and flexible governance in view of technological advancements. To illustrate, by using artificial intelligence, algorithmic issues, bias, and data quality problems must be addressed properly. Likewise, in the case of the Internet of Things, there is a need to address challenges related to data collection and sharing. This entails that both the quality and governance of data play a crucial role in the successful implementation of the SDGs.[15]

The 2030 Agenda represents an interdisciplinary approach and acknowledges the private sector as a key element given innovation. One must note that digitalization itself and innovation-driven technologies play a crucial role in achieving SDG 8, 9 and 16. Even though the 2030 Agenda pays attention to voluntary efforts to attain the SDGs, there is also an increasing need for more specific regulations in terms of digitalization. Indeed, it is intended to ensure innovation through the protection of intellectual property rights and e-commerce, among others. Besides, there is a trend towards recognizing the right to a sustainable and healthy environment as a human right.[16]

Issue 12023 CEPANI Rules, https://www.cepani.be/wp-content/uploads/2022/12/Cepani_Brochure_03_EN-80-web.pdf.

14 L.G. de Magalhães Santos, S.B. Dhaou, *Opena Data and Emerging Technologies: Connecting SDG Performance and Digital Transformation*, https://sdgs.un.org/sites/default/files/2023-05/A13%20-%20Magalh%C3%A3es%20-%20Open%20Data%20and%20Emerging%20Technologies%20Connecting%20SDG%20Performance%20and.pdf, p. 2.

15 *Ibidem*, p. 3.

16 Z. Meskic, M. Albakjaji, N. Jevremovic, E. Omerovic, J. Adams, *Digitalization and Innovation ...*, p. 1.

In addition, the rule of law alongside the SDGs are interconnected and they even reinforce each other. Through the recognition of access to justice and the rule of law, the 2030 Agenda, most notably in terms of SDG 16th, acknowledges its role in promoting sustainable development. The rule of law is widely recognized as ensuring equal treatment for everyone, upholding human rights, and promoting the fulfilment of social, economic, and cultural needs. It also plays a crucial role in shaping public policies along with governing competent institutions.[17]

Indeed, the use of ICTs is helpful to speed up the process of achieving all 17 UN SDGs. International Telecommunication Union (ITU), which is a specialized agency for information and communication technologies within the UN framework, has the aim to facilitate international connectivity through communications networks.[18] ITU plays a significant role in achieving all the SDGs, most notably SDG 9 (that is improved infrastructure). To realize this goal, it is important to create a robust infrastructure, promote inclusive and sustainable industrialization and stimulate innovation. Therefore, countries could make use of such efficient and cost-effective ICT infrastructure to participate actively in the digital economy. Consequently, they could improve their economic competitiveness and well-being. One must note that ICTs provide products and services in many different areas, including health care, education, finance, commerce, governance, and agriculture, among others. They could also be useful in terms of reducing poverty and hunger, mitigating climate change, improving energy efficiency, and promoting sustainable cities and communities.[19]

Considering the 9th SDG, ITU's primary goal is to improve both the scope and quality of the ICT infrastructure, most notably in terms of radiocommunication and backbone networks as well as to provide such networks to underdeveloped, rural areas. Importantly, through the implementation of the ITU's standards, the energy efficiency and performance of ICT networks are improved in multifarious networks, including backhaul, wireline, and radiocommunication.[20]

---

17 L. Boisson de Chazournes, *The Sustainable Development Goals (SDGs) and the Rule of Law: A Propos SDG 6 on Access to Water and Sanitation*, "ASIL Proceedings. Sustainable Development and International Law" 2020, p. 143.

18 Since 1865 ITU is responsible for assigning both global radio spectrum and satellite orbits. In addition, ITU introduces technical standards to guarantee that networks and technologies are interconnected. One of the most important aims of this agency is to enhance access to ICTs to underserved communities globally. See: *About International Communication Union (ITU)*, https://www.itu.int/en/about/Pages/default.aspx. Accessed on 11.04.2023.

19 *Digital technologies to achieve the UN SDGs*, https://www.itu.int/en/mediacentre/backgrounders/Pages/icts-to-achieve-the-united-nations-sustainable-development-goals.aspx. Accessed on 11.04.2023.

20 *Ibidem*. See: *Sustainable Development Goal 9: Investing in ICT access and quality education to promote lasting peace*, "United Nations" 20.06.2017, https://www.un.org/sustainable

In addition, the 16th SDG concerning peace, justice and strong institutions is also based on the improvement of ICTs. Given the e-government services, the relationship between citizens and the state is enhanced alongside the delivery of government services becoming more efficient. ITU contributes significantly to driving citizen empowerment. This goal is achieved through ITU's work on smart sustainable cities and key performance indicators (KPIs). Indeed, the latter refers to voter participation or the number of government services which are delivered electronically.[21]

Nonetheless, it is noteworthy that Internet-driven solutions generate a relatively huge amount of non-personal data. This begs the question whether of who is the owner of such data and how they should be used. This paves the way for governments to develop the right to balance. This means that they should address and solve problems related to privacy concerns without damage to the use of beneficial Internet-driven innovations.[22]

The term "access to justice" is mostly regarded as a synonym of access to the courts. Therefore, it focuses on providing less expensive, cost-effective, and relatively fast and simple proceedings.[23] Obviously, there are still some doubts about whether the remote hearings could be classified in terms of access to justice. These types of hearings also raise the question of whether disputes would be settled within a reasonable time as stipulated by Article 6 of the European Convention of Human Rights. This also begs "Whenever the parties have agreed to a remote hearing, can the arbitral tribunal ignore or override that agreement if they had agreed before the pandemic started?".[24] This means that there are many concerns and practical issues that need to be addressed.

3 From "Smart Courts" to "Smart Arbitration"

Digitalization of international dispute resolution resulted in a need for a new reinterpretation of international law to adjust it to a new normal. On the one hand, both the 1958 New York Convention, the UNCITRAL Model Law and the 1965 Washington Convention should be in line with the new trends. On the other hand, international arbitral tribunals (both commercial and investment)

development/blog/2017/06/sustainable-development-goal-9-investing-in-ict-access-and-quality-education-to-promote-lasting-peace/. Accessed on 11.06.2023.

21 *Digital technologies to achieve ...*

22 K. Szubert, *The Future is Digital ...*, p. 22.

23 E. Katsh, O. Rabinovich-Einy, *Digital justice ...*, p. 40.

24 B.O. Giupponi, *"Virtual" Dispute Resolution ...*, p. 78.

adjust their rules to comply with the current challenges and facilitate the possibility of handling remote arbitral proceedings.

Digitization of the courts has become a key issue for resolving all ongoing litigation. It can be seen as a solution to the inefficiency of traditional courts, the weakness of judicial credibility as well as an inconvenience to the parties. Max Weber once said that "a modern judge is a vending machine into which the pleadings are inserted together with the fee, and which then disgorges the judgment together with the reasons mechanically derived from the code".[25] Max Weber's statement should be understood as a metaphor regarding the vital connotation of intelligence. Therefore, people, data and technology are considered key elements of intelligence. This begs the question, how we can make use of these elements within the judiciary? Currently, many courts benefit from new technologies, including artificial intelligence and blockchain, in their everyday work. This entails the use of innovation-driven technologies in case filing, investigation, collecting of evidence and court trials, among others. Overall, this approach refers to the "smart justice" concept emerging across the globe. It is worth adding that China has paved the way in the development of this concept by introducing "smart courts".[26]

The emergence of so-called "smart courts" is widely regarded as a key project within the "smart justice" strategy in China and thus a necessary step in the development of courts. It is notable that the Chinese experiences and accomplishments in the digitalization process of the court system may be useful both in crisis times, such as a worldwide pandemic with which we currently

25 Liao Ting, How Emerging Technologies Shape the Face of Chinese Courts?, "Conflict of Laws.net" 10.11.2021, https://conflictoflaws.net/2021/how-emerging-technologies-shape-the-face-of-chinese-courts%ef%bc%9f/.

26 *Ibidem*. See: Luo Xiulan, *A Study on the Disputes Settlement Mechanism in Online Transactions – Based on the Visual Angle of Complementation between Folk Law and State Law*, "Hebei Law Science" 2010, Vol. 8, p. 60; Gu Weixia, *Dispute Resolution in China: Litigation, Arbitration, Mediation, and Their Interactions*, Routledge, New York 2021, p. 92; Gu Weixia, *The Developing Nature of Arbitration in Mainland China and Its Correlation with the Market: Institutional, Ad Hoc, and Foreign Institutions Seated in Mainland China*, "Contemporary Asia Arbitration Journal" 2017, Vol. 10(2), p. 261; Gu Weixia, *When Local Meets International: Mediation Combined with Arbitration in China and Its Prospective Reform in a Comparative Context*, "Journal of Comparative Law" 2016, Vol. 10, no. 2, pp. 85–86; Jia Zuo, *One Belt One Road Disputes: Does China Have Dispute Resolution Methods Fit for Purpose?*, "LSE Law Review" 2020, Vol. 5, pp. 107–108; M. Łągiewska, *Arbitraż w Chinach – uwagi wstępne*, „Gdańskie Studia Azji Wschodniej" 2020, Vol. 17, p. 42; M. Łągiewska, 中国与波兰关于国际商事仲裁效力的比较研究, [Effectiveness of the arbitration agreement under Chinese and Polish law: A Comparative Study] Toruń 2022, pp. 218.

struggle, and in the hereafter. The examples analyzed offer insights into the entire court digitization process.

The aim of this section is thus to outline solutions adopted in the People's Republic of China (PRC) given the digitalization of the court system. First and foremost, this study outlines previous achievements in digitizing Chinese courts, with a special focus on the "smart courts" concept. Further, it brings attention to the challenges linked to cybersecurity and data protection. The analysis concludes that there are still many loopholes that need to be addressed because technology itself develops much faster than the law.

First, there is a new global phenomenon, including online dispute resolution mechanisms (hereafter referred to as ODR) and online courts. Based on the Chinese approach, "smart justice" consists of "smart courts", "smart judicial administration" and "smart procuratorates".[27] Therefore, one could even say that the emergence of "smart courts" in China is part of a global strategy for restructuring the judiciary. Many new innovation-driven technologies are widely used in online courts. Furthermore, the Chinese government actively promotes information and communication technologies (ICT).[28] Such technologies are crucial in terms of judicial reforms in China. These reforms aim to build "a judicial mechanism that is open, dynamic, transparent, and convenient and improving public understanding, trust, and supervision of the judicature".[29]

It is noteworthy that Chinese scholars and practitioners have widely discussed the digitalization of courts. Additionally, the Supreme People's Court (SPC) in China issued its "Opinions on Accelerating the Construction of Smarts Courts". The SPC seeks to encourage the Chinese people's courts to make use of artificial intelligence (AI) in the judiciary. Therefore, through the adoption of such technologies, the Chinese judiciary could easily provide not only smarter litigation but also legal literacy services. The entire "smart courts" system in

27 Liao Ting, How Emerging Technologies...

28 G.G. Zheng, China's Grand Design of People's Smart Courts, "Asian Journal of Law and Society" 2020, pp. 1–3.

29 Zou Mimi, "Smart courts" in China and the future of personal injury litigation, "Journal of Personal Injury Law" (forthcoming, June 2020), https://papers.ssrn.com/sol3/papers.cfm?abstract_id=3552895, pp. 1–2. See more: Xu (Lu) Alison, *Chinese judicial justice on the cloud: a future call or a Pandora's box? An analysis of the 'intelligent court system' of China*, "Information & Communications Technology Law" 2017, Vol. 26, issue 1, pp. 59–71, DOI: 10.1080/13600834.2017.1269873.

China is based on more than 3,000 people's courts, together with more than 10,000 detached tribunals and more than 4,000 collaborative departments.[30]

The digitalization of courts relates to litigation proceedings. In other words, this includes online litigation activities such as filing a case, the court trial, the execution of the judgement, etc. Currently, along with the dynamic development of modern technologies, it seems inevitable for online courts to use big data, cloud computing and artificial intelligence more frequently. This means that digitalization resulted as a natural consequence of the development and improvement of judicial efficiency. Furthermore, the entire judicial process is much more convenient for people who can make use of it, even while at home.[31]

It should be noted that the COVID-19 pandemic only sped up the process of online trials. In fact, the PRC launched its smart courts before the COVID-19 pandemic, basing the idea of smart courts on the Internet courts. This means that offline litigation activities were changed into online activities. Following this new trend, it was possible to not only reduce the flow of personnel but also to keep trials in working order. One could even say that the smart court system succeeded by implementing the entire full-service online processing. Hence, the Chinese authorities launched a comprehensive and multi-functional online litigation platform. In addition, the Supreme People's Court (SPC) in China was also active and quickly adjusted to the new reality. To illustrate, the SPC promulgated the so-called "Notice on Strengthening and Standardizing Online Litigation during the COVID-19 Prevention and Control Period". This legal act is widely considered to be a basis for the functioning of smart courts, including "online court hearings, electronic service, identity authentication, and material submission".[32]

Based on the available data, between 3 February and 4 November 2020, the people's courts in China (including four levels) filed more than 6.5 million online cases, 778,000 online court sessions, 3.23 million online mediations and 18.15 million electronic services.[33]

30 Liao Ting, *How Emerging Technologies...*

31 Peng Junlin, Xiang Wen, *The Rise of Smart Courts in China: Opportunities and Challenges to the Judiciary in a Digital Age*, "Nordic Journal of Law and Social Research" 2019, no. 9, p. 245.

32 Wei Bin, Kuang Kun, Sun Changlong, Feng Jun, Zhang Yating, Zhu Xinli, Zhou Jianghong, Zhai Yinsheng, Wu Fei, *A full-process intelligent trial system for smart court*, "Frontiers of Information Technology & Electronic Engineering" 2022, Vol. 23(2), pp. 186–187.

33 *Ibidem.*

It is noteworthy that the Zhejiang Higher People's Court, together with the Alibaba group, launched a full-process intelligent trial system, aka FITS. This system is recognized as a strong technical support for the establishment of the smart court system in the Zhejiang province and more specifically in the Zhejiang Provincial People's Court. In fact, the FITS is responsible for conducting the following tasks:

> (1) extracting essential information from the legal text (indictment, lending contract, court debate transcript, etc.), to help the judge promptly grasp the key case information; (2) summarizing the controversy focuses from the court debate transcript recorded during the trial; (3) verifying the authenticity, legality, and relevance of the evidence; (4) recommending candidate questions to the judges to assist in the necessary trial procedures and discover facts related to the case; (5) retrieving the most similar cases from the historical data, and leveraging the knowledge of legal experts to predict case facts and help judges make judicial decisions; (6) generating a judgment document with complete structure, complete elements, and rigorous logic after confirming the facts of the case and applying laws and regulations.[34]

The FITS further develops smart courts. First, it serves as the primary phase of the trial procedure. This system changes the central judicial tasks pertaining to the trial procedure into natural language processing (NLP). To achieve this goal, the FITS system adopts a certain combination of knowledge-based and data-driven models. Aside from the aforementioned innovations, the FITS system also allowed the development of an artificial intelligence judge assistant robot. Such a robot, widely known as Xiaozhi (micro intelligence), seems to be helpful for judges. This AI tool was used mostly in Zhejiang province, both in financial lending and private lending cases.[35]

To better understand tools within the smart court system, their functionality should be explained. Information extraction (IE) aims to obtain structured information from unstructured documents. In fact, considering legal information extraction, the process focuses on the extraction of legal ontology as well as the legal relations and legal named entities. IE is possible based on the support vector machine (SVM) and other algorithms which help to extract the correlation between ongoing cases and precedent. In addition, the transfer learning approach turned out to be useful when a neural network was trained for the sake of linking named entities with some legal documents. Now, there

34 *Ibidem*, p. 187.
35 *Ibidem*.

is a BiLSTM-CRF neural structure. This innovation-driven tool allows performing many sequence-labelling tasks with a relatively high robustness and not too much computational complexity. In fact, this tool is based upon 70 million judgments. These documents served as corpus and consider over 360,000 court records and 100,000 evidence samples.[36]

There are currently three online courts functioning within the territory of the PRC in Beijing, Hangzhou and Guangzhou respectively. Since April 2015, the High People's Court of Zhejiang Province has introduced special online e-commerce tribunals. Those tribunals handle cases, mainly relating to online monetary claims, copyright infringement and transaction disputes. It was, in fact, the first online court operating in China. Bearing in mind its latest experiences, China established the Hangzhou Internet Court in August 2017.[37] In addition, Beijing and Guangzhou Internet Courts were launched in September 2018. There are currently eight specialized divisions functioning within these Internet courts. It is worth adding that those courts function with success. Until 31 October 2019, they accepted almost 120,000 Internet-related cases and completed 88,000. Compared to the classic pattern, the court conducted 45-minute online hearings and issued a decision within 38 days on average. Accordingly, the Chinese judiciary saved time in online hearings by three-fifths and in issuing a judgment by half. Besides, the online courts are remarkably effective because the parties acknowledged first-instance judgments in the majority of cases (up to 98% handled by the online courts). There were practically no appeals to judgements issued by the Chinese online courts. Given these statistics, the online courts represent a high quality of the Chinese judiciary.[38]

In addition, it is worth highlighting that Internet courts should introduce innovative mechanisms in different areas of their activities. Such tools have the aim of improving both judicial efficiency and accessibility. One of these tools concerns innovating online preservation mechanisms and special platforms for the authentication of e-evidence. The Chinese judiciary took some efforts to cure the shortcomings in this field and initiated a new approach. Hence, courts began to apply the so-called blockchain technology associated with big data and cloud storage. Importantly, the blockchain has unique features like traceability, post-audit, data-tampering prevention and high security. Those

36 *Ibidem.*

37 See more: Shu Shang Carrie, Guo Wenli, *The Rise of Online Dispute Resolution-led Justice in China: An Initial Outlook*, "Australian National University Journal of Law and Technology" 2020, pp. 29–30.

38 中华人民共和国最高人民法院编, 中国法院的互联网司法, 北京 2019, pp. 63–64. See more: M. Łągiewska, *The New Landscape of Arbitration in View of Digitalization* [in:] *The Impact of Covid on International Disputes. International and Comparative Business Law and Public Policy*, ed. Lalani, S.G. Shapiro, Brill 2022, pp. 208–217.

features are significantly important given the credibility and authenticity of pieces of evidence stored online. To illustrate, until 31 October 2019, courts operating within 22 provinces across China made use of new technologies by interconnecting their services with national e-evidence platforms supported by blockchain. This national e-evidence platform is extensively connected to 27 sites such as Diversified Dispute Resolution platforms, notary offices and forensic-science centres, among others. There have been over 194 million pieces of e-evidence collected this way (中国法院的互联网司法).[39]

As discussed above, it is noteworthy to address the judicial blockchain example concerning three Internet courts operating in China. The first, the Beijing Internet Court, introduced a permissioned blockchain, also known as Libra Chain (Tianping Lian 天平链), that was "incorporated into the first blockchain units filed at the Cyberspace Administration of China (CAC)".[40] As a result, this chain linked over 100 organizations, with the evidence stored on the court server's nodes. In fact, more than 4.72 million pieces of evidence have been collected online in such a way. Another example is the Hangzhou Internet Court. It was actually the first court that stored evidence on a blockchain. Therefore, it is worth recalling the Huatai versus Daotong case, when "the plaintiff stored a screen clip showing the defendant's copyright violation on a blockchain".[41]

This case is particularly important because the Hangzhou Internet Court admitted the authenticity of a screen clip. In addition, it was the first time that the Chinese court reviewed a piece of electronic evidence in a trial that had been stored in a blockchain. Thus, this type of activity shows the direction of the development of the judiciary in China. Finally, the Guangzhou Internet Court was a pioneer in the intelligent trust ecosystem, also known as the Law Network Chaintong Falian (*wang tong fa lian* 网通法链). This initiative joined over 50 local institutions such as judicial-administration authorities, Internet enterprises and some telecommunications operators. According to available data, over 5.45 million pieces of evidence were collected and preserved in that matter. Based on these positive experiences, other courts functioning within the territory of the PRC created their own blockchain networks.

Furthermore:

> [a]s of 31 October 2019, courts in Beijing, Shanghai, Tianjin, Jilin, Shandong, Shaanxi, Henan, Zhejiang, Guangdong, Hubei, and other provinces

39 中华人民共和国最高人民法院编, 中国法院的互联网司法, 北京 2019, p. 75.
40 *Ibidem.*
41 G.G. Zheng, *China's Grand Design...*, p. 18.

> had interconnected with a national e-evidence platform underpinned by a blockchain, which is linked to 27 sites including the National Time Service Centre, Diversified Dispute Resolution platforms, notary offices, and forensic-science centres.[42]

Apart from the blockchain, since 2016 the SPC in China has promoted the application of digitized files. To illustrate, until 31 October 2019, over 3,300 courts across China had already taken measures to build up the "simultaneous generation system". Thanks to this solution, the Chinese judiciary achieved a paper-free goal in two-thirds of cases. By way of example, the Kunshan Primary People's Court, situated in Jiangsu Province, launched a special paper-free handling process widely known as the Qiandeng Model. This process enables pre-filing documents via scanning, one-click archiving and tracking, among others. Therefore, smarter solutions and automatization concern not only case handling but also the whole range of litigation services, including case management. Recent developments launched by the Kunshan Primary People's Court improved the effectiveness of the court. The number of concluded cases has increased significantly, and long-term pending cases have decreased by almost 20%.[43] This example confirms that Chinese courts function more effectively due to digitalization.

Another example concerns the artificial intelligence used in Chinese courts. Importantly, AI fulfils three principal functions in the judiciary. Foremost, artificial intelligence takes part in judicial decision-making. From this perspective, it is noteworthy that there were some experiments in China with "AI judges". They were responsible for adjudicating basic, relatively easy and uncomplicated legal cases, such as contracts of low-value or negligence disputes. In fact, such a solution aimed at ensuring more consistent judgements issued within the territory of the PRC. Besides, "AI judges" could also play a key role in mitigating any gaps related to judicial expertise. Therefore, a judge may decide to submit relevant information concerning the legal case to a special AI-enabled system that would automatically present the outcome of similar cases. Thus, the judge could easily refer to another comparable case. In addition, it is also possible, in certain courts, that this AI system could launch the so-called "deviation analysis" of the draft judgements. This analysis compares relevant evidence presented in the legal case with those mentioned in previously issued

42 *Ibidem.*

43 中华人民共和国最高人民法院编, 中国法院的互联网司法, 北京 2019, pp. 79–80.

court decisions.[44] This means that the AI system can easily reduce the number of errors in court judgments and speed up the entire litigation process. As such, "AI judges" represent a new value in the judiciary.

It is worth adding, however, that such innovation-driven technologies relating to the "AI judges" are also controversial, most notably in the criminal law field.

Huang has suggested for example that government policies should be introduced to prevent the use of AI-judge in the criminal justice area. Zhang has also noted that while automated judgments may improve efficiency, the process could impact judges and may cause them to be reluctant to elaborate on their reasoning or to craft decisions. As a result, some AI-generated judgments are issued without human judge input and may be unclear and difficult to understand.[45]

Apart from the above-mentioned use of AI, there are also some human-like holograms functioning in the Beijing Internet Court. They are responsible for giving some essential information to the parties about the common laws, some regulations as well as the applicable court procedure. In other words, such a hologram can easily inform parties about the appropriate jurisdiction or even the types of dispute resolution that are most suitable to their case. However, there are some limits to the functioning of those human-like holograms. They can only answer up to 140 questions. It seems to be a particularly interesting solution adopted in some local courts situated in nine provinces across China. Beijing, Shanghai and Guangzhou were pioneers in making use of new AI-powered robots. They were launched in court halls as a tool providing public access both to manuals concerning litigation proceedings and to judicial procedures. In fact, some more advanced AI robots can even predict the potential outcome of a legal case prior to its filing in court.[46] This example touches upon more complex and developed technologies that can support judges in their ordinary work. Hence, human-like holograms or AI-powered robots can easily assist people by sharing basic knowledge about court proceedings. Thanks to this solution, there is no need to duplicate posts, and thus the human being can be more effectively employed in the courts. It seems to

44 Zou Mimi, "*Smart courts" in China...*, p. 1–2.

45 Shi Changqing, Sourdin T, Li Bin, *The Smart Court – A New Pathway to Justice in China?*, "International Journal for Court Administration" 2021, Vol. 12(1), p. 10.

46 Zou Mimi, *Smart courts" in China ...*, pp. 1–2.

be an interesting approach, showing how to benefit from new technologies and how to effectively use them in the judiciary.

4 Green Arbitration

The COVID-19 pandemic has also increased human consciousness concerning natural environmental issues. Therefore, there is a growing perception of the relationship between infectious diseases and excessive (mis)utilization of the natural environment by human beings. To tackle these challenges, international arbitration takes some initiatives to promote environmentally sustainable arbitration proceedings, widely recognized as "green arbitrations". The term "green arbitration" refers to:

> several practices that could contribute to reducing carbon emissions associated with the conduct of arbitrations, such as reducing long-haul travel by flight or otherwise, eliminating the use of disposables such as coffee cups and eliminating hard copy filings and exchanges altogether.[47]

The discussion over greener arbitrations was handled even before the COVID-19 pandemic. To illustrate, the ICC's Commission on Arbitration and Alternative Dispute Resolution launched the so-called Task Force on the Use of Information Technology at the beginning of the 2000s. The first report dates to 2004 and concerned "Operating Standards for Using IT in International Arbitration". Interestingly, this report referred to "paperless arbitration"[48] which requires that each participant in the arbitral proceedings:

> converts all documents that it normally would submit only in hard copy form (e.g. submissions, letters, witness statements, transcripts) into the machine-readable and processable file format(s) and attempts

47 P. Panjwani, *The Impact of the COVID-19 Pandemic on International Arbitration Practices*, [in:] *The Impact of Covid on International Disputes*, eds. S. Lalani, S.G. Shapiro, "International and Comparative Business Law and Public Policy" Vol. 2, Leiden-Boston 2022, pp. 50–51.

48 See more: W. Brillat-Capello, L. Canet, Lemaire Gilian Carmichael et al., *Paperless Arbitration: The New Trend?*, "International Journal of Online Dispute Resolution" 2020, Vol. 7, no. 2.

submitting documents in such electronic file format(s) as opposed to in physical hard-copy form.[49]

Following this ICC IT Task Force, the ICC introduced the NetCase platform.[50] In addition, many arbitral institutions worldwide also focused on paperless arbitrations. Prior to ICC Rules 2017, it was needed to submit preliminary submissions, including the request for arbitration and the answer thereto in a certain "number of copies" which were further transferred to each party, arbitrator, and the ICC's Secretariat. It is noteworthy, however, that given the ICC IT Task Force report from 2017, paperless arbitration was substituted by electronic submissions while becoming commonplace. On the other hand, some arbitrators are traditional, and they are not convinced to work truly in a paperless environment. The situation has changed alongside the ICC Rules 2021 which opt for paperless preliminary submissions which must be filed merely electronically by default, "unless the party filing the submission wishes transmission thereof by courier in hard copy".[51] In the wake of the new trend in international arbitration, other well-recognized institutions followed the same idea by introducing even all communications between the arbitral tribunals and the parties only in electronic form (i.e. LCIA Arbitration Rules 2020, the Belgian Centre for Arbitration and Mediation Rules, aka CEPANI Rules 2020[52]). It should be noted that the LCIA Arbitration Rules 2020 even focus on rendering awards which are "signed electronically and/or in counterparts and assembled into a single instrument".[53]

One could even say that there is a new practice aiming at introducing arbitration proceedings as environmentally sustainable. It is also reflected by the 2019 Campaign for Greener Arbitration (CGA) established by Lucy Greenwood for the sake of raising "awareness of the significant carbon footprint of the arbitration community".[54] Such a sustainable change is based upon pragmatic

49 P. Panjwani, *The Impact of the COVID-19 ...*, p. 51. Cf. ICC Commission on Arbitration and Alternative Dispute Resolution, Task Force on the Use of Information Technology, "Operating Standards for Using it in International Arbitration," in Special Supplement 2004: Using Technology to Resolve Business Disputes, ICC's Digital Library, sec. 2, p. 3.

50 See more: M. Łągiewska, *New Technologies in International Arbitration: A Game-Changer in Dispute Resolution?*, "International Journal for the Semiotics of Law" 2024, Vol. 37, pp. 851–864, https://doi.org/10.1007/s11196-023-10070-7.

51 ICC Rules 2021, Articles 3(1), 4(4), and 5(3).

52 "Rules of CEPANI," The Belgian Centre for Arbitration and Mediation, in effect as of January 1, 2020, Article 8(2) ("CEPANI Rules 2020"), https://www.cepani.be/wp-content/uploads/2020/04/RULES-ENG-2020.pdf. Accessed on 12.05.2024.

53 LCIA Rules 2020, Article 26.2.

54 P. Panjwani, *The Impact of the COVID-19 ...*, p. 54.

solutions adopted in Guiding Principles. Aside from these Principles, CGA also issued a set of Green Protocols, which is a set of directives with the aim to decrease the negative impact of international arbitrations on the natural environment. Given Green Protocols, there are three chief areas of concern. Primarily, there is a need to change some behavioural practices of arbitrators themselves to reduce carbon emissions. Further, this initiative seeks to convince to adopt clean forms of energy, decrease the number of long-haul travel and minimize waste, including hard copies in case of arbitral proceedings. Even though the Green Protocols represent a voluntary commitment for the arbitrators.[55]

To illustrate, there are different types of Green Protocols which can be summarizes as follows: Protocol for Arbitral Proceedings and the Model Green Procedural Order, Protocol for Law Firms, Chambers and Legal Service Providers Working in Arbitration, Protocol for Arbitrators, Protocol for Arbitral Institutions, Protocol for Arbitration Conferences and Protocol for Arbitration Hearing Venues.

The first protocol refers to the arbitral proceedings and is widely considered a guide to introducing environmental-friendly procedural order. Interestingly, the initiative to benefit from this protocol can be undertaken by both parties or arbitral tribunals. Some recommendations included in this protocol concern remote proceedings, reduction of hard copies documents and unnecessary travel.

The second protocol concerning law firms, chambers and legal service providers working in arbitration provides some rules on the day-to-day operations of organizations. To comply with such rules, different types of organizations are encouraged to select the so-called "Green Arbitrators" who would be responsible for developing green policies and best practices within their units.

The third type of protocol includes some practical suggestions for arbitrators themselves, namely saving energy, travel, and waste of paper in case of hard copy documentation.

The next protocol for arbitral institutions suggests improving the working habits both within the organization itself and in case management. Practically, the arbitral tribunal should also encourage parties to benefit from remote hearings instead of traditional ones.

55 L. Greenwood, C. Falcicchio, C. Foty, *The Campaign for Greener Arbitration's Green Protocols: Actions Not Words*, "Kluwer Arbitration Blog" 22.04.2021, https://arbitrationblog.kluwerarbitration.com/2021/04/22/the-campaign-for-greener-arbitrations-green-protocols-actions-not-words/. Accessed on 16 February 2023.

Considering the protocol for arbitration conferences, there are some recommendations with regard to the event planning and implementation (through the selection of venues till the follow-up measures). One could note that the organizers are even encouraged to cooperate with "green" organizations while launching such an event. Therefore, sustainable behaviours and practices would become a new normal providing virtual events instead of in-person at times.

The last protocol for arbitration hearing venues pays attention to the use of new innovation-driven technologies in arbitral proceedings, mostly concerning the technology platforms promoting digital presentations and file sharing. Therefore, given these solutions, it would be possible to reduce paper during the entire proceedings. In addition, powering venues with green energy seems to be a very interesting solution as well.[56]

It is noteworthy that these protocols were preceded by a public consultation period. Such a global launch and even a campaign conducted for the sake of changing attitudes towards "green arbitration" indicate new trends worldwide. For instance, the "Green Pledge" program focuses on workspaces with electronic communications instead of hard copies.

Finally, according to the 2021 Queen Mary and White&Case Survey on International Arbitration, respondents have already presented their open attitude towards paperless practices in arbitral proceedings. Therefore, they are much more willing to make use of electronic copies of documents instead of hard copies and provide submissions, evidence, and correspondence electronically. Interestingly, parties even expect more "green guidance" from both arbitral tribunals and soft law regulations.[57] This survey has already confirmed that a new trend focusing on sustainable development is of crucial importance also for the parties involved in international arbitration.

In addition, based on this survey, respondents have also revealed reasons behind participation in remote hearings. Interestingly, the so-called environmental benefits of such a solution cannot be recognized as a primary motivation. By contrast, the need to follow "greener" practices is much more important. As such, "the reduction of environmental impact is a welcome side-effect of their choices throughout the arbitral process, rather than a priority in and of itself".[58]

56 *Ibidem.*

57 *2021 International Arbitration Survey* ..., p. 3.

58 *Ibidem.*

5 AI-arbitrators: Pipe Dream or Realistic Future?

AI-judges have been already introduced in China. To illustrate, a judge called Xiaozhi handled a lending dispute case in Hangzhou in 2019. Indeed, Xiaozhi conducted all the proceedings within thirty minutes not only by questioning the parties but also analyzing evidence and issuing a decision. One must note that Xiaozhi is not a person. In turn, it represents an intelligent trial system which is widely recognized as a "robot judge".[59]

Apparently, the development of AI has become a target for China. It is just at the centre of the "smart courts" initiative. Estonia has decided to delegate small complaints to be handled by an algorithm. As such "the literature that predicts or otherwise assumes a future populated by robo-judges is growing fast".[60] Likewise, the so-called robot mediator was used instead of human mediation in Canada. Indeed, it even resolved a three-month dispute within less than one hour. As such, it has also proved that AI systems would play an important role in international arbitration as well. One could even say that the process of replacing the secretariat of arbitral tribunals with AI tools is on the way of implementation. Therefore, such an AI is already responsible for both legal research and the summary of both legal submissions and evidence in many arbitral institutions worldwide.[61]

Arbitrators are widely considered indispensable in the course of the decision-making process in view of arbitral proceedings. No one has ever challenged that arbitration should be a human being. On the contrary, many questions arise as a result of the application of artificial intelligence (AI) in arbitral proceedings. One could even say that such AI-supported technologies are seen in terms of threat in the entire process. It is incontrovertible in international commercial law that an arbitrator is a human neutral who has a certain capacity, impartiality, independence, and ability to handle a case and issue an arbitral award.[62]

Recently, much more debate arose concerning the role and even the junction of arbitration and technology. This begs the question of the scope and degree of such reform as well as of whether AI would be appropriate in the case of a stand-alone arbitrator. On the one hand, AI likewise other IT tools

59 D. Horton, *Forced Robot Arbitration*, "Cornell Law Review" 2023 [forthcoming], Vol. 109, p. 2.

60 *Ibidem*, p. 5; see: D. Freeman Engstrom & Jonah B. Gelbach, Legal Tech, Civil Procedure, and the Future of Adversarialism, "U. PA. L. REV." 2021, p. 1099.

61 G.I. Zekos, *Advanced Artificial Intelligence ...*, p. 323.

62 M.S. Abdel Wahab, E. Katsh, *Revolutionizing Technologies and the Use ...*, p. 48.

could certainly improve not only the efficiency of the arbitral proceedings but also reduce its costs. On the other hand, it also points out some questions on the issuance of reasonable and fair decisions by AI-powered arbitrators. In addition, there are more specific and detailed challenges that need to be addressed, namely the question of whether such an AI arbitrator[63] would be able to capture some nuances and social cues[64] during arbitral proceedings.[65] Apparently, by using AI in arbitral decision-making, the expectations of the consumers of such legal services would be naturally changed.

Nonetheless, it is also worthwhile to differentiate AI applications to assist arbitrators in their daily work from AI applications to replace arbitrators. Zekos stresses that "lawmakers must increase the efficiency and quality of arbitrations, fully realizing the potential of AI-powered arbitration. First, blockchain applications for arbitrations endure efficiency in executing human decisions. By contrast, AI systems assist humans in decision-making or even replace humans as decision-makers altogether".[66]

Although the use of AI-powered tools mostly increases both performance and productivity, the concerns relate to the implications of such AI in arbitration. One could even ask whether machines could simply replace human

63 See more: V. Pavlovskaya, *Machine Arbitrators: Technology and Ethics in International Arbitration*, "Biuletyn Arbitrażowy. Nowe technologie w arbitrażu instytucjonalnym" 2020, no. 26; Kasap Gizem H, *Can Artificial Intelligence ("AI") Replace Human Arbitrators? Technological Concerns and Legal Implications*, "Journal of Dispute Resolution" 2021, Vol. 2021, issue 2; G. Bayraktaroğlu-Özçelik, Ş. Barış Özçelik, *Use of AI-Based Technologies in International Commercial Arbitration*, "European Journal of Law and Technology" 2021, Vol. 12, no. 1.

64 "Empathy is a valuable skill, because without empathy humans would be incapable of relating to one another. With arbitration, an arbitrator's ability to empathize cognitively is a crucial skill […]. Empathy is often defined as understanding another person's experience by imagining oneself in that other person's situation. Emotional empathy requires an individual to feel the same emotion as the affected party. Cognitive empathy, also referred to as empathetic accuracy, requires an individual to have a 'more complete and accurate knowledge about the contents of another person's mind, including how the person feels'. Emotional empathy is a natural reaction to the plight of another, whereas cognitive empathy is a skill that allows an individual to rationally understand the plight of another without being emotionally swayed or affected by the plight of another person. Knowing how another person feels without being impacted by emotions is an incredibly useful skill, especially for arbitrators who must make impartial decisions". See: C. Dorsey, *Hypothetical AI Arbitrators: A Deficiency in Empathy and Intuitive Decision-Making*, "Arbitration Law Review" 2021, Vol. 13, pp. 10–11.

65 J.B. Rajendra, A.S. Thuraisingam, *The deployment of artificial intelligence in alternative dispute resolution: the AI augmented arbitrator*, "Information & Communications Technology Law" 2022, Vol. 31, issue 2, p. 178.

66 G.I. Zekos, *Advanced Artificial Intelligence …*, p. 325.

arbitrators. How properly ensure data protection and confidentiality of the arbitral proceedings? Fully up to date, there is no regulatory framework for AI implementation in arbitration. To address all the questions and challenges, the United Nations Commission on International Trade Law (UNCITRAL) should amend its rules alongside procedural and institutional laws to fully allow AI implementation in arbitration. In addition, the successful deployment of AI in the case of arbitration cannot be achieved without the legal framework. Therefore, the first step should be to establish such a legal background and then reduce the complexity and ambiguity concerning their application.[67]

In fact, the arbitrator should be very conscious while using AI for the sake of avoiding unintended biases, data privacy infringement along with some ethical concerns. Although AI-augmented arbitrators could be potentially implemented in the future, there is still a need for human supervision to fully ensure equitable dispensation in terms of arbitral proceedings. Even though machine-based AI can accomplish basic tasks, some problems arise when someone expects to execute a purpose which has not been explicitly stated either in its coding or in data series. Given this situation, the AI systems simply are not able to provide an equitable solution. On the one hand, it is also worthwhile to note that computer systems, including AI can produce accurate results, but on the other hand, they are not resistant to errors. This means that errors could even result from bad programming in algorithm codes. Therefore, human programmers once made a mistake could lead to erroneous and even inaccurate conclusions. Importantly, to avoid such situations and thus decrease the potential risks, human arbitrators are needed. In consequence, arbitrators who are equipped with AI-supported tools are merely complemented to better perform and deliver their services in arbitration. Nonetheless, a hybrid approach is more appropriate. Given this perspective, arbitrators could co-work with AI-supported systems to provide more efficient and better services in terms of arbitral proceedings.[68]

Would it be possible that AI arbitrators work instead of human arbitrators? It is crucial to remember that the legal decision-making process requires both cognitive and emotional capabilities which are beyond the scope of AI tools. In addition, binding laws and regulations opt for natural persons to fulfil their duties as arbitrators and they even do not allow the functioning of an AI arbitrator.[69] Some jurisdictions are very strict in confirming the universal presumption that an arbitrator must be a human. To illustrate, according to the

67 J.B. Rajendra, A.S. Thuraisingam, *The deployment of artificial* ..., p. 178.
68 *Ibidem*, p. 184.
69 G.I. Zekos, *Advanced Artificial Intelligence* ..., p. 324.

French law on arbitration, namely Decree No. 2011-48 of 13 January 2011 and the French Code of Civil Proceedings, "only a natural person having full capacity to exercise his or her rights may act as an arbitrator. If the arbitration agreement names a legal person, the latter has only the power to organize the arbitration". This entails that French law represents a strict and traditional approach to the nature of arbitrators. Therefore, it does not even allow the possibility that the arbitrator is non-human. As such, AI cannot fully act as an arbitrator.[70]

In addition, parties are willing to comprehend the reasons behind the issuance of a certain arbitral award. Under Article 31(2) of the UNCITRAL Model Law, "The award shall state the reasons upon which it is based unless the parties have agreed that no reasons are to be given or the award is an award on agreed terms".[71]

Hence, "AI cannot satisfy this requirement of giving reasons for the award, as it is better suited to provide a binary response based on probabilistic interference, which would lack legitimacy which means that reasoning will always be inherently and uniquely a human task".[72] The code can only solve the disputed case, most notably in the case of self-executing blockchain arbitration. One could even stress that this solution would infringe upon the requirement of reasoning stipulated by the UNCITRAL Model Law.

Given the binding legal framework, there is no legal system allowing robots or computer codes to act as arbitrators. Zekos argues that even though:

> there is no express obligation as to the status of the arbitrator, it would be legal for a machine to perform this function. Nevertheless, the arbitrator should have legal aptitude as a natural or legal person, which is presently not the case for a robot. Thus, a robot arbitrator would not have an existence of its own but would have to be connected to the existence of a legal entity or an individual, apparently the robot's owner or administrator. So, it would not be possible to name a given system as an arbitrator which means that the arbitrator would be the person or entity controlling the AI system.[73]

One must note that the current legal framework of international commercial arbitration does not allow fully AI/robotized arbitration based on constitutional limits and legal encounters concerning the enforcement of such issued

70 M.S. Abdel Wahab, E. Katsh, *Revolutionizing Technologies and the Use …*, p. 49.

71 UNCITRAL Model Law, Article 31(2).

72 G.I. Zekos, *Advanced Artificial Intelligence …*, p. 324.

73 *Ibidem*, p. 332.

arbitral awards. Indeed, robotized arbitration poses challenges in view of the constitutional considerations, mostly by questioning whether this type of dispute resolution could be classified as a proper system of justice. Therefore, it also challenges the human rights convention.[74]

Even though the UNCITRAL Model Law does not explicitly cover issues related to the personality of the arbitrator, it is implicitly acknowledged that an arbitrator must be a natural person. Such a deduction stems from the human-associated pronouns used throughout the UNCITRAL Model Law[75] such as "he" and "his". As such, bearing in mind the influence of the UNCITRAL Model Law on national arbitration law, it is noteworthy that many countries follow solutions adopted in Model Law. This entails that most arbitration legislation opts for recognizing an arbitrator as a human being. One could even stress that it is almost impossible to admit that an arbitrator is an artificial being or even non-human-based intelligence although the AI-supported tool has been launched by the human being.[76]

Likewise, in many other AI-powered tools, AI arbitrators would rely greatly on the amount of uploaded data. This entails that sufficient historical data must be properly analyzed by such an AI arbitrator for establishing a certain new rule that could be applied in new situations. In addition, the key issue is the quantity of data, namely training cases that would have an impact on future predictions.[77]

Interestingly, one must note that the machines are aimed at generalizing. In the case of international arbitration, the AI arbitrator is deemed to generalize the so-called decision-making patterns based on pieces of training through previous cases. Nonetheless, such an ideal scenario may be challenged or even difficult to achieve given certain limits of machine learning, namely the so-called "overfitting". Yet, the "overfitting" happens while "the algorithm learns the idiosyncratic features of the data, so much so that the machine starts to create patterns and rules that fit the data exactly, thereby failing to generalize when applied to other data sets".[78]

---

74 *Ibidem*, p. 331.

75 See more: B. Gessel-Kalinowska vel Kalisz, *UNICTRAL Model Law: Composition of the Arbitration Tribunal Reconsidering the Case upon Setting Aside of the Original Arbitration Award*, "Journal of International Arbitration" 2017, pp. 17–33.

76 M.S. Abdel Wahab, E. Katsh, *Revolutionizing Technologies and the Use ...*, p. 49.

77 G.H. Kasap, *Can Artificial Intelligence ("AI") Replace Human Arbitrators? Technological Concerns and Legal Implications*, "Journal of Dispute Resolution" 2021, Vol. 2021, issue 2, pp. 221–222.

78 *Ibidem*, p. 224.

Practically, it may cause many problems, most notably if an AI arbitrator becomes capable of analyzing document metadata (i.e. file size). Therefore, AI arbitrators may produce outcomes given the file size instead of features of the disputed case. Indeed, "overfitting" should be seen as a challenging problem in the development of a machine arbitrator due to the fact that "AI is prone to overfitting if the number of input features is high, and a small dataset is used for training".[79]

AI algorithms may also reflect some bias, either in favour of or against a particular person or group of people. Therefore, there are many types of biases associated with AI algorithms. Briefly, they can be summarized as follows: 1. biases introduced by data (meaning that an AI system cannot be better than the data uploaded to train it); 2. biases introduced by developers (which can be either conscious or unconscious); 3. biases introduced by training on a relatively small amount of data; 4. biases due to trust (regarding AI algorithms in the sense of 'black boxes', whereas users are assumed to trust the results provided). Apart from biases, AI algorithms can also pose some challenges in terms of ethics and social consequences related to algorithmic decision making. It should be noted that, unlike humans, AI algorithms cannot rely on the concept of "conduct". Obviously, it is also worth remembering that the risks generated by AI, including errors, failures and malicious interference, could lead to a serious miscarriage of justice.[80]

This brings us to the conclusion that AI arbitrators will need a relatively huge amount of input elements to effectively handle both complex and multilayered disputes. Nonetheless, it is worth acknowledging that a lack of data poses a challenge in international arbitration due to the principle of confidentiality. This means that there is a lack of arbitral awards available to the public. In fact, both a low number of arbitrations per year and a wide range of arbitration disputes may lead to concerns about the availability of data itself.[81]

Another practical issue refers to the decision that has been rendered by a machine. Such an arbitral award would have challenges to be qualified as an award in general. Therefore, it also raises the question of whether such an award could be recognized and enforced internationally. To illustrate, French law requires that an arbitral award must be signed by the arbitrators and thus refers to the arbitrator's legal personality. Under Article 1513 of the French Code

79 *Ibidem.*

80 J. Barnett, P. Treleaven, F.I. Lederer, N. Vermeys, J. Zeleznikow, *JudicialTech supporting Justice* (October 10, 2023). Available at SSRN: https://ssrn.com/abstract=4597917 or http://dx.doi.org/10.2139/ssrn.4597917, p. 15.

81 G.H. Kasap, *Can Artificial Intelligence* ..., p. 225.

of Civil Procedure, “In the silence of the arbitration agreement, the award is rendered by the majority. All arbitrators shall sign the arbitral award. However, if a minority of arbitrators refuse to sign it, the president specifies this in the award signed by him alone [...]”.

By contrast, the organization which is responsible for the robot itself could also be the signatory of the arbitral award. For instance, an award issued by ICC during the robotized arbitration could be signed in twofold manners: by an administrator of the “ICC’s AI dispute system” acting in his/her capacity or by the ICC itself. This entails that the administrator of the system would bear legal responsibility for both the award and its signature. Nonetheless, it is worth adding that in the case of the AAI (Advanced Artificial Intelligence) system, the entire process of issuing and signing arbitral awards would be made by the AAI entity. In addition, such AAI would be empowered with legal personality. Therefore, it would bear both full responsibility and accountability in view of the entire processes undertaken by the AAI system in a robot world.[82]

6 Blockchain-based Arbitration

6.1 *Definition of Blockchain-based Arbitration*

As a result of the decentralized global economy, the already well-known, conventional methods of dispute settlement may become outdated given their speed, high costs, and lack of reliability. Therefore, there are already a few decentralized applications (the so-called DApps), including Kleros Court which is based on blockchain technology. This Court has been launched for the sake of decision-making and arbitration with the aim of addressing commercial disputes. Even though the so-called blockchain-based arbitration shares similarities with traditional, conventional arbitration, it occurs on blockchains such as Ethereum. In addition, the arbitration agreement is a part of the smart contract. Considering arbitrators, they are chosen through random numbers stemming from the blocks in the blockchain. Finally, the arbitral award is rooted in a special self-executing smart contract.[83]

One of the most challenging issues is to ensure due process in the case of blockchain-based arbitration. Apparently, due process belongs to the fundamental assumption of international arbitration itself. One must note that this

82 G.I. Zekos, *Advanced Artificial Intelligence ...*, p. 333.

83 J. Tirado, G. Cosio, *Lex Cryptographia: Guidelines for ensuring due process in transnational blockchain-based arbitration*, “IBA” 04.03.2022, https://www.ibanet.org/lex-cryptographia-due-process-blockchain-based-arbitration. Accessed on 05.06.2023.

concept is confirmed in the New York Convention. Under Article V(1)(b) of the New York Convention:

> recognition and enforcement of the award may be refused, at the request of the party against whom it is invoked, only if that party furnishes to the competent authority where the recognition and enforcement is sought, proof that the party against whom the award is invoked was not given proper notice of the appointment of the arbitrator or of the arbitration proceedings or was otherwise unable to present his case.[84]

Nonetheless, the aforementioned sanction cannot be applied in the case of arbitral awards that have been rendered through self-executable smart contracts. In such cases, the enforceability is applied automatically.[85]

Indeed, such constraints have stronger implications in the case of due process in blockchain-based arbitration DApps. These limitations could be classified into the following three categories:

> First, there is a jurisdictional challenge inherent to the decentralized nature of the applications, which limits the effects of national and international laws in safeguarding due process in blockchain-based arbitration. Then, whilst social norms provide for due process when upholding fairness and equality as regarded principles in society, there is no real or immediate sanction imposed by society in the case of blockchain-based arbitration.[86]

In view of due process in blockchain-based arbitration, it seems that the conventional framework becomes irrelevant given the mutual interests of all parties involved in the arbitral proceedings. Indeed, the right to due process could be opposed to the right to an efficient process. Although at first sight, it could be seen as a contradiction. Nonetheless, "due process is in fact linked to the right of the parties to an efficient process, i.e., it is not a matter of sacrificing one for the other, but rather upholding both rights in careful balance in order to assure that the parties have an equal and effective right to fully present their

84 Article V(1)(b) of the 1958 New York Convention, https://uncitral.un.org/sites/uncitral.un.org/files/media-documents/uncitral/en/new-york-convention-e.pdf.

85 J. Tirado, G. Cosio, *Lex Cryptographia: Guidelines ...*

86 *Ibidem.*

case".[87] Therefore, "due process and efficiency can be seen as the two sides of the same coin".[88]

6.2 *Types of Blockchain-based Arbitration*

6.2.1 Kleros Court

At the outset, it is worth analyzing the features of the Kleros Court built on Ethereum. Indeed, it is an open-source online dispute resolution protocol. In addition, it makes use of both blockchains and crowdsourcing to provide a fair solution in handling disputes.[89] This Court can easily adjudicate either simple or highly complex disputes. It has been designed in such a way to provide services in every kind of dispute. Interestingly, the Kleros Court provides automated services, including each stage of the arbitration proceedings such as securing evidence, selecting arbitrators, etc. Instead of relying on individuals, this tool is based on game-theoretical economic incentives. Some scholars even point out that this Court:

> is based on a fundamental insight from legal epistemology: a court is an epistemic engine, a tool for ferreting out the truth about the events from a confusing array of clues. An agent (jury) follows a procedure where an input (evidence) is used to produce an output (decision). Kleros leverages the technologies of crowdsourcing, blockchain and game theory to develop a justice system that produces true decisions in a secure and inexpensive way.[90]

Practically, it is crucial to remember that Kleros which is an opt-in court system must be designated in smart contracts as an arbitrator. Afterwards, the so-called contract creators decide on the number of arbitrators and which court would be eligible to handle a case. Indeed, a court specializing in the topic of the contract should be chosen.[91]

---

87 *Ibidem.*

88 *Ibidem.*

89 *Kleros*, https://kleros.io/about. Accessed on 05.06.2023. See more: L. Bergolla, K. Seif, C. Eken, *Kleros: A socio-legal case study of decentralized justice & blockchain arbitration*, "Ohio State Journal on Dispute Resolution" 2021, Vol. 37, no. 1; T.M. Evans, *The Role of International Rules in Blockchain-Based Cross-Border Commercial Disputes*, "Wayne Law Review" 2019, Vol. 65, issue 1, pp. 1–16.

90 C. Lesaege, F. Ast, W. George, *Kleros*, "Short Paper v1.0.7.", p. 1., https://kleros.io/static/whitepaper_en-8bd3a0480b45c39899787e17049ded26.pdf. Accessed on 05.06.2023.

91 *Ibidem*, p. 3.

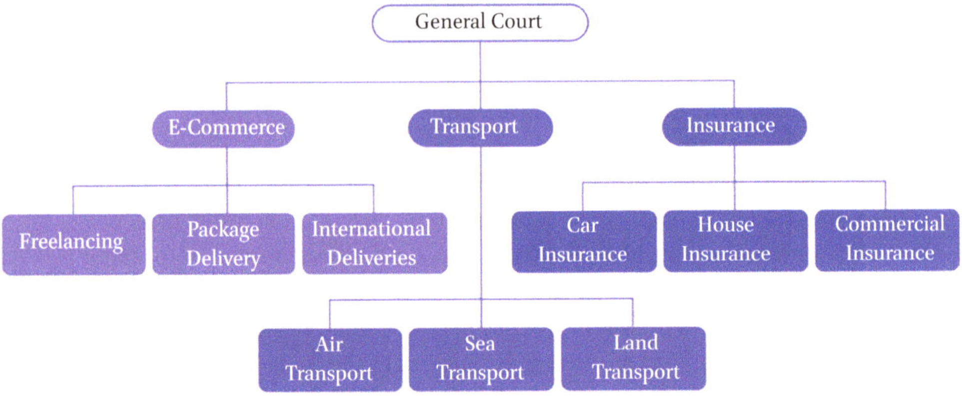

FIGURE 4 Idea of selecting a court by smart contract creators
SOURCE: C. LESAEGE, F. AST, W. GEORGE, *KLEROS*, "SHORT PAPER V1.0.7.", P. 4, HTTPS://KLEROS.IO/STATIC/WHITEPAPER_EN-8BD3A0480B45C39899787E17049DED26.PDF. ACCESSED ON 05.06.2023

Briefly, the Kleros Court provides that once the claimant explains their claim, the Court notifies the respondent about the dispute being raised. Further, the process of appointing arbitrators starts. Therefore, each juror receives an email including the following information: "You have been selected as a juror on a website quality dispute. Download the evidence here. You have three days to submit your decision".[92] This means that the AI tool helps to select a juror amongst 3000 candidates. Interestingly, given the features of the Kleros Court, such jurors do not know each other before the dispute. Instead, they are only deemed to collaborate with each other to handle the disputed case. If someone would like to be appointed as a juror, he or she must have to stake pinakion (PNK). Practically, this entails that "The more tokens they stake, the more likely it is that they will be selected. For the random selection of jurors to be resistant to manipulation, the random numbers used to select jurors are drawn from numbers for a block in the blockchain known as block hashes".[93]

In view of evidence, the Kleros Court provides a specification, widely known as "Evidence standard-1497". Indeed, such specification provides some criteria that must be met to comply with the Kleros Court DApps. Therefore, in the case of smart contracts, they must adhere to the standard. Afterwards, jurors

92 J. Tirado, G. Cosio, *Lex Cryptographia: Guidelines ...*
93 *Ibidem.*

from Kleros Court would have access to both the information and context resulting from the smart contracts.[94]

Lastly, it is worth mentioning the appeals mechanisms provided by such blockchain-based arbitration. Once the party disagrees with the award, it can appeal several times. One must note however that "only each time the number of jurors would be doubled, and an additional juror would be added".[95] Interestingly, the appealing party must pay the costs of such proceedings which increase substantially alongside each appeal. This solution was introduced for the sake of preventing excessive use of appeal in unreasonable situations by the parties.[96]

6.2.2 Juris

Juris is another type of blockchain-based arbitration. Juris is widely recognized as providing a decentralized dispute resolution system based on both blockchain technology and the Juris token (JRS). It is possible to apply this system once parties have incorporated the so-called Juris code in their smart contract. Therefore, in case of any dispute, the parties can easily freeze the contract and thus make use of the Juris dashboard to access the system. One must note that the system guides the parties through a multi-step dispute resolution process. At the outset, parties should go through "SELF Mediation" which encompasses different types of tools intending to facilitate a mutually agreed-upon resolution.[97]

If the parties fail to reach a consensus, they could continue with a "SNAP" (Simple Neutral Arbitration Pool) judgement. Given this system, the parties receive a judgment anonymously voted by neutral jurors. In addition, such a group of jurors is deemed to provide a concise opinion on the matter. After receiving a judgment from jurors, the parties may return smoothly to the "SELF" stage to achieve a consensual agreement. The parties should provide the necessary details concerning the case within the specified timeframe. Afterwards, the case is sent to jurors with JRS tokens for review. They are deemed to provide one of three justifications alongside brief reasoning. Overall, "all judgements remain concealed until the deadline for submission. After this time, the information becomes public and a discussion among SNAP jurors ensues, and

94 *Ibidem.*

95 *Ibidem.*

96 *Ibidem.*

97 O. Rabinovich-Einy, E. Katsch, *Blockchain and the Inevitability of Disputes: The Role for Online Dispute Resolution*, "Journal of Dispute Resolution" 2019, issue 2, p. 61.

legal experts actively participate by asking questions, providing relevant information and justifications".[98]

Afterwards, there is another vote when jurors explain their reasoning. Indeed, each legal expert pertains to a certain group which must form a "final opinion". Once shaped, such opinions are shared with the concerned parties who can make use of them during the consensual tools.[99]

Lastly, the so-called "PANEL" (Preemptory Agreement for Neutral Expert Litigation) judgment stage applies. During this specific stage, the most experienced jurors would be responsible for handling the most complex disputes or these disputes where parties are willing to reach a legally binding award under the 1958 New York Convention. Even though these procedures are more expensive compared to the SNAP, it provides parties with an award which holds both legal validities and can be enforced worldwide. In addition, jurors can make use of all materials that have been collected during the SNAP stage. They can also ask for more detailed information, if needed, prior to the rendering of the award. Given the PANEL stage, the final decision must be reached within a period of thirty days, and once such a decision is rendered, the smart contract between the parties is cancelled and the award is enforced automatically.[100]

To sum up, the Juris system involved different types of jurors, namely high jurists, good standing jurists, and novice jurists. The first one represents professional arbitrators who have already experience on the platform. Based on their proficiency, they are deemed to handle the most extensive and rewarding cases. The second, good-standing jurists, are not only well-experienced with the platform itself but also have the ability to vote on SNAP cases. By obtaining higher ratings, they can be easily upgraded to the rank of high jurists. The last, novice jurors, are relatively new users who can take part merely in discussions. Besides, they can assess SNAP cases without having the right to make final decisions. This entails that Juris adopts a reputational system given jurors. Therefore, the quality of the decision-making process is evaluated.[101]

6.3 *Challenges Related to Blockchain-based Arbitration*

Although blockchain-based arbitration seems to be an interesting solution, there are many challenges concerning its proper functioning. One of the most significant challenges refers to the legitimacy of blockchain arbitration. Indeed, it has decentralized nature compared to the territoriality stipulated by

98 *Ibidem*, p. 62.
99 *Ibidem.*
100 *Ibidem.*
101 *Ibidem.*

the 1958 New York Convention. One must stress that most blockchain-based platforms do not have a seat of arbitration.[102]

On the other hand, through the development of blockchain technology, arbitration itself has become more open in view of the possibility of automatically enforcing arbitral awards. Therefore, there is no need to rely on the authority of the state courts. Given the legal theories and principles of international arbitration, it represents the concept of delocalized arbitration which leaves room for developing a new form of arbitration, namely the so-called "decentralized arbitration".[103]

There are many differences between blockchain-based arbitration and the traditional one. In the case of on-chain arbitration, coded evidence is submitted. This entails that there is no requirement for oral hearings which is one of the key elements of the arbitral proceedings handled conventionally. This modern approach to resolving disputes does not fully respect the principles of natural justice. Indeed, it even undermines an integral part of the adjudication process. Regardless of the nature of the case itself, every person has the right to receive a fair trial. To make it possible, it is crucial to follow the principles of natural justice. Therefore, "due to the nature of the strict functionality of blockchain that eliminates the presence of third parties, the possibility of procurement and admission of evidence from third parties is completely ruled out".[104]

Confidentiality is a significant principle in arbitration. Even though blockchain technology provides a strong protection, there are some concerns regarding data privacy which arise when an independent third-party acts as an oracle in dispute resolution. Indeed, it is noteworthy that GDPR does not cover issues pertaining to the use of blockchain arbitration. This entails that it is difficult to hold data controllers accountable. In addition, the traceable feature of blockchain contradicts the requirement stipulated by the GDPR, that is the "right to be forgotten".[105]

102 M. Chevalier, *From Smart Contract Litigation to Blockchain Arbitration, a New Decentralized Approach Leading Towards the Blockchain Arbitral Order*, "Journal of International Dispute Settlement" 2021, Vol. 12, issue 4, p. 558.

103 *Ibidem*.

104 D. Bhora, A. Raj, *Blockchain Arbitration – The Future of Dispute Resolution Mechanisms?*, "Cambridge International Law Journal" 16.12.2020, http://cilj.co.uk/2020/12/16/blockchain-arbitration-the-future-of-dispute-resolution-mechanisms/. Accessed on 09.06.2023.

105 *Ibidem*.

7 Conclusion

This analysis brings us to the conclusion that here again there are no specific regulations at international level to cover issues relating to green arbitration, blockchain-based arbitration, among others. Instead, many international arbitral institutions worldwide adopt their own rules to comply with the ongoing changes which result from the development of innovation-driven technologies. Likewise, "soft law" solutions are also commonly used in this context.

In addition, the entire concept of "smart courts" once established in China may be an example for "smart arbitration". Many solutions that result from the digitalization along with innovation-driven technologies also lead to the fulfilment of the UN sustainable development goals. It is noteworthy, however, that such a process of going online should properly balance both advantages with disadvantages.

Final Conclusions and Recommendations

New technologies are promoted in international arbitration as a way to improve and enhance not only efficiency but also lower expenses. They also allow arbitration to reach new market segments. Interestingly, various legal systems have already recognized efficiency and cost management as priorities for arbitration. Indeed, the widespread use of emerging innovation-driven technologies will lead to many new and complicated disputes based on the unique features of the technology or the slow development of regulations covering these issues.[1]

The process of digitization and the use of new technologies have become a reality. International arbitration, as an alternative dispute resolution method, has proven to be highly adaptable to these new realities. It is worth noting that the international community itself plays a significant role and shows a keen interest in using such technologies in ongoing arbitration proceedings. The first chapter discusses terminological issues aimed at organizing the issues related to the discussed subject matter. Importantly, the first chapter already refers to the legal framework for the functioning of international arbitration. From the conducted analysis, it can be inferred that the most important international legal instruments in this regard are the 1958 New York Convention and the UNCITRAL Model Law. Nonetheless, they only provide a framework for the functioning of international arbitration, and many issues remain unregulated thus far.

One must note, however, that the 1958 New York Convention, also known as the Convention on the Recognition and Enforcement of Foreign Arbitral Awards, was adopted far before the digital era. This entails that during its enactment, the Internet had not yet been invented. In addition, various long-distance communication methods alongside tools did not even exist. Even though the Convention merely acknowledges telegraph as a recognized means of communication, international arbitration has demonstrated its flexibility to the changing times. As a result of such ongoing changes, it has embraced multifarious technolog-driven developments that facilitate long-distance communication. It is noteworthy that such openness towards innovation-driven technologies is chiefly observed among arbitrators and the international community, while the fundamental principles of international commercial arbitration remain largely unchanged.

1 F. Uribarr Soares, *New Technologies and Arbitration*, "Indian Journal of Arbitration Law" 2018, Vol. 7, issue 1, pp. 84–85.

 | DOI:10.1163/9789004700710_008

Notably, the binding rules and regulations in international arbitration were established and put into practice long before the rise of technology-driven advancements. As a result, it becomes crucial to assess the suitability of these technologies and determine if any changes are required to accommodate them. Consequently, it becomes imperative to examine the adaptability of the current legal framework to identify any necessary adjustments that may be needed.

This legal gap is filled by the arbitration institutions themselves, which adapt their rules to the changing reality. On the one hand, this approach is admirable as it demonstrates the recognition of the need for legal grounding in this matter. On the other hand, there are significant discrepancies among the arbitration institutions. For example, the issue of filing a case with an arbitral tribunal varies depending on the institution involved. This means that at this preliminary stage, there are different requirements regarding the acceptable format of documents, whether it should be paper-based documents, electronic ones, or a hybrid solution that offers greater flexibility to the parties. In practice, this can pose a considerable challenge for parties who have chosen this method of dispute resolution, most notably these parties who prefer a more traditional way of handling their disputes.

To illustrate, let's imagine a situation where parties have successfully entered into a legally binding arbitration agreement under institutional arbitration. In addition, they have chosen a specific arbitration institution that will be competent to handle their case. At the time of entering into such an agreement, they had certain expectations in choosing that particular arbitration institution. Nonetheless, the dynamic technological progress and the resulting changes in the rules of the arbitration institutions could significantly impact future proceedings. If one of the parties is flexible and easily adapts to the new reality, the more dynamic progress of digitization and the use of increasingly advanced technologies would not be a problem. However, the situation would be more complicated for a party that prefers a more traditional approach. It should be noted that especially the older generation may be less familiar with the use of technological innovations. Meeting the strict requirements, mostly in the form of "soft law", could be a challenging task. Technological progress and the pace of changes, however, lead to the reflection that this direction is inevitable. It is important to consider how to protect the interests of a party that, due to objective reasons, could be in a less privileged position.

The existing discrepancy among the various rules of arbitration institutions worldwide creates a certain "chaos". Furthermore, digitization and the use of new technologies in international arbitration present many new challenges that did not exist at the time when international legal instruments were enacted. Therefore, it is worth emphasizing the significant role played by the international community. Arbitral tribunals themselves often take positions that, on the one hand, aim to respect the parties' autonomy. On the other hand, they establish new frameworks for the functioning of the tribunals and the conduct of arbitration proceedings. This is an advantage of arbitration compared to traditional courts, which cannot afford such flexibility. However, there are many discrepancies in the interpretation of provisions, which result from the diversity of legal systems and jurisdictions.

For example, the issue of concluding an arbitration agreement in electronic form is problematic. The mere recognition of whether an electronic signature is necessary or not is already a challenge. The situation is similar when it comes to issuing awards in electronic form. Some jurisdictions recognize that such a digital award, following the provisions of the 1958 New York Convention, should be issued in writing and signed. Here, practical problems arise once again - how to effectively sign such a document? Is it necessary to print the arbitration award and handwrite sign it? Is it sufficient to provide a scanned signature? It turns out that in some legal systems, a scanned document with a signature is not equivalent to meeting the mentioned requirements. Furthermore, it is necessary to sign such an award with an electronic signature that must meet specific conditions. Failure to comply with the specified requirements may undermine the validity of the award and ultimately lead to its challenges.

Another issue is paying attention to the conduct of arbitration proceedings in line with fundamental principles that apply to international commercial arbitration, such as due process and the right to be heard. The use of remote proceedings (which, as proven in the work, even terminologically poses many difficulties - there is a distinction between online, virtual, and remote proceedings) and the use of new technologies also requires finding a "golden mean" and balancing how to effectively conduct such proceedings. Often, the parties to the proceedings may be unaware of potential risks and challenges. The lack of appropriate safeguards by arbitral tribunals can lead to numerous problems, such as when documents and evidence are hacked.

Another important yet underestimated issue in the literature is the use of artificial intelligence. On the one hand, it is worth noting that intelligently used artificial intelligence can be an effective tool in the daily work of arbitral tribunals and arbitrators. Artificial intelligence could expedite many processes. Nonetheless, there is a lack of more in-depth analysis regarding ethical issues and the upper limits of its usage. Another problem relates to the accountability of any mistakes or damages caused by such artificial intelligence.

This book aimed to examine how international law regulates digitization and the use of new technologies in international arbitration. The conducted analysis led us to the conclusion that the current legal framework for arbitration as a method of international dispute resolution only contains regulations of a soft law nature and guidelines. Nonetheless, it lacks an international convention that would comprehensively address this issue. Despite its amendment in 2006, the UNCITRAL Model Law does not reflect the latest trends in international arbitration law. It is worth emphasizing that the changes occurring in the legal sphere as a result of technological progress are not as dynamic. In other words, adapting international law to the new reality of digitization and the use of new technologies in international arbitration is a laborious process. The adoption of an international convention requires extensive consultations between the international community. Therefore, given the numerous discrepancies and ever-increasing challenges posed by new technologies, it is worthwhile to present a list of recommendations for current issues.

The first recommendation concerns the creation of comprehensive legal framework for digitization and the use of new technologies in international arbitration. This is particularly important in the context of the increasing use of artificial intelligence. As an example, it is worth mentioning ChatGPT, which is increasingly being used in the legal field. While it serves only as an auxiliary function in everyday work, improving language precision, it seems to be permissible. Nonetheless, outlining the parameters for the use of such artificial intelligence is problematic. Already today, ChatGPT plays a role in drafting arbitration awards (mostly in the reasoning section of such awards). It is important to remember, though, that various practices for the use of such artificial intelligence can exist. The legal gap resulting from technology's rapid development compared to the law in general (and international law in particular) means that arbitrators and arbitral institutions' secretariats increasingly employ this tool without paying too much attention to potential risks and problems that may arise. In my opinion, an arbitral award should be exclusively drafted by a human arbitrator who, relying on his knowledge, engages in proper reasoning. Therefore, artificial intelligence should only serve as an auxiliary function, rather than a replacement for arbitrators.

The second recommendation pertains to paying attention to and establishing ethical frameworks for the use of new technologies and artificial intelligence in international arbitration. It is important, therefore, to consider to what extent an arbitrator could make use of such new technologies, including artificial intelligence, during arbitral proceedings. We are referring to a situation in which an arbitrator, guided by ethical principles, conscience, and his own knowledge, can make a decision that further uses new technologies. Hence, the lack of clear legal prohibitions and regulations in this regard could lead to negative consequences, such as disregarding the fundamental principles of conducting the arbitration proceedings themselves. It is worth noting, however, that while unethical conduct in the "real world" can result in legal consequences, it is more challenging on one hand to identify irregularities arising from the unethical use of new technologies in the "digital world". On the other hand, proving that such unethical behaviour has occurred also presents difficulties. Additionally, holding such individuals accountable remains another matter to consider.

The third recommendation concerns the harmonization of existing principles regarding online proceedings, the admissibility of blockchain evidence, and the method of electronically signing arbitral awards, among others. The analysis conducted indicates that an arbitral tribunal has significant discretion in making decisions on matters that are not regulated. Consequently, in the absence of specific internationally recognized regulations or appropriate provisions stemming from the rules of the arbitral tribunal, there is considerable freedom in decision-making. This is evident, for example, in the acceptance of blockchain evidence, which has only been regulated within the context of general courts. To illustrate, China was the first country to admit blockchain evidence, followed by the United States. Nonetheless, there is a lack of equivalent regulations in international arbitration law. It is worth noting that arbitrators generally admit the possibility of presenting such evidence, partly due to concerns about the potential for challenging the award otherwise. While new technologies can contribute to the advancement of arbitration, it is vital to recognize the need for both a legal framework and a technical infrastructure to protect the integrity of evidence and detect potential manipulation.

It is noteworthy that the incorporation of innovation-driven technology in international arbitration holds both advantages and risks. Numerous technology-driven innovations and IT tools not only allow long-distance communication but also significantly facilitate the transmission of evidence and reduce overall costs in arbitral proceedings. Nonetheless, the use of technology also introduces new risks, most notably in the case of privacy and confidentiality. Therefore, such a risk of information leakage is considerably raised in contemporary international arbitration. As such, there is no longer a matter of "if" a security breach will take place but rather a question of "when" it will occur. Cyberattacks are prevalent in everyday life, and international arbitration is not resistant to such threats.

The use of new technologies, although interesting, also requires knowledge of their proper implementation. Similarly, there is a lack of harmonization regarding standards for cybersecurity and data protection. Almost every arbitral institution uses its own platforms, providing different tools that vary in their level of protection for the parties and the data transmitted. Nonetheless, there is a lack of specific internationally recognized legal regulations that directly govern the minimum level of such protection. Due to this legal gap, as only non-binding recommendations currently exist, many cases of abuse can occur. It is important to recognize that issues of cybersecurity and data protection in the virtual world should be a priority in light of one of the fundamental principles of arbitration, namely confidentiality.

Indeed, arbitrators along with arbitral tribunals benefit from the authority to issue necessary orders for safeguarding confidential information and documents. This entails that arbitrators have broad procedural powers. Therefore, such power enables them to issue orders about the storage, use, and transfer of data generated during arbitral proceedings. On one hand, protocols and recommendations addressing cybersecurity risks for parties and arbitral tribunals are mostly considered positive improvements and should be embraced by the international arbitration community. Nonetheless, once implemented by the arbitral tribunal, such measures may have limited both scope and enforceability. Indeed, some arbitrators have a broad knowledge of cybersecurity issues, whereas others may not be well-familiar with IT tools. Therefore, having confidence merely in arbitrators to enhance cybersecurity might not grant sustainable and satisfactory outcomes in the foreseeable future.

In summary, notwithstanding contemporary threats and risks, various arbitral institutions worldwide remain consistent in using relatively insecure storage and communication systems. In addition, institutional rules frequently neglect to effectively address cybersecurity concerns, allowing electronic communication and data transfer through remote means without adequate levels of safeguards. Notably, many arbitral institutions worldwide do not pay sufficient attention to cybersecurity issues and thus they make use of commercially available cloud data repositories and unencrypted email methods.

References

Legal Sources

2017 Arbitration Rules," International Chamber of Commerce, adopted March 1, 2017, ("ICC Rules 2017"), http://www.arbiter.com.sg/pdf/rules/ICC%20Arbitration%20(2017)%20and%20Mediation%20(2014)%20Rules%20(ENG).pdf.

2020 LCIA Arbitration Rules, https://www.lcia.org/Dispute_Resolution_Services/lcia-arbitration-rules-2020.aspx.

2021 IBA Rules on the Taking of Evidence in International Arbitration adopted by a resolution of the IBA Council, 17 December 2020, International Bar Association, https://www.ibanet.org/MediaHandler?id=def0807b-9fec-43ef-b624-f2cb2af7cf7b.

2021 ICC Rules, https://iccwbo.org/dispute-resolution/dispute-resolution-services/arbitration/rules-procedure/2021-arbitration-rules/#block-accordion-26.

2021 International Dispute Resolution Procedures (Including Mediation and Arbitration Rules), https://www.icdr.org/sites/default/files/document_repository/ICDR_Rules_1.pdf?utm_source=icdr-website&utm_medium=rules-page&utm_campaign=rules-intl-update-1mar.

AAA-ICDR Model Order and Procedures for a Virtual Hearing via Videoconference, "American Arbitration Association", https://go.adr.org/rs/294-SFS-516/images/AAA270_AAA-ICDR%20Model%20Order%20and%20Procedures%20for%20a%20Virtual%20Hearing%20via%20Videoconference.pdf.

Convention on the Recognition and Enforcement of Arbitral Awards (1958 New York Convention), https://uncitral.un.org/sites/uncitral.un.org/files/media-documents/uncitral/en/new-york-convention-e.pdf.

Directive 2000/31/EC on Certain Legal Aspects of Information Society Services, in Particular Electronic Commerce, in the Internal Market, OLEC, July 17, 2000, L 178/1, Dalloz 2000, leg., https://eur-lex.europa.eu/legal-content/EN/TXT/?uri=CELEX%3A32000L0031.

Draft Convention on Electronic Evidence, https://www.google.com/url?sa=i&rct=j&q=&esrc=s&source=web&cd=&ved=0CAIQw7AJahcKEwjI3r3m67r_AhUAAAAAHQAAAAAQAg&url=https%3A%2F%2Fjournals.sas.ac.uk%2Fdeeslr%2Farticle%2Fdownload%2F2321%2F2245%2F0&psig=AOvVaw310dubAlYP-321nVKGGiKU&ust=1686559757235749.

European General Data Protection Regulation, https://gdpr-info.eu/. Accessed on 12.05.2024.

Geneva Protocol, https://www.trans-lex.org/511300/_/protocol-on-arbitration-clauses-signed-at-a-meeting-of-the-assembly-of-the-league-of-nations-held-on-the-twenty-fourth-day-of-september-nineteen-hundred-and-twenty-three/.

IBA Rules on the Taking of Evidence in International Arbitration adopted by a resolution of the IBA Council (29 May 2010), https://www.international-arbitration-attorney.com/wp-content/uploads/2018/09/IBA-Rules-Document-Production-Arbitration.pdf.

ICC Checklist for a Protocol on Virtual Hearings and Suggested Clauses for Cyber-Protocols and Procedural Orders Dealing with the Organisation of Virtual Hearings, https://iccwbo.org/publication/icc-checklist-for-a-protocol-on-virtual-hearings-and-suggested-clauses-for-cyber-protocols-and-procedural-orders-dealing-with-the-organisation-of-virtual-hearings/.

ICCA-NYC Bar-CPR Protocol on Cybersecurity in International Arbitration (2022 Edition) with the assistance of the Permanent Court of Arbitration, Peace Palace, the Hague, "ICCA Reports" 2022, No. 6, https://static.cpradr.org/docs/Cybersecurity%20ICCA-NYC%20Bar-CPR-protocol-international-arbitration-2022.pdf.

ICSID Convention, https://icsid.worldbank.org/sites/default/files/ICSID_Convention_EN.pdf.

Postanowienie Sądu Najwyższego z dnia 13 września 2012 r., sygn. akt V CSK 323/11, https://www.sn.pl/sites/orzecznictwo/Orzeczenia2a/V%20CSK%20323-11-1.pdf. Accessed on 17.02.2023.

Postanowienie Sądu Najwyższego z dnia 28 listopada 2018 r., sygn. akt III CSK 406/16, https://www.sn.pl/sites/orzecznictwo/Orzeczenia3/III%20CSK%20406-16-1.pdf. Accessed on 17 February 2023.

Rules for Expedited Arbitration, SCC, https://sccarbitrationinstitute.se/sites/default/files/2022-12/scc_expedited_arbitration_2023_english.pdf.

Rules of CEPANI, The Belgian Centre for Arbitration and Mediation, in effect as of January 1, 2020, Article 8(2) ("CEPANI Rules 2020"), https://www.cepani.be/wp-content/uploads/2020/04/RULES-ENG-2020.pdf.

SAKIG Arbitration Rules, https://sakig.pl/wp-content/uploads/2022/06/ARBITRATION-RULES-in-force-1-January-2015-with-changes-from-8-november-2021-in-force-1-april-2022-1-1.pdf.

Seoul Protocol on Video Conferencing in International Arbitration, http://www.kcabinternational.or.kr/static_root/userUpload/2020/03/18/1584509782805DD02R.pdf.

Swiss Chambers' Arbitration Institution Rules, https://www.swissarbitration.org/wp-content/uploads/2024/03/Swiss-Arbitration-Centre_International-Swiss-Rules-2021-EN.pdf.

UNCITRAL Model Law on Electronic Commerce with Guide to Enactment 1996 with additional article 5 *bis* as adopted in 1998, https://uncitral.un.org/sites/uncitral.un.org/files/media-documents/uncitral/en/19-04970_ebook.pdf.

UNCITRAL Model Law on International Commercial Arbitration (1985) with amendments as adopted in 2006, https://uncitral.un.org/sites/uncitral.un.org/files/media-documents/uncitral/en/19-09955_e_ebook.pdf.

UNCITRAL Notes on Organizing Arbitral Proceedings 2012, https://uncitral.un.org/sites/uncitral.un.org/files/media-documents/uncitral/en/arb-notes-e.pdf.

UNICTRAL Model Law on Electronic Signatures with Guide to Enactment 2001, https://uncitral.un.org/sites/uncitral.un.org/files/media-documents/uncitral/en/ml-elecsig-e.pdf.

United Nations Convention on International Settlement Agreements Resulting From Mediation (Singapore Mediation Convention), https://uncitral.un.org/sites/uncitral.un.org/files/singapore_convention_eng.pdf.

最高人民法院关于互联网法院审理案件若干问题的规定, "The Supreme People's Court of the People's Republic of China", https://www.court.gov.cn/zixun-xiangqing-116981.html. Accessed on 25.06.2023.

Articles and Books

《国际商事仲裁》刘晓红、袁发强主编, 北京 2015 年 [*Guójì shāngshì zhòngcái*, Liú Xiǎohóng, Yuán Fāqiáng zhǔbiān, Běijīng 2015].

Abdel Wahab M.S., Katsh E., *Revolutionizing Technologies and the Use of Technology in International Arbitration: Innovation, Legitimacy, Prospects and Challenges* [in:] *Arbitration in the Digital Age: The Brave New World of Arbitration*, ed. M. Piers, C. Aschauer, Cambridge University Press 2018.

Al Dalaien M.N., Al Enizi Z., Al Dalaien A., *Problems of Proving the Electronic Arbitration Agreement in Applicable International Laws and Agreements*, "Journal of Applied Security Research" 2021, Vol. 18, issue 3.

Alessa H., *The role of Artificial Intelligence in Online dispute Resolution: A brief and critical overview*, "Information & Communications Technology Law" 2022, Vol. 31, issue 3.

Allsop Ao J., *Technology and the future of the courts*, "University of Queensland Law Journal" 2019, Vol. 38, issue 1.

Aouidef Y., Ast F., Deffains B., *Decentralized Justice: A Comparactive Analysis of Blockchain Online Dispute Resolution Projects*, "Frontiers in Blockchain" 2021, Vol. 4.

Barnett J., Treleaven P., *Algorithmic Dispute Resolution – The Automation of Professional Dispute Resolution Using AI and Blockchain Technologies*, "The British Computer Society" 2017.

Barnett J., Treleaven P., Lederer F.I., Vermeys N., Zeleznikow J., *JudicialTech supporting Justice* (October 10, 2023). Available at SSRN: https://ssrn.com/abstract=4597917 or http://dx.doi.org/10.2139/ssrn.4597917,

Bayraktaroğlu-Özçelik G., Barış Özçelik Ş., *Use of AI-Based Technologies in International Commercial Arbitration*, "European Journal of Law and Technology" 2021, Vol. 12, no. 1.

Becker D., Marques R.D., *Why the use of technology in arbitrators' selection process – although fostered – must still be handled carefully*, "Comitê Brasileiro de Arbitragem", https://cbar.org.br/site/why-the-use-of-technology-in-arbitrators-selection-process-although-fostered-must-still-be-handled-carefully/. Accessed on 06.06.2023.

Bergolla L., Seif K., Eken C., *Kleros: A socio-legal case study of decentralized justice & blockchain arbitration*, "Ohio State Journal on Dispute Resolution" 2021, Vol. 37, no. 1.

Beyea L.L., *The Rise of ChatGPT: Why Arbitrators Need to Take Notice: Potential Impact of ChatGPT in ADR*, "American Arbitration Association" 17.03.2023, https://www.adr.org/blog/The-Rise-of-ChatGPT-Why-Arbitrators-Need-to-Take-Notice. Accessed on 31.05.2023.

Bhora D., Raj A., *Blockchain Arbitration – The Future of Dispute Resolution Mechanisms?*, "Cambridge International Law Journal" 16.12.2020, http://cilj.co.uk/2020/12/16/blockchain-arbitration-the-future-of-dispute-resolution-mechanisms/. Accessed on 09.06.2023.

Biukovic L., *International Commercial Arbitration in Cyberspace: Recent Developments*, "Northwestern Journal of International Law & Business" 2002, Vol. 22.

Błaszczak Ł., Ludwik M. *Sądownictwo polubowne (arbitraż)*, Warszawa 2007.

Boisson de Chazournes L., *The Sustainable Development Goals (SDGs) and the Rule of Law: A Propos SDG 6 on Access to Water and Sanitation*, "ASIL Proceedings. Sustainable Development and International Law" 2020.

Born G.B., *Annulment of International Arbitral Awards* [in:] G.B. Born, *International Commercial Arbitration*, Kluwer Law International 2020.

Born G.B., *International Commercial Arbitration*, Wolters Kluwer 2014.

Brenner S.W., *Law in an Era of "Smart" Technology*, Oxford 2007, p. 7. Cf. *Black's Law Dictionary*, Minnesota 2004.

Brillat-Capello William , Canet Laura , Lemaire Gilian Carmichael et al., *Paperless Arbitration: The New Trend?*, "International Journal of Online Dispute Resolution" 2020, Vol. 7, no. 2.

Brownsword R., *Law, Liberty, and Technology* [in:] *The Oxford Handbook of Law, Regulation and Technology*, ed. Roger Brownsword et al., Oxford 2016.

Budniak-Rogala A., *Charakter prawny zapisu na sąd polubowny w postępowaniu cywilnym*, Wrocław 2015.

Bull C., *An Effective Platform for International Arbitration: Raising the Standards in Speed, Costs and Enforceability* [in:] *International Organizations and the Promotion of Effective Dispute Resolution. AIIB Yearbook of International Law 2019*, ed. P. Quayle, Gao Xuan, Leiden-Boston 2019.

Camacho L., *Sustainable Development Goals: kinds, connections and expectations*, "Journal of Global Ethics" 2015, Vol. 11, no. 1.

Carneiro D., Novais P., Neves J., *Conflict Resolution and its Context. From the Analysis of Behavioural Patterns to Efficient Decision-Making*, "Law, Governance and Technology Series" vol. 18, Series Editors: P. Casanovas, G. Sartor, Springer 2014.

Carpentier C.L., Braun H., *Agenda 2030 for Sustainable Development: A powerful global framework*, "Journal of the International Council for Small Business" 2020, Vol. 1, no. 1.

Carrara C., *Chapter IV: Science and Arbitration, The Impact of Cognitive Science and Artificial Intelligence on Arbitral Proceedings Ethical issues*, "Austrian Yearbook on International Arbitration" 2020, eds. K. Christian et al.

Cavalcanti A. Andrade de Araújo, *Connecting Law to New Technologies: Perspectives and Challenges*, [in:] *Internet and New Technologies Law. Perspectives and Challenges*, eds. D. Szostek, M. Załucki, Nomos 2021.

Ceil C., *Theory of Delocalization in International Commercial Arbitration*, available at SSRN: https://papers.ssrn.com/sol3/papers.cfm?abstract_id=3521053.

Centner D., Ford M., *A Brief Primer on the history of arbitration*, [in:] *Arbitration and the surety*, eds. A. Belleau, L. McGrew Brewer, L.P. Jortner, M. Oertel, Chicago 2020.

Chaisse J., Bauer C., *Cybersecurity and the Protection of Digital Assets: Assessing the Role of International Investment Law and Arbitration*, "Vanderbilt Journal of Entertainment and Technology Law" 2020, Vol. 21.

Chan V., Koo A.M., *Blockchain Evidence in Internet Courts in China: The Fast Track Evidence Collection for Online Disputes*, "Lexology" 15.07.2020, https://www.lexology.com/library/detail.aspx?g=1631e87b-155a-40b4-a6aa-5260a2e4b9bb. Accessed on 25.06.2023.

Chen Lei, *Regulating Smart Contracts and Digital Platforms: A Chinese Perspective* [in:] *The Cambridge Handbook of Smart Courts, Blockchain Technology and Digital Platforms*, ed. L.A. DiMatteo, M. Cannarsa, C. Poncibò, Cambridge 2019.

Chen Meng, *The Reforming Chinese Chapter of International Dispute Resolution under the Belt and Road Initiative*, "The Pacific Review" 2021, Vol. 34, no. 3, https://www.tandfonline.com/doi/abs/10.1080/09512748.2019.1677749.

Chevalier M., *From Smart Contract Litigation to Blockchain Arbitration, a New Decentralized Approach Leading Towards the Blockchain Arbitral Order*, "Journal of International Dispute Settlement" 2021, Vol. 12, issue 4.

Cohen S., *Draft Zoom Hearing Procedural Order*, "Transnational Dispute Management", https://www.transnational-dispute-management.com/journal-advance-publication-article.asp?key=1815.

Concise Oxford English Dictionary, New York 2002.

de Magalhães Santos L.G., Dhaou S.B., *Opena Data and Emerging Technologies: Connecting SDG Performance and Digital Transformation*, https://sdgs.un.org/sites/default

/files/2023-05/A13%20-%20Magalh%C3%A3es%20-%20Open%20Data%20and%20Emerging%20Technologies%20Connecting%20SDG%20Performance%20and.pdf.

Dietz T., *The Rule of Law Effects of Commercial Arbitration from a Socio-Legal Perspective* [in:] *The Oxford Handbook of International Arbitration*, ed. T. Schultz, F. Ortino, Oxford 2020.

Dorsey C., *Hypothetical AI Arbitrators: A Deficiency in Empathy and Intuitive Decision-Making*, "Arbitration Law Review" 2021, Vol. 13.

Durban M., *„Protokół seulski" dotyczący wideokonferencji w międzynarodowym arbitrażu handlowym,* "Biuletyn Arbitrażowy. Nowe technologie w arbitrażu instytucjonalnym" 2020, no. 26.

El Ahdab J., Berenguer P., Chik M., Choo J. et al., *Approaches to Evidence across Legal Cultures*, [in:] *The Guide to Evidence in International Arbitration*, ed. A.C. Kläsener, M. Magál, J.E. Neuhaus, London 2021.

Evans T.M., *The Role of International Rules in Blockchain-Based Cross-Border Commercial Disputes*, "Wayne Law Review" 2019, Vol. 65, issue 1.

Fernández Arroyo D., Sousa Rodrigues B., *An Arbitrator's Perspective: Between Equal Treatment and the Good Administration of Transnational Justice in Online Arbitration* [in:] *Online Dispute Resolution. New Challenges*, ed. D. Moura Vicente, E. Dias Oliveira, J. Gomes de Almeida, Baden-Baden 2022.

Ferreira D.B., Gromova E.A., *Electronic evidence in arbitration proceedings: empirical analysis and recommendations*, "Digital Evidence and Electronic Signature Law Review" 2023, Vol. 20.

Ferreira Lousa N., *A Lawyer's Perspective: Guarantees of a Fair Trial and Online Dispute Resolution* [in:] *Online Dispute Resolution. New Challenges*, ed. D. Moura Vicente, E. Dias Oliveira, J. Gomes de Almeida, Baden-Baden 2022.

Finizio S.P., *Remote hearings in international arbitration* [in:] *Specialized arbitration: Emerging international trends and practices*, eds. C. Balyan. Y. Samant, Gurgaon 2022.

Fortier Y., *The Occasionally Unwarranted Assumption of Confidentiality*, "Arbitraion International" 1999, no. 15.

Freeman Engstrom D., Gelbach J.B., *Legal Tech, Civil Procedure, and the Future of Adversarialism*, "U. PA. L. REV." 2021.

Fry J., Greenberg S., Mazza F., The Secretariat's Guide to ICC Arbitration, 2012.

Garg P.K., *Overview of Artificial Intelligence* [in:] *Artificial Intelligence. Technologies, Applications, and Challenges*, ed. L. Sharma, P.K. Gard, Oxon 2022.

Gauke D., Lord Chancellor and Sec'y of State for Just., House of Commons, Statement at The Artificial Intelligence in Legal Services Summit (June 4, 2019).

Gaultier T., *Cross-Border Mediation: A New Solution for International Commercial Dispute Settlement?*, „NYSBA International Law Practicum" 2013, Vol. 26, no. 1.

Gearing M., Liu J., *The Contributions of the Hong Kong International Arbitration Centre to Effective International Dispute Resolution* [in:] *International Organizations and the Promotion of Effective Dispute Resolution. AIIB Yearbook of International Law 2019*, ed. P. Quayle, Gao Xuan, Leiden-Boston 2019.

Gessel-Kalinowska vel Kalisz B., *UNICTRAL Model Law: Composition of the Arbitration Tribunal Reconsidering the Case upon Setting Aside of the Original Arbitration Award*, "Journal of International Arbitration" 2017.

Gessel-Kalinowska vel Kalisz, *Wyrok arbitrażowy w czasie pandemii – dopuszczalność współczesnych form elektronicznych (skrót artykułu opublikowanego w „Przeglądzie Prawa Handlowego")*, "Biuletyn Arbitrażowy. Nowe technologie w arbitrażu instytucjonalnym" 2020, no. 26.

Gicquello M., *Artificial Intelligence in International Arbitration*, [in:] *The Oxford Handbook of International Arbitration*, ed. T. Schultz, F. Ortino, Oxford 2020.

Gifford D., *Law and Technology: Interactions and Relationships*, "Minnesota Journal of Law, Science & Technology" 2007, Vol. 8, issue 2.

Giupponi B.O., *"Virtual" Dispute Resolution in International Arbitration. Mapping Its Advantages and Main Caveats in the Face of COVID-19*, [in:] *The Impact of Covid on International Disputes*, eds. S. Lalani, S.G. Shapiro, "International and Comparative Business Law and Public Policy" Vol. 2, Leiden-Boston 2022.

Gómez K.F., *The Role of Mediation in International Commercial Disputes. Reflections on some Technological, Ethical, and Educational Challenges* [in:] *Mediation in International Commercial and Investment Disputes*, ed. C. Titi, K.F. Gómez, Oxford 2019.

Grabowska-Łysyszyn, *Rozprawa w postępowaniu przed sądem polubownym w dobie* pandemii *COVID-19. Doświadczenia Sądu Arbitrażowego przy Krajowej Izbie Gospodarczej w Warszawie*, "Biuletyn Arbitrażowy. Nowe technologie w arbitrażu instytucjonalnym" 2020, no. 26.

Gu Weixia, *Dispute Resolution in China: Litigation, Arbitration, Mediation, and Their Interactions*, Routledge, New York 2021.

Gu Weixia, *Hybrid Dispute Resolution Beyond the Belt and Road: Toward a New Design of Chinese Arb-Med.(-Arb) and Its Global Implications*, "Washington International Law Journal" 2019, Vol. 29, no. 1.

Gu Weixia, *The Developing Nature of Arbitration in Mainland China and Its Correlation with the Market: Institutional, Ad Hoc, and Foreign Institutions Seated in Mainland China*, "Contemporary Asia Arbitration Journal" 2017, Vol. 10(2).

Gu Weixia, *When Local Meets International: Mediation Combined with Arbitration in China and Its Prospective Reform in a Comparative Context*, "Journal of Comparative Law" 2016, Vol. 10, no. 2

Gulyamov S., Bakhramova M., *Digitalization of International Arbitration and Dispute Resolution by Artificial Intelligence*, "World Bulletin of Management and Law" 2022, Vol. 9.

Hague Conference on Private International Law, *Guide to Good Practice on the Use of Video-Link under the Evidence Convention.*

Halla S., *Arbitration going online - new challenges in 21st Century?*, “Masaryk University Journal of Law and Technology” 2011, Vol. 5, issue 2.

Hatami Alamdari B., *The Question of Remote Hearings in International Commercial Arbitration,* [in:] *The Impact of Covid on International Disputes,* eds. S. Lalani, S.G. Shapiro, “International and Comparative Business Law and Public Policy” Vol. 2, Leiden-Boston 2022.

Hay E., *Data protection and international arbitration: never the twain shall meet?*, [in:] *International Arbitration and Technology,* ed. P. Ortolani, A. Janssen, P. Wolters, Kluwer Law International 2022.

Henry M., *An Arbitrator's Perspective: Confidentiality – Privacy – Security in the Eye of the Arbitrators or the Story of the Arbitrator who Became a Bee* [in:] *Online Dispute Resolution. New Challenges,* ed. D. Moura Vicente, E. Dias Oliveira, J. Gomes de Almeida, Baden-Baden 2022.

Hill J., *Determining the Seat of an International Arbitration: Party Autonomy and the Interpretation of Arbitration Agreements,* “International & Comparative Law Quarterly” 2014, Vol. 63.

Hörne J., *Online Dispute Resolution: The Emperor's New Clothes? Benefits and Pitfalls of Online Dispute Resolution and its Application to Commercial Arbitration,* “International Review of Law Computers & Technology” 2003, Vol. 17, no. 1.

Hörnle J., *Online Dispute Resolution – More Than The Emperor's New Clothes,* “Proceedings of the UNECE Forum on ODR” 2003.

Horton D., *Forced Robot Arbitration,* “Cornell Law Review” 2023 [forthcoming], Vol. 109.

Huang Jie, *Conflicts and Tentative Solutions to Protecting Personal Data in Investment Arbitration*¸” The European Journal of International Law” 2021, Vol. 32, no. 4.

Jia Zuo, *One Belt One Road Disputes: Does China Have Dispute Resolution Methods Fit for Purpose?*, “LSE Law Review” 2020, Vol. 5.

Judkiewicz M., *Wady i zalety zdalnego postępowania arbitrażowego,* “Biuletyn Arbitrażowy. Nowe technologie w arbitrażu instytucjonalnym” 2020, no. 26.

Kasap G.H., *Can Artificial Intelligence (“AI”) Replace Human Arbitrators? Technological Concerns and Legal Implications,* “Journal of Dispute Resolution” 2021, Vol. 2021, issue 2.

Katsh E., Rabinovich-Einy O., *Digital justice,* Oxford 2017.

Kauflmann-Kohler G., Potestà M., *Special Issue: Investor-State Dispute Settlement and National Courts. Current Framework and Reform Options. European Yearbook of International Economic Law,* Springer 2020.

Kaufmann-Kohler G., Schulz T., *The Use of Information Technology in Arbitration* (December 5, 2005), JusLetter, December 2005, available at SSRN: https://ssrn.com/abstract=924878. Access on 11.03.2023.

Koulu K., *Law, Technology and Dispute Resolution. Privatisation of Coercion*, New York 2019.

Łągiewska M., *Arbitraż w Chinach – uwagi wstępne*, „Gdańskie Studia Azji Wschodniej" 2020, Vol. 17.

Łągiewska M., Łukasiewicz J.M., *Chińskie prawo rodzinne. Zagadnienia wybrane*, Toruń 2020.

Łągiewska M., *New Technologies in International Arbitration: A Game-Changer in Dispute Resolution?*, "International Journal for the Semiotics of Law" 2024, Vol. 37, https://doi.org/10.1007/s11196-023-10070-7.

Łągiewska M., *Prawo arbitrażowe Chińskiej Republiki Ludowej na tle ustawy modelowej UNCITRAL o międzynarodowym arbitrażu handlowym – zagadnienia wybrane*, „Folia Iuridica Universitatis Wratislaviensis" 2023, Vol. 12(1), DOI:10.34616/149315.

Łągiewska M., *The New Landscape of Arbitration in View of Digitalization*, [in:] *The Impact of Covid on International Disputes*, eds. Shaheeza Lalani, Steven G. Shapiro, "International and Comparative Business Law and Public Policy" Vol. 2, Leiden-Boston 2022.

Łągiewska M., 中国与波兰关于国际商事仲裁效力的比较研究, [Effectiveness of the arbitration agreement under Chinese and Polish law: A Comparative Study] Toruń 2022.

Lal H., Kaiding J., Defranchi L., *Virtual Hearings in International Construction Arbitration: Evolution or Mitigant?*, "Construction Law Journal" 2021, Vol. 37, no. 2.

Liang Wenwen, *The World Bank and the Creation of the International Center for Settlement of Investment Disputes: Legality and Legitimacy* [in:] *International Organizations and the Promotion of Effective Dispute Resolution. AIIB Yearbook of International Law 2019*, ed. P. Quayle, Gao Xuan, Leiden-Boston 2019.

Liao Ting, How Emerging Technologies Shape the Face of Chinese Courts?, "Conflict of Laws.net" 10.11.2021, https://conflictoflaws.net/2021/how-emerging-technologies-shape-the-face-of-chinese-courts%ef%bc%9f/.

Luo Xiulan, *A Study on the Disputes Settlement Mechanism in Online Transactions – Based on the Visual Angle of Complementation between Folk Law and State Law*, "Hebei Law Science" 2010, Vol. 8.

Mandel G.N., *Legal Evolution in Response to Technological Change* [in:] *The Oxford Handbook of Law, Regulation and Technology*, ed. R. Brownsword et al., Oxford 2016.

Márquez A.S., *Can Artificial Intelligence be used to appoint arbitrators?*,"AVANI" 2020, no. 1.

Marrow P.B., Karol M., Kuyan S., *Artificial Intelligence and Arbitration: The Computer as an Arbitrator – Are We There Yet?*, "Dispute Resolution Journal" 2020, Vol. 74, no. 4.

Mason S., *Introduction* [in:] *International Electronic Evidence*, ed. S. Mason, London 2008.

Menezes T., *Remote Hearings in International* Arbitration, "Jus Corpus Law Journal" 2022, Vol. 2, no. 3.
Menon S., *Arbitration's Blade: International Arbitration and the Rule of Law*, "Journal of International Arbitration" 2021, Vol. 38, issue 1.
Nasser Agil H., *Electronic Arbitration: The new mechanism for dispute resolution*, "The Arbitrator & Mediator" December 2016.
Ortolani P., *The Judicialization of Blockchain* [in:] *Regulating Blockchain: Techno-Social and Legal Challenges*, ed. P. Hacker et al., Oxford 2019.
Paisley K., Sussman, E., *Artificial Intelligence Challenges and Opportunities for International Arbitration*, "Special Feature: Artificial Intelligence and New Arbitration Data Sources. NYSBA New York Dispute Resolution Lawyer" 2018, Vol. 11, no. 1.
Palmerini E., *The interplay between law and technology, or the RoboLaw project in context*
Panjwani P., *The Impact of the COVID-19 Pandemic on International Arbitration Practices. Greener Arbitrations with Reduced Due Process Paranoia?*, [in:] :] *The Impact of Covid on International Disputes*, eds. Shaheeza Lalani, Steven G. Shapiro, "International and Comparative Business Law and Public Policy" Vol. 2, Leiden-Boston 2022.
Panjwani P., *The Present and Near Future of New Technologies in Arbitration* (Report on the Club Español de Arbitraje's Third Annual Conference), 2018 Spain Arb. Rev.
Paulsson M., *The 1958 New York Convention in Action*, New York 2016.
Pavlovskaya V., *Machine Arbitrators: Technology and Ethics in International Arbitration*, "Biuletyn Arbitrażowy. Nowe technologie w arbitrażu instytucjonalnym" 2020, no. 26.
Peng Junlin, Xiang Wen, *The Rise of Smart Courts in China: Opportunities and Challenges to the Judiciary in a Digital Age*, "Nordic Journal of Law and Social Research" 2019, no. 9.
Perales Viscasillas P., *An Arbitrator's Perspective: Online hearings in Arbitration: the taking of Evidence* [in:] *Online Dispute Resolution. New Challenges*, ed. D. Moura Vicente, E. Dias Oliveira, J. Gomes de Almeida, Baden-Baden 2022.
Perlman A., *The Implications of OpenAi's Assistant for Legal Services and Society*, "The Practice. Harvard Law School" 2023, https://clp.law.harvard.edu/knowledge-hub/magazine/issues/generative-ai-in-the-legal-profession/the-implications-of-chatgpt-for-legal-services-and-society/. Accessed on 15.06.2023.
Pfadt, *Blockchain*, [in:] *Leksykon prawa nowych technologii. 100 podstawowych pojęć*, ed. A. Krasulski, Warszawa 2021.
Pfadt W., *Cyfryzacja* [in:] *Leksykon prawa nowych technologii. 100 podstawowych pojęć*, ed. A. Krasulski, Warszawa 2021.
Piers M., C. Aschauer, eds. *Arbitration in the Digital Age: The Brave New World of Arbitration*, Cambridges 2018.
Piers M., Aschauer C., *Foreword* [in:] *Arbitration in the Digital Age. The Brave New World of Arbitration*, eds. M. Piers, C. Aschauer, Cambridge 2018.

Pires de Sousa L.F., *A Judge's Perspective: Online Hearings, especially the Gathering and Assessment of Evidence* [in:] *Online Dispute Resolution. New Challenges*, ed. D. Moura Vicente, E. Dias Oliveira, J. Gomes de Almeida, Baden-Baden 2022.

Pogge T., Sengupta M., *The Sustainable Development Goals: a plan for building a better world?*, "Journal of Global Ethics" 2015, Vol. 11, no. 1.

Polański P., Gołaczyński J., *Online Dispute Resolution and the Form of an Arbitration Agreement*, , [in:] *Internet and New Technologies Law. Perspectives and Challenges*, eds. D. Szostek, M. Załucki, Nomos 2021.

Protopsaltou D., Schultz T., Magnenat-Thalmann N., *Taking the Fourth Party further? Considering a shared virtual workspace for arbitration*, "Information & Communications Technology Law" 2006, Vol. 15, issue 2.

Puertas Álvarez O., Valentí i Vidal O., Díaz Vallespinós L., *Unlocking Blockchain Evidence in International Arbitration*, "Spain Arbitration Review, Revista del Club Español del Arbitraje", Wolters Kluwer España 2022, Vol. 2022, issue 43, https://www.cuatrecasas.com/resources/unlocking-blockchain-evidence-in-international-arbitration-636a8db7a3d02887902120.pdf?v1.42.2.20230126.

Qureshi A.H., *The World Trade Organization and the Promotion of Effective Dispute Resolution: In Times of a Trade War* [in:] *International Organizations and the Promotion of Effective Dispute Resolution. AIIB Yearbook of International Law 2019*, ed. P. Quayle, Gao Xuan, Leiden-Boston 2019.

Rabinovich-Einy O., Katsch E., *Blockchain and the Inevitability of Disputes: The Role for Online Dispute Resolution*, "Journal of Dispute Resolution" 2019, issue 2.

Rajendra J.B., Thuraisingam A.S., *The deployment of artificial intelligence in alternative dispute resolution: the AI augmented arbitrator*, "Information & Communications Technology Law" 2022, Vol. 31, issue 2.

Reinert K.A., *From Sustainable Development Goals to Basic Development Goals*, "Ethics & International Affairs" 2020, Vol. 34, no. 2.

Ribeiro Mendes S., *A Lawyer's Perspective: Confidentiality, Privacy and Security in Arbitration in Times of Covid* [in:] *Online Dispute Resolution. New Challenges*, ed. D. Moura Vicente, E. Dias Oliveira, J. Gomes de Almeida, Baden-Baden 2022.

Roos H., *Arbitration Tech Toolbox: Let's Chat Some More about ChatGPT and Dispute Resolution*, "Kluwer Arbitration Blog" 08.04.2023, https://arbitrationblog.kluwerarbitration.com/2023/04/08/arbitration-tech-toolbox-lets-chat-some-more-about-chatgpt-and-dispute-resolution/. Accessed on 26.06.2023.

Rothe F-F., Audenhove L.V., Loisen J., *ICT for development and the novel principles of the Sustainable Development Goals*, "Third World Quarterly" 2022, Vol. 43, issue 6.

Rothe F-F., *Rethinking positive and negative impacts of 'ICT for development' through the holistic lens of the sustainable development goals*, "Information Technology for Development" 2020, Vol. 26, issue 4.

Ryšavý L., *Form of Arbitration Agreement in a Comparative Perspective*, "ICLR" 2020, Vol. 20, no. 2.

Sanders P., *New York Convention on Recognition and Enforcement of Foreign Arbitral Awards*, "Netherlands International Law Review" 1959, Vol. 6, issue 1.

Sanderson B., Scott M., Croft S., *Hearings in International Arbitration. What Has the Pandemic Taught Us about Virtual Hearings and What They Cn Offer in the Future?*, [in:] *The Impact of Covid on International Disputes*, eds. S. Lalani, S.G. Shapiro, "International and Comparative Business Law and Public Policy" Vol. 2, Leiden-Boston 2022.

Santos Abrantes Geraldeas A., *A Judge's Perspective: Guarantess of a Fair Trial and Online Dispute Resolution* [in:] *Online Dispute Resolution. New Challenges*, ed. D. Moura Vicente, E. Dias Oliveira, J. Gomes de Almeida, Baden-Baden 2022.

Schaumann P., Burger-Scheidlin M., *The Security and Reliability of Electronic Communication With a Critical Note on the Human Factor*, [in:] *Arbitration in the Digital Age: The Brave New World of Arbitration*, ed. M. Piers, C. Aschauer, Cambridge University Press 2018.

Scherer M., *Artificial Intelligence and Legal Decision-Making: The Wide Open?*, "Journal of International Arbitration" 2019, Vol. 36, issue 5.

Scherer M., *Remote Hearings in International Arbitration: An Analytical Framework*, "Journal of International Arbitration" 2020, Vol. 37, issue 4.

Serralda Hierro J., *An Arbitration Center's Perspective: Due Process in Online Dispute Resolution* [in:] *Online Dispute Resolution. New Challenges*, ed. D. Moura Vicente, E. Dias Oliveira, J. Gomes de Almeida, Baden-Baden 2022.

Shi Changqing, Sourdin T, Li Bin, *The Smart Court – A New Pathway to Justice in China?*, "International Journal for Court Administration" 2021, Vol. 12(1).

Shu Shang Carrie, Guo Wenli, *The Rise of Online Dispute Resolution-led Justice in China: An Initial Outlook*, "Australian National University Journal of Law and Technology" 2020.

Soares F.U., *New Technologies and Arbitration*, "Indian Journal of Arbitration Law" 2018, Vol. 7, issue 1.

Stewart F., *The Sustainable Development Goals: a comment*, "Journal of Global Ethics" 2015, Vol. 11, no. 3.

Susskind R., *Online courts and the future of justice*, New York 2019.

Susskind R., Susskind D., *Future of the Professions: How Technology Will Transform the Work of Human Experts*, Oxford 2015.

Swain R.B., Yang-Wallentin F., *Achieving sustainable development goals: predicaments and strategies*, "International Journal of Sustainable Development & World Ecology" 2020, Vol. 27, issue 2.

Szubert M., *The Future is Digital*, [in:] *Internet and New Technologies Law. Perspectives and Challenges*, eds. D. Szostek, M. Załucki, Nomos 2021.

Szumański A., *Pojęcie, rodzaje i charakter prawny arbitrażu handlowego* [w:] *Arbitraż handlowy. System Prawa Prywatnego. Tom 8*, red. A. Szumański, Kraków 2015.

Tao Jingzhou, M. Zhang, *Resolving Disputes in China: New and Sometimes Unpredictable Development* [in:] *International Organizations and the Promotion of Effective Dispute Resolution. AIIB Yearbook of International Law 2019*, ed. P. Quayle, Gao Xuan, Leiden-Boston 2019.

Tasca P., Piselli R., *The Blockchain Paradox* [in:] *Regulating Blockchain: Techno-Social and Legal Challenges*, ed. P. Hacker et al., Oxford 2019.

The Admissibility of Blockchain as Digital Evidence, "Concord Law School" 23.03.2019, https://www.purduegloballawschool.edu/blog/news/admissibility-blockchain-digital-evidence. Accessed on 26.06.2023.

Torres Vouga R., *A Judge's Perspective: Privacy and Confidentiality in Voluntary Commercial Arbitration* [in:] *Online Dispute Resolution. New Challenges*, ed. D. Moura Vicente, E. Dias Oliveira, J. Gomes de Almeida, Baden-Baden 2022.

Tranter K., *From Law and Technology to Law as Technology* [in:] K. Tranter, *Living in Technical Legality*, Edinburgh 2018.

van der Velden M., *Digitalisation and the UN Sustainable Development Goals: What role for design*, "Interaction Design and Architectures(s) Journal" 2018, no. 37.

van Haersolte-van Hof J., Holland R., *What makes for Effective Arbitration? A Case Study of the London Court of International Arbitration Rules* [in:] *International Organizations and the Promotion of Effective Dispute Resolution. AIIB Yearbook of International Law 2019*, ed. P. Quayle, Gao Xuan, Leiden-Boston 2019.

Virtual Assistant, https://www.virtualassistantassistant.com/x-ai/. Accessed on 12.03.2023.

Wade S. , *Practical implications of ChatGPT in the arbitration proceedings*, "LexisNexis" 02.02.2023, https://www.lexisnexis.co.uk/legal/news/practical-implications-of-chatgpt-in-the-arbitration-proceedings. Accessed on 25.06.2023.

Wahab M.A., *The Global Information Society and Online Dispute Resolution: A New Dawn for Dispute Resolution*, "Journal of International Arbitration" 2004, Vol. 21, issue 2.

Wang F.F., *Online arbitration*, Routledge 2018.

Wang Jia, Chen Lei, *Will Innovative Technology Result in Innovative Legal Frameworks? – Smart Contracts in China*, "European Review of Private Law" 2018, Vol. 26, issue 6.

Waqar M., *The Use of AI in Arbitral Proceedings*, "Ohio State Journal on Dispute Resolution" 2022, Vol. 37, no. 3.

Wei Bin, Kuang Kun, Sun Changlong, Feng Jun, Zhang Yating, Zhu Xinli, Zhou Jianghong, Zhai Yinsheng, Wu Fei, *A full-process intelligent trial system for smart court*, "Frontiers of Information Technology & Electronic Engineering" 2022, Vol. 23(2).

Weir G.R.S., Mason S., *The sources of electronic evidence*, [in:] *Electronic evidence*, ed. S. Mason, D. Seng, London 2017.

Westrum R., *Technologies & Society: The Shaping of People and Things*, Belmont 1990.

Wiśniewski A.W., *Międzynarodowy arbitraż handlowy w Polsce. Status prawny arbitrażu i arbitrów*, Warszawa 2011.

Wolff R., *E-arbitration agreements and e-awards – arbitration agreements concluded in an electronic environment and digital arbitral awards* [in:] *Arbitration in the Digital Age: The Brave New World of Arbitration*, ed. M. Piers, C. Aschauer, Cambridge 2018.

Wronkowska S., Ziembiński Z., *Zarys teorii prawa*, Poznań 2001.

Xu (Lu) Alison, *Chinese judicial justice on the cloud: a future call or a Pandora's box? An analysis of the 'intelligent court system' of China*, "Information & Communications Technology Law" 2017, Vol. 26, issue 1, DOI: 10.1080/13600834.2017.1269873].

Young K.M., Ivers J.A., Schroeder K., *The Impact of Covid-19 on International Arbitration Procedure*, [in:] *The Impact of Covid on International Disputes*, eds. S. Lalani, S.G. Shapiro, "International and Comparative Business Law and Public Policy" Vol. 2, Leiden-Boston 2022.

Yun Zhao, *The Singapore mediation convention: A version of the New York convention for mediation?*, „Journal of Private International Law" 2021, Vol. 17, issue 3.

Zekos G.I, *Development on courts' involvement in arbitration. Volume 2: the rule of law*, New York 2019.

Zekos G.I., *Advanced Artificial Intelligence and Robo-Justice*, Cham 2022.

Zekos G.I., *Development on courts' involvement in arbitration. Volume 1: the rule of law*, New York 2019.

Zhang Yanan, *Alternative Dispute Resolution System in the People's Republic of China*, „Polski Proces Cywilny" 2012, nr 3(8).

Zhen Qin, *The Use of New Technologies in International Arbitration*, "The American Review of International Arbitration. Columbia Law School" 25.02.2019, https://aria.law.columbia.edu/the-use-of-new-technologies-in-international-arbitration/. Accessed on 20.06.2023.

Zheng G.G., *China's Grand Design of People's Smart Courts*, "Asian Journal of Law and Society" 2020.

Zou Mimi, "Smart courts" in China and the future of personal injury litigation, "Journal of Personal Injury Law" (forthcoming, June 2020), https://papers.ssrn.com/sol3/papers.cfm?abstract_id=3552895.

Zwolankiewicz A., Sachan A., *Big Data, Bigger Disruption: In Institutional Arbitration Ready?*, "Biuletyn Arbitrażowy. Nowe technologie w arbitrażu instytucjonalnym" 2020, no. 26.

Internet Sources

"ICSID Makes Electronic Filing its Default Procedure," ICSID, last modified March 16, 2020, https://icsid.worldbank.org/news-and-events/news-releases/icsid-makes-electronic-filing-its-default-procedure.

"SCC Virtual Hearing Survey," Arbitration Institute of the Stockholm Chamber of Commerce, October 2020, https://sccinstitute.com/media/1773182/scc-rapport_virtual_hearing-2.pdf.

2021 International Arbitration Survey: Adapting arbitration to a changing world, "Queen Mary and White&Case" 2021, https://arbitration.qmul.ac.uk/media/arbitration/docs/LON0320037-QMUL-International-Arbitration-Survey-2021_19_WEB.pdf.

AAA WebFile. New Hearing Exhibits Feature , "American Arbitration Association", https://www.adr.org/aaa-webfile-hearing-exhibits?utm_source=website-adr&utm_medium=tech-services-software-and-online-tools-page&utm_campaign=website_hearing-exhibits-webfile. Accessed on 11.06.2023.

AAA-ICDR Technology Services, "American Arbitration Association", https://www.adr.org/TechnologyServices/aaa-icdr-software-and-online-tools. Accessed on 11.06.2023.

About International Communication Union (ITU), https://www.itu.int/en/about/Pages/default.aspx. Accessed on 11.04.2023.

Amado L., Griffiths D., *Improving transparency in international arbitration: digital solutions*, "Osborne Clarke" 19.05.2021, https://www.osborneclarke.com/insights/improving-transparency-international-arbitration-digital-solutions. Accessed on 12.03.2023.

Annex I, *Checklist for a protocol on virtual hearings*, "ICC Checklist for a Protocol on Virtual Hearings and Suggested Clauses for Cyber-Protocols and Procedural Orders Dealing with the Organisation of Virtual Hearings", https://iccwbo.org/publication/icc-checklist-for-a-protocol-on-virtual-hearings-and-suggested-clauses-for-cyber-protocols-and-procedural-orders-dealing-with-the-organisation-of-virtual-hearings/. Accessed on 21.01.2023.

Association for Computing Machinery, Statement on Algorithmic Transparency and Accountability (Jan. 12, 2017), https://www.acm.org/binaries/content/assets/public-policy/2017_usacm_statement_algorithms.pdf.

Baetens K., *Cyber hack challenges in international arbitration*¸ "Linkaters" 22.04.2021, https://www.linklaters.com/en/insights/blogs/arbitrationlinks/2021/april/cyber-hack-challenges-in-arbitration. Accessed on 04.04.2023.

Baetens K., Suschinski J., *Cyber hack challenges in international arbitration – Part 2*, "Linklaters" 13.05.2021, https://www.lexology.com/library/detail.aspx?g=b350fa18-ad82-4828-a21e-e5aed590512f. Accessed 07.04.2023.

Bienvenu P., Grant B., *Data protection and cyber-risk issues in arbitration: regulation, cyberattacks and hacked evidence*, "Lexology" 17.10.2019, https://www.lexology.com/commentary/arbitration-adr/international/norton-rose-fulbright/data-protection-and-cyber-risk-issues-in-arbitration-regulation-cyberattacks-and-hacked-evidence#cyberattacks. Accessed on 03.04.2023.

Case Filing Guidelines, "World Intellectual Property Organization", https://www.wipo.int/amc/en/arbitration/filing/#pd. Accessed on 19.02.2023.

Case management, "SCC Arbitration Institute" https://sccarbitrationinstitute.se/en/case-management. Accessed on 20.06.2023.

CaseShield. Cyber threaths are on the rise. Is your case information safe?, "American Arbitration Association", https://go.adr.org/Case-Shield. Accessed on 11.06.2023.

Course on Dispute Settlement: International Commercial Arbitration, UN Conference on Trade and Development, New York and Geneva, UNCTAD/EDM/Misc.232/Add.20.

Decision Tree Model: *Value Your Legal Case with TreeAge Pro*, https://www.treeage.com/legal/. Accessed on 12.03.2023.

Digital technologies to achieve the UN SDGs, https://www.itu.int/en/mediacentre/backgrounders/Pages/icts-to-achieve-the-united-nations-sustainable-development-goals.aspx. Accessed on 11.04.2023.

Dispute Settlement. International Commercial Arbitration: Electronic Arbitration, "United Nations Conference on Trade and Development" 2003.

Dobry T.R., Napoli T.M., *Beyond E-Discovery: The Ethical & Legal Use of Machine Learning Technologies*, "Lexology" 09.03.2021, https://www.lexology.com/library/detail.aspx?g=cbbc81c3-c0cb-4999-8bc1-b86a85463d16. Accessed on 26.06.2023.

Douglas-Henry J.P. et al., "Virtual Hearings 2021: Virtual hearings," DLA Piper, September 21, 2021, 8, https://www.dlapiper.com/en/uk/insights/publications/2021/07/virtual-hearings-2021/ ("DLA September 2021 Report").

Ethics guidelines for trustworthy AI, "European Commission" 08.04.2019, https://digital-strategy.ec.europa.eu/en/library/ethics-guidelines-trustworthy-ai. Accessed on 12.06.2023.

File your Request via ICC Case Connect, "ICC International Court of Arbitration", https://iccwbo.org/dispute-resolution-services/arbitration/file-your-request-via-icc-case-connect/#case-before-2022. Accessed on 19.02.2023.

García-Perrote G., *Admissibility of 'Hacked Evidence' in International Arbitration*, "Kluwer Arbitration Blog" 07.07.2021, https://arbitrationblog.kluwerarbitration.com/2021/07/07/admissibility-of-hacked-evidence-in-international-arbitration/. Accessed on 07.06.2023.

Green Protocols. Campaign for Greener Arbitration, https://www.greenerarbitrations.com/green-protocols. Accessed on 30 April 2023.

Greenwood L., Falcicchio C., Foty C., *The Campaign for Greener Arbitration's Green Protocols: Actions Not Words*, "Kluwer Arbitration Blog" 22.04.2021, https://arbitrationblog.kluwerarbitration.com/2021/04/22/the-campaign-for-greener-arbitrations-green-protocols-actions-not-words/. Accessed on 16 February 2023.

Hafez M., *Remote hearings and the use of technology in arbitration*, "Global Arbitration Review" 21.04.2023, https://globalarbitrationreview.com/review/the-middle-eastern-and-african-arbitration-review/2022/article/remote-hearings-and-the-use-of-technology-in-arbitration. Accessed on 20.06.2023.

Hangzhou Internet Court Province of Zhejiang People's Republic of China (Judgment), https://go.dennemeyer.com/hubfs/blog/pdf/Blockchain%2020180726/20180726_BlogPost_Chinese%20Court%20is%20first%20to%20accept%20Blockchain_Judgment_EN_Translation.pdf. Accessed on 27.06.2023.

Hayes A., *Blockchain Facts: What Is It, How It Works, and How It Can Be Used?*, "Investopedia" 27.09.2022, https://www.investopedia.com/terms/b/blockchain.asp. Accessed on 20.03.2023.

Hong J., Hwang J.H., *Safeguarding the Future of Arbitration: Seoul Protocol Tackles the Risks of Videoconferencing*, "Kluwer Arbitration Blog" 06.04.2020, https://arbitrationblog.kluwerarbitration.com/2020/04/06/safeguarding-the-future-of-arbitration-seoul-protocol-tackles-the-risks-of-videoconferencing/. Accessed on 09.01.2023.

ICC Commission on Arbitration and Alternative Dispute Resolution, Task Force on the Use of Information Technology, "Operating Standards for Using it in International Arbitration," in Special Supplement 2004: Using Technology to Resolve Business Disputes, ICC's Digital Library, sec. 2, https://iccwbo.org/news-publications/arbitration-adr-rules-and-tools/information-technology-international-arbitration-report-icc-commission-arbitration-adr/. Accessed on 19.02.2023.

ICC launches ICC Case Connect: Secure online case management made easy, "ICC International Court of Arbitration" 12.10.2022, https://iccwbo.org/media-wall/news-speeches/icc-launches-icc-case-connect-secure-online-case-management-made-easy/. Accessed on 19.02.2023.

ICSID Makes Electronic Filing its Default Procedure, "ICSID News & Events" 13.03.2020, https://icsid.worldbank.org/news-and-events/news-releases/icsid-makes-electronic-filing-its-default-procedure. Accessed on 19.02.2023.

Jain N., *Can an Arbitral Tribunal Admit Evidence Obtained through a Cyber-Attack?*, "Kluwer Arbitration Blog" 27.01.2019, https://arbitrationblog.kluwerarbitration.com/2019/01/27/can-an-arbitral-tribunal-admit-evidence-obtained-through-a-cyber-attack/. Accessed on 06.06.2023.

Kisielińska-Garncarek J., Ostas Ł., *Concluding an Arbitration Agreement via Means of Remote Communication under Polish Law: A Short Guide for Practitioners*, "Kluwer Arbitration Blog" 13.11.2022, https://arbitrationblog.kluwerarbitration.com/2022/11/13/concluding-an-arbitration-agreement-via-means-of-remote-communication-under-polish-law-a-short-guide-for-practitioners/. Accessed on 17.02.2023.

Kleros, https://kleros.io/about. Accessed on 05.06.2023.

Larkin K., Sherman J., Renehan K., Patel A., *Using Technology and e-Disclosure*, "Global Arbitration Review" 03.09.2021, https://globalarbitrationreview.com/guide/the-guide-evidence-in-international-arbitration/1st-edition/article/using-technology-and-e-disclosure. Accessed on 13.04.2023.

Lesaege C., Ast F., George W., *Kleros*, "Short Paper v1.0.7.", https://kleros.io/static/whitepaper_en-8bd3a0480b45c39899787e17049ded26.pdf. Accessed on 05.06.2023.

Leveraging Technology for Fair, Effective and Efficient International Arbitration Proceedings, "ICC Dispute Resolution Services, Commission on Arbitration and ADR", Paris 2022, https://iccwbo.org/wp-content/uploads/sites/3/2022/02/icc-arbitration-and-adr-commission-report-on-leveraging-technology-for-fair-effective-and-efficient-international-arbitration-proceedings.pdf.

Morel de Westgaver C., *Cybersecurity in International Arbitration – A Necessity And An Opportunity For Arbitral Institutions*, "Wolters Kluwer" 06.10.2017, https://arbitrationblog.kluwerarbitration.com/2017/10/06/cyber-security/. Accessed 07.04.2023.

Note from the Working Group, Draft Prague Rules of 1 September 2018, https://praguerules.com/upload/medialibrary/b2e/b2e26123ac310b644b26d4cd11dc67d8.pdf. Accessed on 10.06.2023.

Online arbitration. Club des jurists report. Working group chaired by Thomas Clay, Professor at the Faculty of Law at the Sorbonne (Paris-I University), Paris 2019.

Online Litigation Rules of the People's Courts, https://cicc.court.gov.cn/html/1/219/199/201/2208.html. Accessed on 26.06.2023.

Oral Hearing – UNCITRAL Arbitration, "International Centre for Settlement of Investment Disputes", https://icsid.worldbank.org/procedures/arbitration/uncitral/oral-hearing. Accessed on 07.01.2023.

Publication of ICC Arbitral Awards with JUS MUNDI, "ICC", https://iccwbo.org/dispute-resolution/resources/publication-of-icc-arbitral-awards-jus-mundi-not-icc-publication/. Accessed on 10.06.2023.

Schäfer E.G.W., *Managing Data Privacy and Cybersecurity Issues*, "Global Arbitration Review" 03.09.2021, https://globalarbitrationreview.com/guide/the-guide-evidence-in-international-arbitration/2nd-edition/article/managing-data-privacy-and-cybersecurity-issues. Accessed on 07.04.2023.

Singarajah F., *Unconscious Bias in International Arbitration*, "Thomson Reuters. Practical Law Arbitration Blog" 21.06.2021, http://arbitrationblog.practicallaw.com/unconscious-bias-in-international-arbitration/#:~:text=This%20is%20a%20subtle%20bias,the%20arbitrator%20is%20accustomed%20to. Accessed on 01.06.2023.

Singh Chauhan A., *Future of AI in Arbitration: The Fine Line Between Fiction and Reality*, "Wolters Kluwer" 26.09.2022, https://arbitrationblog.kluwerarbitration.com/2020/09/26/future-of-ai-in-arbitration-the-fine-line-between-fiction-and-reality/. Accessed on 12.03.2023.

Soley F.V., *Signing the Arbitral Award in Wet Ink: Resistance to Technological Change or A Reasonable Precaution?*, "Kluwer Arbitration Blog" 06.11.2020, https://arbitrationblog.kluwerarbitration.com/2020/11/06/signing-the-arbitral-award-in-wet-ink-resistance-to-technological-change-or-a-reasonable-precaution/.

Souza-McMurtrie L.F., *Arbitration Tech Toolbox: Will ChatGPT Change International Arbitration as We Know It?*, "Kluwer Arbitration Blog" 26.02.2023, https://

arbitrationblog.kluwerarbitration.com/2023/02/26/arbitration-tech-toolbox -will-chatgpt-change-international-arbitration-as-we-know-it/. Accessed on 31.05 .2023.

Sustainable Development Goal 9: Investing in ICT access and quality education to promote lasting peace, "United Nations" 20.06.2017, https://www.un.org/sustainable development/blog/2017/06/sustainable-development-goal-9-investing-in-ict -access-and-quality-education-to-promote-lasting-peace/. Accessed on 11.06.2023.

Sustainable Development Goals kick off with start of new year, "United Nations" 30.12.2015, https://news.un.org/en/story/2015/12/519172. Accessed on 11.06.2023.

The Arbitration Court of the Blockchain and New Technologies Chamber of Commerce, https://www.blockchaintribunal.org/. Accessed on 05.01.2023.

Thirgood R., *Remote hearings: storm clouds and silver linings*, "International Bar Association" 27.09.2022, https://www.ibanet.org/clint-september-2022-feature-5. Accessed 15.04.2023.

Three takeaways on how digital technologies are transforming arbitration, "ICC" 30.08.2017, https://iccwbo.org/media-wall/news-speeches/three-takeaways-digital -technologies-transforming-arbitration/, Accessed on 10.03.2023.

Tirado J., Cosio G., *Lex Cryptographia: Guidelines for ensuring due process in transnational blockchain-based arbitration*, "IBA" 04.03.2022, https://www.ibanet.org /lex-cryptographia-due-process-blockchain-based-arbitration. Accessed on 05.06 .2023.

WIPO eADR, "World Intellectual Property Organization", https://www.wipo.int/amc /en/eadr/wipoeadr/. Accessed on 19.02.2023.

Index

access to justice 5, 83–85, 93, 153, 154
AI 1, 2, 5, 8, 14, 22, 26, 27, 42, 64–80, 82, 85, 148, 152, 156, 158, 161, 162, 167–173, 176, 189, 192, 194, 197, 199, 202, 204
AI-arbitrators 2, 5, 148, 167
arbitral tribunal 1, 3, 5, 13, 22, 36, 42, 44, 47, 48, 50–56, 58, 59, 62, 63, 70, 73, 76, 79, 86, 102, 105, 106, 111–118, 126, 129, 133, 136–140, 142, 144, 154, 165, 182, 185, 186
artificial intelligence 5, 8, 14, 27, 31, 42, 73, 82, 87, 105, 118, 146, 152, 155–158, 161, 167, 183, 184, 197

blockchain 2, 5, 24, 108–111, 117–121, 146, 148, 152, 155, 159–161, 168, 170, 173–180, 185, 190, 197, 205
blockchain-based arbitration 2, 5, 148, 173–175, 177–180, 205

case management 33, 36, 37, 40, 43, 126, 136, 138, 161, 165, 203
ChatGPT 75–80, 184, 190, 197, 199, 204
China 6, 46, 110, 119, 120, 132, 135, 155–157, 159–162, 167, 180, 185, 189, 191, 193, 194, 196, 198–200, 203
confidentiality 26, 32, 38–40, 45–47, 72, 75, 77, 84–86, 113, 127–129, 131, 133, 134, 140, 147, 169, 172, 185, 186
COVID-19 pandemic 1–4, 11, 17, 29, 33, 34, 41, 43, 47, 50, 53, 54, 67, 97, 130, 139, 150, 157, 163
cybersecurity 1, 5, 31, 34, 38, 39, 46, 47, 94, 127–130, 132–135, 137–141, 147, 156, 185, 186

data protection 1, 5, 31, 37, 38, 94, 134–136, 138, 140–142, 144, 156, 169, 185
delocalized arbitration 22, 101, 179
digital arbitral award 5, 94, 122, 126
digitalization 2, 7, 8, 15, 31, 83, 93, 94, 111, 146, 152, 155–157, 161, 180
digital technologies 2, 94, 205
due process 1, 5, 12, 13, 29, 45–47, 69, 80, 83, 103, 113, 115, 126, 145, 173, 174, 183, 205

e-evidence 5, 94, 106, 111–113, 116, 120, 145, 159, 161
effectiveness 5, 9, 13, 15, 20, 22, 56, 90, 91, 94, 138, 141, 161
efficiency 5, 12, 13, 15, 17, 26, 30, 37, 53, 58, 59, 68, 69, 72, 77, 87, 88, 91, 93, 105, 118, 153, 157, 159, 162, 168, 175, 181
electronic arbitration agreement 5
electronic evidence 106, 192, 199
e-proceedings 5, 94, 104, 105, 106

flexibility 5, 26, 87, 88, 92, 93, 128, 181–183

green arbitration 2, 5, 148, 163, 166, 180

international arbitration 2–7, 11, 12, 17–20, 25, 26, 28, 31, 33, 41–43, 45–48, 61–63, 66, 69, 72–76, 78, 81–83, 85, 87, 92–95, 99, 101, 104, 111, 112, 118, 119, 122, 125, 128–130, 132, 135, 140, 141, 145, 146, 148, 163, 164, 166, 167, 171–173, 179, 181–186, 192, 194, 201
international commercial arbitration 2, 3, 18–21, 27, 41, 72, 74, 86, 100, 102, 103, 140, 145, 170, 181, 183
international dispute resolution 1–4, 7, 15, 17, 29, 30, 94, 111, 154, 184
international investment arbitration 3, 23
IT tools 3, 4, 11, 31, 32, 81, 82, 87, 89– 92, 129, 167, 185, 186

law 2–10, 14, 16, 19, 21, 29, 38, 46, 48, 62, 65, 69, 72, 73, 75, 77, 78, 82–84, 86, 93, 95, 96, 98, 102–104, 106, 108, 111, 112, 117, 119, 121, 123–125, 128, 140, 141, 146, 149, 153, 154, 156, 162, 165–167, 170–172, 180, 182–185, 195, 196, 200

machine learning 64, 67–71, 171
mediation 13, 23–25, 36, 40, 72, 167, 200

new technologies 1–8, 10, 11, 14, 16, 25–27, 29–31, 49, 57, 66, 73, 81, 82, 90, 93, 94, 99, 118, 126, 141, 148, 155, 160, 163, 181–185

New York Convention 4, 20, 21, 52, 55, 58, 71, 82, 94, 97, 98, 100, 103, 118, 122–126, 145, 146, 154, 174, 178, 179, 181, 183, 187, 196, 198

ODR 13, 15, 16, 27, 40, 42, 156, 194
online arbitration 4, 7, 13, 28–30, 104
online courts 42, 156, 157, 159

remote hearings 1, 4, 11, 17, 31, 41–45, 47–60, 70, 82, 84, 87–90, 92, 93, 103, 130, 144, 147, 154, 165, 166
right to a hearing 48, 52
rule of law 72, 83, 153

seat of arbitration 5, 11, 38, 51, 94, 101–103, 179
Seoul Protocol 4, 45–47, 82, 188, 203
smart courts 154–158, 167, 180
sustainable development goals 2, 148, 180, 197, 198

transparency 5, 12, 13, 26, 80, 85, 86, 107, 129, 201

UNCITRAL Model Law 4, 5, 21, 69, 78, 82, 83, 97, 102, 103, 112, 123–125, 146, 154, 170, 171, 181, 184, 188

videoconferencing 26, 32, 33, 41, 43, 45–47, 60, 61, 90, 104, 106, 126, 144
virtual hearings 42, 60, 88, 201

www.ingramcontent.com/pod-product-compliance
Lightning Source LLC
Chambersburg PA
CBHW070248260926
51849CB00001BA/35
9789004700703